MEDIATING
MORALITY

Mediating Morality

THE POLITICS OF TEEN PREGNANCY
IN THE POST-WELFARE ERA

CLARE DANIEL

University of Massachusetts Press
Amherst and Boston

ISBN 978-1-62534-267-6 (paper); 266-9 (hardcover)

Designed by Jack Harrison
Set in Adobe Minion Pro
Printed and bound by The Maple-Vail Book Manufacturing Group

Cover design by Jack Harrison

Library of Congress Cataloging-in-Publication Data
Names: Daniel, Clare, 1981– author.
Title: Mediating morality : the politics of teen pregnancy in the post-welfare era / Clare Daniel.
Description: Amherst : University of Massachusetts Press, [2017] |
Includes bibliographical references and index.
Identifiers: LCCN 2017001734| ISBN 9781625342676 (pbk. : alk. paper) |
ISBN 9781625342669 (hardcover : alk. paper)
Subjects: LCSH: Teenage pregnancy—Prevention. |
Teenage pregnancy—Social aspects. | Teenagers—Sexual behavior. | Poverty.
Classification: LCC RG556.5 .D37 2017 | DDC 618.200835—dc23
LC record available at https://lccn.loc.gov/2017001734

British Library Cataloguing-in-Publication Data
A catalog record for this book is available from the British Library.

For my parents, James and Therese

Contents

Preface

I was pregnant in 2011, when the seeds of this research were forming, and I found myself watching episode after episode of *16 and Pregnant*. This experience was both fascinating and excruciating, because, although I was twenty-nine at the time, it was my first pregnancy and what I affectionately call "an initially-very-shocking-but-ultimately-awesome surprise." As such, I felt some sense of identification with the characters, however small and imagined, given our drastically different circumstances. It pained me to watch how the show crafted and manipulated their experiences to serve the sometimes converging and often conflicting goals of profit maximization and teen pregnancy prevention.

At the same time, I had the acute sense that *16 and Pregnant* was part of something bigger—a shift in the contours of the public image of teen pregnancy. I first became interested in the politics of teen pregnancy when I worked with adolescent parents who received Temporary Assistance to Needy Families (TANF) in St. Paul, Minnesota, in the mid-2000s. That experience made me want to examine the history and politics of welfare in the United States, which led me to conduct research into the rhetoric of childhood within welfare reform debates of the mid-1990s. From this perspective, it was clear to me that *16 and Pregnant*'s portrayal of pregnant and parenting teens was different than those of the not-too-distant past. These teenagers appeared overwhelmingly white and middle class, rather than impoverished, black, and Latina, and their problems seemed fundamentally personal, rather than economic, geographic, legal, and health-related.

This book is my effort to contextualize programming like *16 and Pregnant* and post-welfare teen pregnancy prevention work within the larger shift that has quietly taken place in teen pregnancy's definition as a social problem. My hope is to reveal the ways that teen pregnancy prevention, even as it appears increasingly distanced from questions of welfare and race, actually furthers the processes by which neoliberalism deepens social inequalities based on race, gender, class, and sexuality.

Mediating Morality is the product of many people's generous support. I wish to extend immense gratitude to my mentors in American studies at the University of New Mexico. Alyosha Goldstein provided endless insight and encouragement. Alex Lubin, Claudia Isaac, and Amy Brandzel also contributed countless rounds of thoughtful feedback on early drafts. I am grateful as well to my mentors, colleagues, and friends at UNM, Tulane University, and beyond, for their companionship and support. In particular, many thanks to Emily Skidmore, Kara McCormack, Jessica A. F. Harkins, Srdjan Smajić, Jake Kosek, Laura Gómez, Scott Morgensen, Bill Dewan, Gina Díaz, Rachel Levitt, Claire-Lise Bénaud, the late Ann Massmann, Karissa Haugeberg, Jana Lipman, Christina Juhasz-Wood, Carolyn McSherry, Emily Cammack, Marisa Potter, Sarah Wentzel-Fisher, Tita Berger, Annette Rodríguez, Heather Cooper, Sarah Montès, Sunanda Vaz, Amjad Ayoubi, Eric Gremillion, and Michael Zapata.

Research for this book was funded by the Office of Graduate Studies at the University of New Mexico. I also received funding for multiple conference presentations from the Department of American Studies, the American Studies Graduate Student Association, and the Graduate and Professional Student Association at UNM, as well as the American Studies Association, the National Women's Studies Association, and Tulane University's Academic Advising Center. Each of these opportunities to present portions of this work provided crucial insights and I thank my fellow panelists and those audience members who shared their thoughts.

An early section of chapter 3 was published in *MTV and Teen Pregnancy: Critical Essays on "16 and Pregnant" and "Teen Mom,"* edited by Letizia Guglielmo (Scarecrow Press, 2013), who provided valuable comments on it. A portion of chapter 2 was published in *Signs: Journal of Women in Culture and Society* (39:4), and I am grateful to Mary Hawkesworth, the editorial team, and anonymous reviewers for their feedback, as well as to the University of Chicago Press for permission to include this revised material.

At the University of Massachusetts Press, I wish to thank Brian Halley for his consistent support and guidance. I am also grateful to the editorial, production, and marketing teams, and to the anonymous reviewers for prodding me toward clearer stakes and bolder claims.

I would also like to thank Micaela Cadena from Young Women United, and Jinx Baskerville and Toni Berg from New Futures High School for meeting with me to discuss their important work with and on behalf of pregnant and parenting teens. Thank you also to Denicia Cadena and others at YWU, Strong Families, Forward Together, and #NoTeenShame for their activism and responsiveness to my inquiries.

Finally, thank you to my parents, Therese (1945–2013) and James Daniel, who enabled my education and research through multiple forms of support; to my sisters, Martine and Andrea, for being excellent role models and friends; and to their families for their love and delightful company. I am indebted to Katherine Minkin, Emily J. Serna, Lou Serna, Lucia Villela Minnerly Kracke, and the late Waud Kracke for their support. My deepest gratitude to Blake and Milo, who have made my life rich and bright in ways I never could have anticipated.

MEDIATING
MORALITY

INTRODUCTION
Preventing Equality

On May 21, 2013, a *Huffington Post* blogger praised billboard campaigns in Milwaukee and Chicago featuring boys with pregnant bellies and teen pregnancy prevention slogans.[1] One Chicago ad pictures a shirtless African American teenage boy with a bulging belly and the words "Unexpected? Most Teenage Pregnancies Are. Avoid unintended pregnancies and STIs. Use Condoms. Or Wait." A 2012 Milwaukee ad shows a pregnant, white, long-haired boy with the words "It should be no less disturbing when it's a girl."[2] The blogger, psychologist, and "parenting expert" Barbara Greenberg writes that these ads are part of an effort to "step out of the box to educate and warn teens" who are prone to getting bored when adults try to communicate with them.[3] She states that they aim to help boys realize that "teenage pregnancy is their responsibility too." The campaigns assume that teenage pregnancy results from teenagers' uninformed responses to their own naturally volatile state. They thus exemplify a surge within the 2000s and 2010s in teen pregnancy prevention that aims to capture teenagers' attention by finding ever more shocking and provocative ways to portray adolescent reproduction as universally unnatural, freakish, and personally dire.

These ads suggest that pregnant boys are deeply "disturbing" in their upheaval of gender and sex norms, suggesting not only that pregnancy is also a boy's responsibility, but that it fundamentally upends that boy's status as properly male and masculine. Liberal-democratic political theorists of the late nineteenth and early twentieth century equated an adolescent boy's lack of control over his sexual urges with a loss of manly virtue. Conversely, they viewed proper self-governing as a necessary precondition for political subjecthood.[4] In keeping with these notions and the corresponding long-standing fears within dominant U.S. culture around the existence and management of adolescent sexuality, these boys' protruding pregnant bellies signal the perverse effects of adolescent sex and reproduction on their development into healthy, male adults and citizens. They suggest that U.S. culture has dangerously normalized the visibly and physically disruptive effects teen pregnancy has on girls' lives, at the same time that the deep and invisible damage it does to American manhood is completely overlooked. As the Albuquerque-based Media Literacy Project points out, these ads also perpetuate "a culture of ignorance, prejudice, and violence around transgender people" by suggesting that the pregnant bodies of transgender boys and men are "disturbing."[5] Moreover, the ads lack any information about differential access to health care, education, and bodily security based on race, class, gender, and sexuality, which conditions the reproductive lives of teens.

These campaigns represent a broader change in the public image of teen pregnancy as a social problem since the dismantling of the U.S. welfare state in 1996. They—along with teen mom–centered television shows, sex education video games, celebrity-infused public service announcements, and more—signal a shift in the dominant methods of teen pregnancy prevention away from previous (if still existing) models of disciplinary welfare policies, school-based abstinence and sex education, and health care provision. These post-welfare prevention efforts mobilize the vocabulary and technologies of popular culture toward a project of social reform in which the regulation of adolescent sexuality appears as the key to individual and national well-being. This book contends that these strategies emerge out of and help consolidate a remaking of notions of citizenship, social welfare, and race in the United States. Specifically, it argues that post-welfare teen pregnancy prevention campaigns promote a politics of multicultural intimate citizenship in which an adolescent's private, sexual, and reproductive behaviors seemingly determine that individual's access to equality and well-being. As such, post-welfare teen pregnancy prevention efforts reinforce the punitive welfare reform policy of 1996 by shifting the discourse of teen pregnancy away from questions of poverty and welfare, thereby upholding the state's material disinvestment in social well-being and equality.

Teen Pregnancy: A Neoliberal Social Problem

Despite the overwhelming consensus around its problematic nature today, teen pregnancy has only been a locus of social reform in the United States since the mid-1970s. Concerns about unwed motherhood intersected with fears about the effects of "teen culture," premarital sex, and juvenile delinquency throughout the 1950s and 1960s.[6] However, it was not until an increased emphasis on education for young women and the rising age of marriage began to restructure the role of adolescent girls that age became a central focus, leading to the naming of a new social problem.[7] While teen pregnancy rates were at their all-time high in the 1950s, the proportion of those pregnancies that either occurred within the context of marriage or resulted in adoption was much higher.[8] Furthermore, other changes occurring throughout the 1960s and 1970s, such as more inclusive welfare eligibility requirements, the legalization of abortion and liberalization of birth control policy, and a longer route to self-sufficiency, contributed to increased concern about the timing of childbirth.[9] In the context of these broad social transformations, large-scale panic surrounding "teen pregnancy" emerged in the United States in the mid-1970s, and soon solidified "children having children" as an issue of national urgency.[10] Adolescent procreative sex was framed as deeply troubling the division between child and adult—thrusting children into premature adulthood and dependency on government assistance rather than parental support—while fueling the discourses of sexual and cultural pathology already central to the racialization of poor people of color.

Teen parenthood has been associated with, if not fully blamed for, a host of other heavily racialized social problems throughout the 1980s, 1990s, and the beginning of the twenty-first century, including poverty, inner-city crime, juvenile delinquency, drug use, poor maternal and child health outcomes, and high school dropout rates. The sociologist Kristin Luker and many others have illustrated that causal connections between adolescent reproduction and the social ills it ostensibly precipitates and exacerbates are tentative at best.[11] Rather than producing such problems, these scholars argue, teenage reproduction actually indexes the social inequalities that result from structural factors, such as the labor market, educational policy, and the social welfare system. This reality begs the question of why teen pregnancy continues to be such a salient social issue, rallying both liberal and conservative politicians, nonprofit advocates, and the popular culture industry, despite ample evidence that it does not beget the nation's problems. In their examination of the social factors involved in the occurrence of adolescent pregnancy, the sociologists Mary Patrice Erdmans and Timothy Black suggest that our tendency within public policy and advocacy to define teen mothers "*as a problem* distracts us from the larger social problems that wreak havoc in the lives of these young women."[12] More than just obscuring structural forces in the lives of pregnant and parenting teens, the problematization of teen pregnancy has been a crucial technology of discipline and dispossession in the United States.

In order to understand how teen pregnancy became and remains such a visible target of public and private concern, it is useful to position its emergence as a social problem within the ascendance of the cultural, political, and economic project of neoliberalism. Neoliberalism is a worldview and governing logic that came to prominence in the United States and Great Britain in the late 1970s and continues to this day. Broadly, neoliberal policies promote economic and political landscapes favoring private corporate interests and self-owning entrepreneurial individuals. They do this at the expense of public expenditure and infrastructure for broad-based social welfare and equality.[13] Neoliberal cultural discourses that guide and support such policies forward individual over collective responsibility and uphold intimate behaviors rather than public acts as the defining realm of citizenship.[14] As many scholars of welfare reform, such as Gwendolyn Mink, Jamie Peck, and Anna Marie Smith, point out, neoliberal social and economic philosophy views the well-being of disadvantaged populations as the responsibility of those individuals and families who have produced their own misfortune by falling into unhealthy patterns and mismanaging their lives.[15] Part of a larger ethos of scaling back government spending and elevating "free market" principles, proponents of welfare reform held that social inequalities were best solved through the infusion of personal responsibility, rather than material resources, into impoverished communities, as these communities purportedly suffered from individual and familial problems, rather than structural societal ones. Teen pregnancy and parenthood—epitomizing the pathological nature of poor people and representing the misguided values and poor choices that substantive government support could produce—were central rhetorical figures in the bipartisan neoliberal project of "end[ing] welfare as we know it."[16]

When the Personal Responsibility and Work Opportunity Reconciliation Act (PRWORA) passed into law in the summer of 1996, it ended the sixty-year-old entitlements-based U.S. welfare state and replaced it with a workfare regime in which public relief became contingent on recipients' participation in preapproved work-related activities. As Jamie Peck argues, the PRWORA instituted "new codes of conduct for those on the edges of the labor market."[17]

Dismantling the federal welfare bureaucracy, the law funds varying state workfare programs through block grants, while guiding them heavily with neoliberal market rationality. The federal government's use of monetary incentives and disincentives operates on states and recipients alike to elicit numerical outcomes and normative behavior. Gwendolyn Mink explains the effects of this new federalism in these terms: "A state *must* do certain things in exchange for its block grant. It also must *not* do certain things even if local majorities want to. A state cannot offer assistance on more generous or more equitable terms than are stipulated in the [PRWORA]."[18]

Some of the guidelines with which states must comply include strict lifetime limits on assistance, aggressive work requirements, and the profuse application of sanctions to penalize noncompliant recipients. States can opt to implement other regulatory initiatives that tend to enhance their numerical outcomes and increase their chances of improved funding. These include certain child support enforcement measures as well as the punitive "family cap" rule.[19] Widely recognized by scholars of welfare as a policy that increases the material instability and bodily vulnerability of the poorest and most marginalized members of society, the PRWORA helps to produce, manage, and maintain a highly flexible, deeply low-wage labor force made up of a population effectively deemed disposable through demonizing and pathologizing cultural and political discourses. It worked in coordination with other policies passed that same year, such as immigration reform, adoption reform, and the Defense of Marriage Act, to carry out the neoliberal agenda of withdrawing state support from the poor while enforcing the norms of the white, middle-class, heterosexual, consumeristic, nuclear family.[20]

This approach to poverty and welfare rests on a notion of citizenship defined by the personal, private, and familial. As scholars of neoliberal citizenship such as Lisa Duggan, Lauren Berlant, and Aihwa Ong argue, a new form of ideal citizenship emerged in the latter half of the twentieth century, solidifying in the 1970s and 1980s, that envisions proper civic behavior through individual responsibility, entrepreneurship, and heteronormative domesticity.[21] According to Lauren Berlant, this privatized, intimate citizenship promotes racial, gender, class, and sexual norms emblematized throughout the 1980s and 1990s by the figures of the young white girl and the fetus.[22] She argues that the ideal citizen becomes an innocent, vulnerable, trusting subject of state protection, rather than an active, informed participant in policy-making and state action. As such, national culture portrays ideal adult citizens as infantile, while children remain a monolithic category of innocence and corruptibility endangered by threatening adults, and public action appears either menacing or idiotic.

The category of adolescence, marking the transition between child and adult, as well as nascent and full citizen, requires examination for its role in neoliberal discourses of intimate citizenship. In his seminal study of the modern family form in bourgeois European society during the seventeenth, eighteenth, and nineteenth centuries, the historian Philippe Ariès traces a transformation in understandings of childhood.[23] He shows how the modern division between child and adult, nonexistent in the ancien régime, formed gradually as part of a middle-class ethic resulting from the emergence of education reform, the importance of privacy, and the development of fields like child psychology and health and hygiene. As the historian Lawrence Stone explains, sixteenth-century British society treated children with relative indifference and formality because of high infant mortality rates and common practices such as sending upper-class youths to wet nurses and boarding schools and middle- and lower-class ones into domestic servitude.[24] Whereas previously young people had been viewed as small adults, they began in the seventeenth and eighteenth centuries to be imbued with a "special nature"[25] and the modern family became centered on the nurturing and protecting of innocent, adored, corruptible children.

The concept of adolescence, resulting from the notion of "long childhood" in which older young people were to be schooled in discipline and morality, solidified in the eighteenth and nineteenth centuries, including at first only boys of the middle and wealthy classes and gradually extending to girls and the poor.[26] These older children came to embody an important transitional period in the production of adult citizens in that they continue to possess a "special nature," by definition, but are in training as adults. As the education scholar Nancy Lesko and the political scientist Claire Rasmussen point out, the construct of adolescence was forged in the context of European colonialism.[27] It formed an integral part of the parallel theorizations of modern civilization and full political subjecthood. While adolescence marked the transitional period between childhood and adulthood, in which individuals must learn proper control over bodily urges, colonizers also used it to characterize colonized people as immature and in need of training for self-governance. Lesko writes that within scientific thought in the late nineteenth and early twentieth centuries, "Adolescence was singled out as a crucial point at which an individual (and a race) leaped to a developed, superior, Western selfhood or remained in a savage state."[28] In this context, a colonized people's relatively early engagement in sexual activity evidenced its backwardness, while the disciplined chastity of idealized white adolescents prepared them for departure from the innocence of childhood and into public political participation. As this book argues, the category of adolescence continues to bear out its colonial legacy within the post-welfare politics of the teen pregnancy.

Historically, the separation between children and adults has informed a great deal of social policy and exclusion in the United States. The American Studies scholar Molly Ladd-Taylor and the historian Sonya Michel have each illustrated the ways that transformations in notions of childhood generated social reform and state policy regulating motherhood.[29] Concern for the well-being and proper rearing of children fueled campaigns for the development of institutionalized child care programs at the turn of the eighteenth century, Mother's Pensions in the Progressive Era, and Aid to Dependent Children in 1935. The movements that occasioned these reforms drew on notions of proper childhood and motherhood that excluded and regulated families based on race, class, gender, and sexuality. In the post–World War II era, anxieties about the effects of unwed motherhood on children and society fueled research in the social sciences that psychologized and pathologized single mothers and their families.[30] At the same time, with the development for the first time of "teenagers" as a target market for consumption of goods and popular culture, fears swelled about the effects of television, film, and youth culture on the proper development (sexual and otherwise) of adolescents.[31] These concerns led to new racially differentiated approaches to unwed motherhood, as well as new attempts at censoring and manipulating the mass media in order to curb adolescent sex and delinquency and cultivate desired familial forms and citizenship conduct.[32]

The problem of teen pregnancy in its various constructions has long registered concerns with the perils of child sexuality. The desexualization inherent in the modern category of "children," as queer theorists and others point out, serves to prop up heteronormativity, fuel sex panics, and sustain sexuality-based persecution.[33] The literary scholar James Kincaid argues that the figure of the "child" is imbued with innocence and purity, and as such, actually calls forth its opposite—corruption and eroticism—thus always referencing a forbidden desire that must be shunned and Othered.[34] Similarly, the childhood studies scholar Kerry H. Robinson argues that children inhabit a form of "difficult citizenship," characterized by extreme regulation and exclusion from rights, in which their apparent innocence in opposition to sexuality results in widespread efforts to "deny their relevance and access to sexual citizenship."[35] Kincaid's and Robinson's analyses of childhood help to explain how teen parents, whose sexuality as children is apparent, have become one of the most widely scrutinized and demonized groups of young people.

As the American studies scholar Julie Passanante Elman argues in her examination of the emergence of "rehabilitative edutainment" aimed at adolescents in the 1970s, teenagers have come to inhabit a fraught position in which the biological narrative of their development paints them as "inevitably sexual," despite their apparently neurological deficiencies.[36] In the wake of the sexual liberation and feminist movements of the 1960s, she explains, the teenager became a figure "whose proper acquisition of self-discipline and 'healthy' sexual development was imagined as particularly crucial to the nation's future."[37] Pregnant and parenting teens thus represent a specific form of difficult citizenship that threatens the health of the nation. In her work on globalization and constructions of childhood, the critical theorist Sue Ruddick discusses youth classified as "juvenile delinquents" who are increasingly tried as adults. Similarly, teen parents become exceptional through their deviant actions; they are attributed adult responsibility without the rights and privileges that adulthood supplies.[38]

Rhetoric surrounding teen pregnancy during welfare reform debates of the 1980s and 1990s mobilized fears about children's too-early sex and corruption, foregrounded adolescence as the volatile transition into adult citizenship, and provided a salient, personal explanation for racialized poverty and social disorder. As such, it rested on and helped to impose intimate, rather than public, forms of citizenship. The widespread denigration of impoverished mothers' choices and behavior during welfare reform debate contributed to the devaluing of their participation in public discourse.[39] Moreover, the increased instability of welfare recipients' lives that results from the PRWORA renders them less able to find the time and resources to participate in public political debate. By extension, impoverished pregnant and parenting teens have been triply excluded from public forms of citizenship. They contend with the stigma of welfare, based on a logic of poor choices and irresponsibility; the material results of a policy that restricts their time and resources for democratic participation; and the assumption that, due to their age, they qualify for neither parenthood nor the self-governance that full citizenship rights and democratic participation requires.

While specific personal and sexual behaviors have defined U.S. citizenship since its inception, pregnant and parenting teens provide a powerful representation of the neoliberal logic of intimate citizenship in which personal choices and behaviors come to eclipse all other expressions of citizenship.[40] Pregnant and parenting teens figure the demise of nascent citizens via premature sex and reproduction. They are viewed as ruined for proper citizenship, never initiated into it because of their failure to behave as innocent, asexual children protected by the nation, or as properly self-governing adults-in-training. In the 1980s and 1990s, ostensibly race-neutral narratives about cycles of teen pregnancy within crime-stricken, inner-city communities of poverty worked within welfare reform debate to help enforce and manage deepening social stratification while discursively and materially undermining agendas for racial, gender, and class equality.[41] If neoliberalism is at least in part, as the geographer David Harvey argues, a project for the "restoration and consolidation of class power," then the politics of teen pregnancy within welfare reform debate was a particularly effective mechanism of neoliberal social and economic policy.[42]

According to its express purpose of decreasing poverty by promoting work, decreasing dependence on public assistance, decreasing out-of-wedlock and teen pregnancy, and promoting marriage, welfare reform has plainly failed. While poverty rates have fluctuated some since 1996, the number of families living in "extreme poverty" has increased substantially. The only outcome in terms of poverty, pregnancy, and marriage directly attributable to the PRWORA is the much larger percentage of poor families who are not receiving welfare under the new law.[43] Temporary Assistance to Needy Families (TANF)—the program created by the PRWORA, which replaced Aid to Families with Dependent Children (AFDC)—can easily be said to have worsened the situation of poor families in the United States.[44] The policy went into effect during a period of economic prosperity that facilitated the churning of people on and off the welfare rolls and into flexible low-wage jobs. However, the economic downturn beginning in 2007 revealed the true shortcomings of TANF as a poverty alleviator. As experts have argued, most states—in large part because of federal regulations—designed TANF programs that could not effectively adjust to the rising unemployment and poverty rates that resulted from the Great Recession.[45] Welfare reform has not only fully abandoned those with the deepest disadvantages—compounded physical, mental, educational, and familial barriers to employment—since its initiation; it also helps to establish a broader and more visible "disconnected" subset of the population.[46]

Likewise, TANF's record of accomplishment on teen pregnancy and parenthood is also poor. Special provisions for teen parents on TANF include specific housing and school requirements meant to discipline parenting teens, prevent subsequent births, and discourage teen pregnancy at large.[47] According to a 2002 survey done by the Center for Law and Social Policy, most TANF programs over-sanction and underserve teen parents.[48] Although teen pregnancy rates have decreased overall since welfare reform, this trend does not appear to result from TANF. A 2004 study by the sociologists Lingxin Hao and Andrew J. Cherlin shows that welfare reform did not decrease teenage fertility rates or high school dropout rates during the years following its passage. Rather, they suggest, TANF programs may slightly increase the likelihood of adolescent pregnancy and high school dropout for teenagers in households receiving TANF.[49] The PRWORA and TANF reauthorization bills included funding for abstinence-only education and comprehensive sex education, as well as a requirement that states spend their own TANF maintenance of effort (MOE) funds on projects that carry out the TANF objectives, including the prevention and reduction of out-of-wedlock pregnancies.[50] Many studies of the effects of welfare reform programs on teen pregnancy show little or no direct effect on the rates, which were falling already for years before 1996.[51]

In this context, with research showing that teen pregnancy is not a causal factor in poverty and that welfare reform continues to fail in achieving its stated goals, it would seem that a serious reevaluation of workfare and teen pregnancy prevention is in order. However, such has not occurred. In fact, the legislature has reauthorized TANF numerous times with only minor revisions since its passage, while teen pregnancy generates increasing attention as social concern. This book asks why this is the case and how neoliberal welfare reform and the politics of teen pregnancy prevention continue to be mutually reinforcing projects.

I argue that, in the post-welfare context, political and popular culture have reformulated the public image of teen pregnancy to extend the project of neoliberalism, further displacing national discussions around structural inequalities and publicly ensured collective well-being. I show how national legislative, popular culture, and advocacy discourses cleanse teen pregnancy of its former heavily race- and class-based associations to make way for the emergence of a multicultural politics of teen pregnancy within the logic of intimate citizenship. Policy makers and pundits once held the supposedly pathological culture of poverty (spurred on by perverse welfare incentives) as the breeding ground for a dysfunctional, self-perpetuating cycle of teen preg-nancy and fatherlessness. They argued that this cycle led to juvenile sex, drug use, crime, high school dropouts, and national social and economic decline. In the post-welfare era, dominant teen pregnancy prevention policy and discourse present it primarily as an issue of sexual irresponsibility that can turn any normal teenager into a social disgrace, underachiever, and failed citizen—thus upending the acquisitive self-owning individual at the center of a properly neoliberal society.

My discussion of neoliberal multiculturalism in the context of teen preg-nancy prevention draws primarily on the literary scholar Jodi Melamed's for-mulation of it in her book *Represent and Destroy*. Charting the production of neoliberal multiculturalism as an "official antiracism" of the 2000s, Melamed argues that it serves as a form of rationalization for the continuance of racial capitalism.[52] She differentiates this official antiracist framework from the earlier "liberal multiculturalism" of the 1980s and 1990s, stating that the latter emphasized a type of cultural recognition that helped legitimize U.S. global capitalist leadership through the projection of the United States as a bastion of racial equality.[53] Rather than bolstering the U.S. nation-state, she argues, neoliberal multiculturalism responds to the weakening of national governments that results from neoliberal capitalism. It does this by valoriz-ing certain forms of global citizenship within an assumed post-racial global society governed by inherently multicultural markets. She writes, "Neoliberal policy has engendered new racial subjects while creating and distinguishing between newly privileged and stigmatized collectivities, yet multiculturalism has coded the wealth, mobility, and political power of neoliberalism's benefi-ciaries as the just desserts of multicultural global citizens while representing those neoliberalism has dispossessed as handicapped by their own monocul-turalism or historico-cultural deficiencies."[54] Many scholars have described the multicultural discourses of the 1980s and 1990s as depoliticizing race and facilitating the corporate management of diversity.[55] By extending her anal-ysis to the newest regime of official antiracism, Melamed illuminates how neoliberal multiculturalism of the 2000s presents neoliberal capitalism itself as inherently multicultural.[56]

As the following chapters illustrate, post-welfare teen pregnancy preven-tion upholds certain forms of consumerism, privatization, sex, and family as valid, enlightened, and universally accessible, while racializing adoles-cent pregnancy and parenthood as pathological, backward, and cyclical. At the same time that teen pregnancy prevention efforts portray the negative consequences of inappropriate sex and reproduction almost entirely in personal and emotional terms—and therefore not directly economic—they forward proper sexual, consumer, and entrepreneurial behavior as the mechanisms of success and happiness. As Melamed suggests, "Neoliberal multiculturalism is the apotheosis of liberal-antiracist discourses, which have valorized specific economic arrangements."[57] Racial difference, such as that represented in post-welfare teen pregnancy prevention, signals the apparent antiracist nature of markets. Good moral behavior enables the effective navigation of such markets, while too-early pregnancy precludes it. If adolescence was once a colonial technology of racialization that differentiated white civilization from backward nonwhite others, it works within the politics of teen pregnancy to enact new forms of racialization that map across traditional racial categories, painting sexual and reproductive teens as modern savages who willingly forgo the liberating powers of the prevailing neoliberal order.

Teen pregnancy prevention in the post-welfare era constructs neoliberal capitalism as the ultimate inclusionary force, while eliding the racialized, exploitable labor force that remains crucial to capital accumulation and was secured by welfare reform (made possible in part through a previous pathologization and racialization of teen pregnancy). As I show through an analysis of coordinated teen pregnancy prevention efforts within federal policy, popular culture, national advocacy, and local initiatives, this new multicultural politics of teen pregnancy normalizes the notion that the privatized cultivation of proper adolescent sexuality and consumption can secure social well-being. This formulation ignores and discounts the potential role of publicly funded and distributed material supports for underprivileged sectors of the population. *Mediating Morality* thus reveals the importance of adolescent sexuality and reproduction to the discourses and policy structures that promote a neoliberal redefinition of the rights, responsibilities, and privileges of U.S. citizenship, and uphold the processes of deepening social inequality under racial capitalism.

The Privatized Public: Entrepreneurial Pregnancy Prevention

Neoliberal discourse hinges on specific definitions of "public" and "private" that obscure the complex relationships between these two co-constitutive realms. Espousers of neoliberalism view the government and its public works purely as tools for the protection and cultivation of private enterprise. While the public/private divide is a defining aspect of liberalism, the neoliberal view of the role of the public sector differs from Progressive Era and New Deal liberalisms. It does so by emphasizing the primacy of entrepreneurial individuals, markets, and market logic, rather than upholding the importance of sustaining a baseline level of public well-being through state laws, programs, and services in order to facilitate broad participation in regulated markets.[58] This emphasis on "markets" versus "government" denies the reality that capitalist economic formations have, from their onset, necessitated and engendered political and social organization in order to exist and persist.[59] Of course, global, federal, state, and local governments more or less determine the economic policy, physical infrastructure, human rights legislation, labor laws, and other frameworks that condition individuals' and corporations' existence and activities. However, neoliberal discourse portrays an inefficient, wasteful, cumbersome government through a specific subset of public works—those aspects that (1) enable the well-being of underprivileged populations by redistributing wealth and resources through taxation and welfare, and (2) regulate industries for the protection of humans and the nonhuman surroundings that sustain them. This discourse ignores the various aspects of historical and contemporary public policies and structures that instantiate class privilege, systemic racism, and other forms of social inequality in the name of deregulation and supporting private enterprise.[60]

In this context, neoliberal "privatization" refers to the specific trend of transferring previously public responsibilities over to private enterprises to manage and execute. This process often occurs through the creation of government contracts to private industries or through the complete or partial termination of a government program or service, leaving concerned citizens and private organizations to address the consequent void without any government support. One could argue that the application of principles, technologies, and strategies of private markets to publicly funded and implemented projects, which frequently involves the funneling of public funds into and through private channels, is also a form of privatization. Governments nominally carry out these processes to allow the efficiency and equilibrating capacities of market forces or market logic to prevail, to lessen the burden of taxation on successful entrepreneurial citizens, and to cultivate responsibility and initiative in those plagued by a bureaucratic mentality or general laziness.

Neoliberal retrenchment and privatization of welfare has not necessarily decreased public monetary expenditure or the government's role in market regulation. For instance, the economists Therese J. McGuire and David F. Merriman argue that social spending by states since welfare reform has not decreased, but rather spending on programs such as the Earned Income Tax Credit, Supplemental Security Income, food stamps, and Medicaid have increased.[61] As the political economist Bob Jessop observes, "while the Keynesian welfare forms of intervention may have been rolled back, privatization, deregulation and liberalization have also been seen to require new or enhanced forms of regulation, reregulation and competition policy."[62] The primary accomplishment of welfare retrenchment and privatization, as is apparent in the example of teen pregnancy prevention, has been to redirect the flows, beneficiaries, and targets of public funds and policies.

Moreover, privatization is a central method through which neoliberalism naturalizes and promotes specific sexual, familial, and economic arrangements. Some scholars have rightly argued that neoliberalism and neoconservatism are separate but overlapping projects.[63] However, neoliberalism is not just a political-economic rationale. It is also, as is evident within scholarship on neoliberal citizenship, a cultural and moral one that hinges on the norms of the white, middle-class, heteronormative, nuclear family. As Lisa Duggan points out, these cultural politics often appear within appeals to "personal responsibility" as the solution to social problems.[64] Neoliberal social policy, such as the PRWORA, uses the logic of privatization via personal responsibility to shift the costs of social reproduction onto the individual, while punishing nonnormative familial arrangements, and upwardly redistributing wealth.

In the years leading up to welfare reform, politicians, social scientists, and other experts understood teen pregnancy primarily through the lenses of poverty, welfare, and reproductive health. They thus aimed to manage it through public policy relating to health, welfare, and education. While such policies continue to affect adolescents' reproductive lives, the most prominent aspects of post-welfare teen pregnancy prevention result from the logic of neoliberal privatization and are often nongovernmental. This privatized teen pregnancy prevention emerges out of the politics of welfare reform, utilizes public and private funds, engages nonprofit and for-profit entities, and relies on market rationality. In order to examine thoroughly the post-welfare politics of teen pregnancy, this book must straddle sites of analysis located within two intertwined zones: privatized public action—federal and state legislation, political debate, and social programs—and the very public private sphere—popular television and film, internet-based advocacy, and local nonprofit work.

The neoliberal emphases on privatization and market rationality designate popular culture and privatized media technologies as crucial mechanisms of social reform. Accordingly, teenagers appear as primary targets of such strategies due to their apparent interests in trends and proclivities toward new media. Moreover, within a multicultural logic of intimate citizenship, teenagers' purportedly natural capacity for wanton consumption and risk-taking behavior defines their rightful expression of citizenship. However, these tendencies threaten to result in pathological sexuality and subsequent too-early pregnancy and parenting, which would in turn curb the reckless abandon that characterizes normal adolescence. The post-welfare politics of teen pregnancy holds that rather than publicly funded support for health and education, the problem requires that teens cultivate their concern with consuming and conforming. Their well-being lies in their ability to purchase the latest trendy goods and participate in the requisite extracurricular activities as practice for their future as "normal" adult citizens and parents. Sex, pregnancy, and parenthood during adolescence, according to dominant prevention discourse, foreclose those opportunities because offspring drain disposable income and leisure time, reorder teens' priorities, and limit the ultimate entrepreneurial and consuming potential of the individual. In this formulation, public well-being does not hinge on access to nutrition, health care, shelter, and other basic needs, but instead appears as a measurement of an individual's ability to participate in equilibrating markets that naturally set the standards of normality, health, and happiness. In this way, teen sexuality forms a most fitting target for the intertwining neoliberal goals of multicultural intimate citizenship, privatization, and welfare retrenchment.

In the following chapters, I utilize historical, discursive, and visual analysis to examine four intertwined arenas—policy debate, popular culture, national advocacy, and local nonprofit work—in which meaning is created, strategies are determined, and action is carried out in relation to teen pregnancy. I assume a complex relationship among these arenas and remain particularly concerned with the newly constructed linkages that are consequences of neoliberal privatization. Past policies and other public conversations influence the field of discourse in which policymakers produce legislation. Similarly, popular culture produces mass-mediated discourses that affect and are affected by political debate, public policy, and advocacy. In the case of teen pregnancy, publicly funded local and national advocacy organizations produce popular culture texts and social media technologies to carry out their prevention missions. These partnerships illustrate how post-welfare teen pregnancy prevention tactics reflect the tenets of neoliberalism and represent a new horizon of neoliberal social reform. At the same time, the disjunctures between national advocacy organizations like the National Campaign to Prevent Teen and Unplanned Pregnancy and the popular texts they promote, such as MTV's *16 and Pregnant,* reveal crucial excesses and pitfalls of these neoliberal strategies. As certain forms of grassroots activism around rights for pregnant and parenting teens gain increasing ground in the battle over representations of and approaches to teen pregnancy, they challenge—but sometimes also converge with—the multicultural politics of intimate citizenship propagated through prevention regimes.

The post-welfare politics of teen pregnancy prevention was born out welfare reform. Thus, in chapter 1, I analyze the legislative debate and political news surrounding welfare reform and teen pregnancy throughout the 1990s and first decade of the 2000s. Examining the shifting national political discourse and federal policy regimes relating to teenage pregnancy within the last two decades, I show how claims about the effects of social structures and inequalities on reproductive behavior gave way to a focus on sex and pregnancy resulting solely from individual choices.

Welfare reform policy of 1996 was accompanied by a new nongovernmental approach to teen pregnancy. In chapter 2, I analyze the work of two organizations that epitomize this approach: the National Campaign to Prevent Teen and Unplanned Pregnancy and the Candie's Foundation. These organizations' social media–based teen pregnancy prevention work helps to publicly redefine the social "safety net" through a vision of citizens distributing vital, attractively packaged information about proper sexual and reproductive behavior among themselves via a privatized cyber-network.

Along with these social media strategies, a surge of prevention-oriented television programming beginning in 2008 and 2009 provides an important example of the so-called innovative prevention tactics encouraged in post-welfare political discourse and carried out by the National Campaign. In chapter 3, I investigate representations of teenage pregnancy within popular culture texts that explicitly claim a prevention agenda. In accordance with the shift in political and advocacy discourse, these television texts forward a multicultural politics of teen pregnancy in which pregnancy appears equally damaging to all teenage girls, regardless of race or class. They comprise the most far-reaching aspect of the post-welfare biopolitics of teen pregnancy, which targets all adolescents in a heteronormative campaign that both complements and obscures the workings of welfare reform.

To convey the complex ways that everyday realities reflect, challenge, and exceed national narratives, I also examine teenage pregnancy prevention at the state and local levels. In chapter 4, I focus my analysis on the politics of teen pregnancy and parenthood in the particular context of New Mexico, a state with one of the highest rates of teenage pregnancy in the nation. I trace differing discourses of neoliberal multiculturalism, racial pathologization, and reproductive justice as they overlap and diverge within the politics of teen pregnancy.

In the conclusion, I take a brief look at former New York City mayor Michael Bloomberg's 2013 teen pregnancy prevention poster and text message campaign and the grassroots responses to it. I discuss the implications of the post-welfare politics of teen pregnancy within the shifting contours of neoliberal social politics and for pregnant and parenting youth in this era. Many scholars and pundits interpret teen pregnancy as an issue primarily about conservative crusades to prevent premarital sex and abortion, liberal championing of contraception and sexual liberation, or a corporate drive to reap profits from scandalous sex and scintillating dysfunction. While all of these elements are certainly at play, the coordinated use of reality television, social media, posters, billboards, text message campaigns, and community-based programs is better understood as generative of a new horizon of neoliberal material disinvestment in social equality and well-being.

Even as Chicago's and Milwaukee's apparently freakish pregnant boys provide a visual attempt at a gender-blind politics of teen pregnancy—one that in fact reifies normative gender categories—it is primarily the real and living impoverished young mothers and their families who bear the brunt of the "problem" of teen pregnancy and the neoliberal social and economic agenda that it serves. In this context, we must look to the transformational grassroots feminist activism in New Mexico, New York, and across the nation. Such work foregrounds a robust model of reproductive justice, developed by feminists of color in the 1990s, which contextualizes sexual and reproductive behavior within social, political, economic, environmental, and cultural factors.[65] This activism advances the notion that everyone needs and deserves substantive access to quality health care, education, a living wage, housing, child care, bodily safety, and a clean environment. Rather than casting judgment on certain sexual and reproductive behaviors and working to thwart them, the framework of reproductive justice aims to create the conditions under which every person has the resources, knowledge, and tools to manage her own sexual and reproductive life. It is my hope that this book will aid such work by prompting us to question critically whether teen pregnancy prevention is indeed an appropriate goal, or if it has only ever primarily served the goals of neoliberalism.

1

Making the Political Personal

Teenage Pregnancy and Policy Discourse

In May 2010, National Public Radio ran a story about a woman whose boyfriend stole her birth control pills, regularly locked her in a room all day, raped and physically abused her, and then, when she became pregnant, threatened the fetus with violence and abandonment. The story, "The Nation: When Teen Pregnancy Is No Accident," focuses on new studies that suggest partner violence to be a significant factor in the occurrence of adolescent pregnancy. Discussing "reproductive coercion," as well as "pregnancy ambivalence," or the frame of mind in which girls and women claim not to want a pregnancy, but do nothing to prevent it, the story proposes that new research into the relationship and personal dynamics of sexually active teenage girls may open doors for more effective ways of preventing teen pregnancy. Quoting advocates for comprehensive sex education who argue that curriculum about healthy relationships must be included in prevention efforts, NPR notes that President Obama had recently allocated $25 million for "research and testing of innovative new approaches" to teen pregnancy prevention. The head of the National Campaign to Prevent Teen and Unplanned Pregnancy, Sarah Brown, is then quoted as lauding the new focus on "the interpersonal complexities of unintended pregnancy."[1] The political problem of teen pregnancy has transformed from one defined in the 1980s and 1990s through a complex combination of economic, political, and personal factors within impoverished communities, to an issue understood in the 2000s and early 2010s as resulting from the interpersonal deficits of average sexually active teenagers.

While politicians and pundits continue to tout teen pregnancy as a chief domestic political concern, the shape of that concern has shifted with the trajectory of neoliberal governance. Welfare reform itself is a prime example of neoliberal social policy based on the tenets of privatization and personal responsibility, resulting in the scaling back of social supports to the poor and the flexibilization of low-wage labor. The post-welfare discourse of teen pregnancy, however, marks a new horizon of neoliberal social politics by reshaping the debate to further support the goals of welfare retrenchment without explicitly engaging with the question of welfare. The post-welfare politics of teen pregnancy proposes that the proper management of adolescent sexual and reproductive behavior secures the production of successful adult American citizens. This framework is grounded in a politics of neoliberal multiculturalism, which, as Jodi Melamed argues, presents capitalist markets as the arbiters of equality, and moral fortitude as the backbone of entrepreneurial spirit.[2] Such a framework thus renders unintelligible all structural forces that shape reproductive politics, such as economic structure, institutional racism, and heteronormativity.

In welfare reform debate of the 1980s and 1990s, the racially coded, class-centered language of teen pregnancy prevention, while perpetuating racist stereotypes and policy, also allowed for the possibility of understanding difference as socially produced rather than natural. The post-welfare formulation, on the other hand, forecloses that opportunity by denying any difference whatsoever and portraying teen pregnancy as a solely personal moral issue. As such, it furthers the neoliberal logic of intimate citizenship in which successful Americanness appears attainable only through a citizen's proper navigation of personal and intimate relations to achieve the characteristics associated with whiteness, marriage, and entrepreneurial prowess. This new understanding brings new disciplinary tactics, involving policy that is less punitive, but with more emphasis on a comprehensive campaign of moral indoctrination, and only a mild increase in resources that enable reproductive freedom. In conjunction with these new approaches, we see the silent preservation of punitive workfare policy and an ongoing public disinvestment in material well-being and reproductive justice. These political transformations lay the groundwork for contemporary teen pregnancy prevention advocates to present popular and social media as the new frontier of effective prevention.

The 1990s: A Cycle of Babies Having Babies

According to welfare reform debate of the mid-1990s, teen pregnancy was a central causal factor in a wide swath of societal ills. In a 1993 *New York*

Times article on a proposed Republican welfare reform bill, Newt Gingrich is quoted as saying, "You can't maintain civilization with 12-year-olds having babies and 15-year-olds killing each other and 17-year-olds dying of AIDS."[3] Aiming to justify the strict work requirements placed on welfare recipients within the proposed legislation, Gingrich suggests that impoverished teenagers would cause the demise of American society. He presents teen (or, in this case, preteen) pregnancy as the first in a series of implicitly connected deviant behaviors. Similarly, in 1995, one year before the passage of the federal welfare reform legislation, Bill Clinton named teen pregnancy and out-of-wedlock births as America's "most serious social problem" in his State of the Union Address.[4]

Teenage pregnancy was a defining and mobilizing issue within welfare reform debate. In the arena of national political debate during the 1990s, teenage pregnancy appeared almost exclusively within discussions of welfare, specifically the purportedly perverse incentives of Aid to Families with Dependent Children (AFDC) and the necessary disciplinary elements of its impending replacement, Temporary Assistance to Needy Families (TANF). Within these discussions, as the political scientist Holloway Sparks notes, politicians across the mainstream political spectrum described the problem of teen pregnancy by pairing it with statistics about African Americans and drawing on racialized imagery of drugs, welfare dependency, school dropouts, delinquency, and unemployment.[5] This racialized discourse built on denigrating stereotypes of black motherhood that have developed over centuries, most recently through social science research and media portrayals.[6] The rhetorician Jenna Vinson analyzes visual representations of teen pregnancy in the early 1970s, showing how images of lone pregnant white girls were used to universalize the issue of teen pregnancy—helping to generate support for increased access to reproductive health services—while images of black teenage mothers with multiple children helped produce concern about the birthrates of poor communities of color.[7] By the early 1990s, teen pregnancy had become a crucial element of welfare reform rhetoric that reflected and generated anxiety about the nation's future by indexing a host of other social ills associated with economic demise and racial upheaval.

Important to the overall construction of teenage pregnancy within national political debate of this period is the positioning of adolescents as volatile nascent citizens. Queer theorists have pointed to the ways that the construction of children as innocent, nonsexual, and in need of protection has fueled multiple moral panics and punitive policy measures.[8] Lauren Berlant argues that the innocent child, endangered by bad parenting and damaged adults, was a powerful figure in national culture of the 1990s, helping to underwrite neoliberal reforms that narrowed definitions of citizenship and further entrenched and protected heteronormativity.[9] Through an analysis of multiple cultural texts, she shows that proper behavior in the "private" domains of life was forwarded as the gateway to state nurturance and protection, as well as to the national future, while public political engagement that framed the nation-state as complex and alterable was demonized as reckless, misguided, self-indulgent, and unpatriotic. As actual state programs and services were being contracted, she suggests, sentimental and patriotic identification with the nation through its increasingly policed norms of intimacy became the primary avenue through which U.S. citizenship was popularly envisioned. Mass-mediated rhetoric accomplished this by revising and replacing fraught national histories with monolithic figures of pure, "virtual" citizens, such as the innocent girl and the American fetus. These figures appeared in need of protection from dangerous adults, such as sex workers, irresponsible parents, and corrupt politicians. These discourses, she argues, served ultimately to underwrite the enforcement of norms that regulate the behavior of actual citizens, perpetuating and deepening the contradictions between the abstract, disembodied notion of liberal citizenship that guides the logic of the nation-state and the embodied experiences of subjugation that this notion helps to carry out.

These insights are useful for understanding the discourse of teen pregnancy during this same period and the role this discourse played in justifying punitive welfare reform. In the context of discussions about teen pregnancy, children represent America's future, requiring protection but also discipline and guidance to help them make choices that will usher them into full adult self-governance, economic and familial responsibility, and appropriate democratic participation. In contrast to the innocent girl and American fetus of Berlant's analysis, teenagers are themselves capable of transgression and thus demand particular forms of discipline and vigilance.

In a 1996 speech, First Lady Hillary Clinton argues that citizens " 'have to do what we can to cut the rate of teen pregnancy and out-of-wedlock births' by developing programs at home and in the schools to help children 'acquire the skills to say no—no to tobacco, no to alcohol, no to drugs, no to early sexual activities, no to things that will undermine their capacity to become the kind of adults and citizens America needs.' "[10] Teen pregnancy, she suggests, results from a tangle of undesirable behaviors to which children are vulnerable as they enter the interstitial zone of adolescence. In discussing the state of education and Republican interest in improving it, Representative Michael Castle writes, "Issues such as youth violence and teen pregnancy have rippling effects—not only do they scar the life of the young person, but that of everyone close to him or her, and the greater society, as well."[11] Thus teen pregnancy both results from vulnerability and perpetuates it. In short, teenagers are dangerous to themselves, others, and the nation.

As the statement by Newt Gingrich makes clear, the category of adolescence evokes fear and anxiety. Whereas the construction of "children" often references hope and innocence, teenagers frequently represent volatility, danger, foolishness, and irresponsibility. In response to a question about teen pregnancies on *Larry King Live* in 1996, presidential candidate Ross Perot claims that teenagers "can't rationalize getting high, getting drunk, getting pregnant" and suggests that the lack of shamefulness associated with teen pregnancy is at the root of the problem.[12] Stating that teens need to repeat to themselves every day that they are not "rabbits," he portrays adolescents as fundamentally irrational beings who require a culture of shame and social pressure to alter their behavior. A variety of news stories recounting horrific episodes of teenage girls getting pregnant and killing their babies, either through sheer irresponsibility or an inexplicable lack of maternal instinct and love, help to convey adolescence as a period of extreme selfishness in which becoming a parent is a perverse act of the severely misguided.[13] In one story exploring the tough love approach of the PRWORA, a fourteen year old described as "slow," the daughter of a former teenage mother herself, becomes pregnant with twins, disregards her doctor's advice about staying on bed rest due to a high-risk pregnancy, and goes into labor early following a trip to the mall. One of her babies dies after a caesarian-section birth, while the other suffers serious and expensive health problems with long-lasting effects.[14] This story suggests that a teenage girl's frivolous concerns with consumption and recreation, otherwise appropriate to her age, are precisely contrary to motherliness.

These teenage horror stories resonate with the broader cultural context of the 1980s and 1990s in which the fetal rights movement, panic over "crack babies," and the growing industry of pregnancy advice solidified a dichotomy of deserving versus undeserving motherhood that centered increasingly on pregnancy. As writers such as the reproductive justice advocate Rachel Roth and the rhetorician Marika Seigel have illustrated, the politics of fetal personhood helped to construct a reality in which pregnant women's purportedly risky bodies and untrustworthy behavior require surveillance and regulation by the government and private industry alike.[15] In this context, teenagers' perceived underdeveloped physical and mental capacities signal their fundamental status as unfit for pregnancy and motherhood, while the social, economic, political, and environmental factors that influence their pregnancy outcomes disappear.

Within welfare reform rhetoric, irrational and irresponsible teenagers are poised to bring down the country through multiple avenues and are therefore positioned as a major target of social engineering. Pregnant and parenting teens especially appear as a parasitic drain on national resources. Numerous accounts of the danger of escalating teen pregnancy rates cite the pressure they exert on already strained public coffers.[16] A 1995 article in the *Washington Post* paints a picture of America's economic future if teen pregnancy and welfare dependency are left unchecked:

> If there was ever a place that could use a free lunch, it is Jefferson County. The community is completely dependent on monthly welfare checks and food stamps. Four of 10 residents live below the poverty line, including more than half the children. The number of unwed teenage mothers has doubled in the past decade. The county's largest employer is the school system, followed by the county government. Were it not for the monthly government checks, Jefferson County would not have an economic reason to exist.
>
> Two of the county's three small manufacturing plants have closed in the last three years—the jobs gone to Mexico. Many of the graduates of the high school who don't get pregnant leave the county for jobs in Houston or Atlanta. It is a county of mothers and children and old people.[17]

In this portrayal, unwed motherhood, teen pregnancy, and pregnancy in general are apparently at the root of the unfortunate county's economic obsolescence, making it wholly dependent on public money, driving away any viable (non-procreative) human resources, and emptying it of private enterprise. Outsourcing of jobs to Mexico is clearly implicated in the economic demise of the county as well, but the article leaves it up to the reader to decide whether this happened as a result of the lack of productive workers in the area, or vice versa.

Political discourse of this period explicitly links the economic implications of teen pregnancy to the particular construction of teenagers as volatile and unreasonable. Another 1995 *Washington Post* article quotes Republican senator Phil Gramm discussing a proposed welfare reform measure to require teens on welfare to live with a parent in order to receive benefits: "It is a 'national policy of suicide,' Gramm said, to continue the system under which a 16 year old can escape her mother by simply having a child and setting up an independent household with taxpayers' money."[18] Here Gramm not only implicates teen pregnancy in the demise of the nation, but attributes a cold and calculating yet immature and impulsive intention to teenage mothers, once again depicting them as devoid of the requisite motherly qualities. As Anna Marie Smith illustrates, the theme of painting mothers on welfare, in general, as motivated solely by economic incentives when deciding whether to bear children permeates welfare reform discourse, despite obvious flaws in the logic undergirding such dehumanizing portrayals.[19] In Senator Gramm's account, disgruntled teenagers, annoyed with their moms and seeking immediate gratification at the expense of responsible adult taxpayers, will bring about the economic death of the United States.

Although a focus on the category of adolescence allows for putative race neutrality, as scholars such as Holloway Sparks and Kristin Luker have noted, teen pregnancy was heavily racialized in the 1990s.[20] Political discourse and news media portrayed teen pregnancy as a distinctly black and Latina problem through repeated associations with other racialized issues such as inner-city poverty, drug use, juvenile delinquency, and welfare dependency. Discussions of teen pregnancy regularly emphasized statistics about black and Latina teen pregnancy rates. Presenting teen pregnancy precisely as in issue of overabundant undesirable reproduction, political debate of the 1990s often included coded references to racial upheaval intertwined with economic and social concerns. Advocating for vocational education, Representative William Ford states,

> America's schools face an unprecedented challenge if we are to have a work force in the 21st century capable of competing effectively in the world economy.
>
> Of the 3.4 million children who began 1st grade last fall, 23 percent were from poverty families, 12 percent were children of teenage mothers, 11 percent were physically or mentally disabled, 15 percent were immigrants who speak a language other than English, 26 percent were children living with only one parent, 40 percent will live with a single parent before they reach age 18, 12 percent have poorly educated parents (neither parent having finished high school), and 25 percent or more will not finish high school.
>
> If we look at the other end of the pipeline, the Hudson Institute's Workforce 2000 tells us that "only 15 percent of the new entrants to the labor force . . . (by the year 2000) will be native white males, compared to 47 percent in that category (in 1987)."
>
> Those entering school and the work force are increasingly from population groups that in the past have had lower levels of achievement and motivation.

The challenge is not only to bring these traditionally hard-to-reach groups up to the level of white males but to raise the level of education and skill of all students and workers.[21]

Teenage pregnancy appears again among a host of other associated social ills that are framed as nonwhite issues, and are producing a potential national crisis by overturning the dominance of "native white males" and replacing them with unmotivated, underachieving women, people of color, immigrants, poor people, people with disabilities, and children of broken (or never intact) homes. Better education policy, Ford suggests, can make these less desirable workers more suitable and cure their associated problems, such as teenage pregnancy. In this way, he claims, a national disaster can be averted.

Discussions of the problem of teenage pregnancy during this period often cite Daniel Patrick Moynihan's 1965 "The Negro Family: The Case for National Action" as an unheeded call to action that described the problem of teenage pregnancy much earlier than other social researchers did.[22] These discussions present teen pregnancy as an issue within black communities that has been ignored and growing rapidly for 30 years. Others blame immigration for raising rates of teen pregnancy. Noting that the majority of immigrants are Hispanic and Asian, and that Hispanic workers in California "lag far behind all other groups in wages and educational attainment, even through the third generation," a 1999 *Washington Post* article states,

> If current levels of immigration remain in place, an estimated 10 million new immigrants will settle in the United States within the next decade, a [Center for Immigrant Studies] report says. Increasing the number of poor people through immigration complicates current anti-poverty efforts, it adds. Moreover, if immigrant children grow up in poverty, they will be more likely to turn to crime, to have higher teenage pregnancy rates and to do poorly in school, the report says. Thus, the report calls for restrictions on the number of "low-skill" immigrants allowed into the country.[23]

In this account, immigration "increase[s] the number of poor people," and poor people are prone to teenage pregnancy, among other things. In order to prevent huge numbers of incoming Hispanics and their offspring from perpetuating these problems, the influx of immigrants must be curbed. Teen pregnancy becomes a symptom of a larger troubling national demographic change.

Particular legislative proposals and outcomes accompanied these depictions of teenage pregnancy. As noted, the pivotal piece of legislation pertaining to teenage pregnancy and parenthood passed in the 1990s was the PRWORA.[24] Widely understood by scholars of the U.S. welfare state as highly regulatory and punitive, this law established specific rules for teenage parents, structuring their eligibility for TANF resources with various regulations of their living situation as well as educational and employment activities.[25] Among the rules included in the enacted law were specifications about school participation hours; a mandate that a teen parent live with a parent or guardian whenever possible; a monetary incentive for states to lower teen pregnancy rates, while not raising abortion rates; a family-cap option for states to refuse to increase support to teens and other welfare recipients who bear more children; child support enforcement measures to discourage nonmarital childbearing; and funding for abstinence-only sex education.[26] Other measures pertaining to teens proposed by congress members, governors, and state legislators included denying pregnant and parenting teens cash benefits altogether, urging them to put their children up for adoption, placing them in group homes, requiring them to have the birth control Norplant implanted under their skin, and rewarding those who avoid subsequent pregnancies with cash or scholarships.[27] As the PRWORA illustrates, a major strategy in shaping the behavior of teen parents and teens in general was the use of economic carrots and sticks. Understood as a problem associated with impoverished and pathological communities of color, teenage pregnancy and parenthood would be dealt with and curbed through the conditional provision of money and support services. "House Republicans," for example, wanted to "[send] a message that unmarried women, especially teenagers, should not bear children."[28] This message would be sent most effectively, in their view, by welfare retrenchment.

Changing Terms: Legislative Debate before and after the PRWORA

National political discourses of teenage pregnancy and parenthood began to change only a few years after the passage of the PRWORA. As early as the first discussions of TANF reauthorization, conceptions of the problem and potential solutions had already begun to shift away from the demonization of welfare recipients. A comparison of legislative hearings on teen pregnancy and its prevention in the mid-1990s with one in the reauthorization context of 2001 presents a striking, if incomplete, change in the discourse. In 2001, a focus on the dangers of teen sex and the need for better cultivation of values in American youth overshadows discussions that were present in the mid-1990s of the broader set of troubles associated with racialized inner-city poverty and the social policy reform that could address it.

Two congressional committee hearings took place in the mid-1990s addressing teen pregnancy and parenthood: *Teen Parents and Welfare Reform,* before the Senate Committee on Finance on March 14, 1995, and *Preventing Teen Pregnancy: Coordinating Community Efforts,* before the House Subcommittee on Human Resources and Intergovernmental Relations on April 30, 1996. These hearings depict teen pregnancy and parenthood first and foremost as a problem about welfare and draining of resources, contributing to possible economic and labor crises and solvable through welfare reform, education policy, and job creation, in addition to family planning, sex education, and media campaigns discouraging teens from having sex and getting pregnant. They promote a wide range of possible policy approaches, including marriage promotion and the cultivation of personal responsibility, as well the reformation of social and educational policy. In keeping with the 1990s legislative debate and news media coverage already discussed, these hearings racialize teen pregnancy and parenthood as a black and Latina problem using both coded and explicit language and imagery. At the same time, their framing of the issue as the result of a broad confluence of social processes allows for a discussion of teenage reproduction and poverty that implicates the economic and political structures of society.

In both of these hearings, welfare and its impending reform provide the context for discussion.[29] In his opening remarks, the chairman of the Committee on Finance, Senator Bob Packwood, states, "If there is anything this Committee has heard about in its welfare hearings, it is teenage pregnancy, teenage pregnancy, teenage pregnancy, and the relation between teenage pregnancy and the likelihood of being on welfare for a long period of time."[30] Teen pregnancy is up for discussion precisely because of its purported linkage with long-term welfare dependency. Likewise, in his opening statement, Representative Edolphus Towns of the Subcommittee on Human Resources and Intergovernmental Relations discusses the cyclical dynamics of generational teen pregnancy. He claims, "These problems are urgent, and they are costly. The fiscal impact of adolescent motherhood in terms of public expenditures, Aid to Families with Dependent Children (AFDC), Medicaid, and food stamps was 34 billion dollars in 1992."[31] The problem of teenage reproduction appears wholly within the frame of welfare and public monetary resources.

This framing is in keeping with the broader public discourse, in which teen pregnancy apparently threatens the economic viability of the nation through both the wasting of public money and the diminishing of the labor force. Representative Nancy Johnson, for example, a panel member in the *Preventing Teen Pregnancy* hearing, refers to the importance of turning teens into "productive workers instead of parents" in her discussion of a teen pregnancy prevention program that "puts the kids to work."[32] Here, as in much welfare reform rhetoric, "work" of any kind (even without a paycheck) is considered the antidote to problems of personal character. In this discussion, teen parenthood is directly opposed to and can be thwarted by productive labor.

Although this construction of the problem of teenage pregnancy both demonizes poor people of color and describes the economic and racial inequality of the United States as a byproduct of personal and familial pathology, it allows for a discussion of social circumstances and policy outcomes that was all but absent only a few years later. In her analysis of the "underclass research" of the 1980s and 1990s, the historian Alice O'Connor writes that, "for all its connotations of pathology, a strong current of underclass research pointed to the need for a far more proactive agenda, of economic investment, labor market intervention, social welfare expansion, and, for some, antidiscrimination enforcement, than [the Bush and Clinton administrations were] willing to contemplate."[33] She goes on to explain that while these aspects of poverty knowledge existed, policymakers primarily took up the research that leant itself to the project of welfare reform. Welfare reform debate surrounding teen pregnancy illustrates the tensions between research that points to the need for public investment in structural changes and policy agendas aimed at public disinvestment geared toward personal behavioral changes.

For example, as Representative Nancy Johnson stated in her testimony before the House Subcommittee on Human Resources and Intergovernmental Relations, "The problem [of teen pregnancy] is rooted in deep-seated social and economic conditions, which require comprehensive interventions. Among the poorest populations, there is often no reason to delay pregnancy and childbirth."[34] She goes on to discuss the low expectations that poor youth have for the future and their resulting lack of motivation to delay childbirth in order to pursue "greater opportunities." This formulation continues a trend within welfare reform discourse of reducing complex decisions about reproduction to economic calculations (in this case, having a child as a teen is no more or less financially savvy than waiting until adulthood); however, it also refers to a difference in the quality and number of opportunities readily apparent to a teenager, depending on socioeconomic class. Nonetheless, Johnson continues by proposing programs that "target and strengthen families" and instill hope for "future life prospects," an approach that clearly locates the solution in personal values instead of structural conditions.[35]

Other hearing participants suggest that creating more opportunities for low-income teens to be hopeful about would curb adolescent pregnancy. In an article submitted to the Senate Committee on Finance, Douglas Besharov, a scholar at the American Enterprise Institute, writes, "Increasing the life prospects of disadvantaged teens is surely the best way to raise the opportunity costs of having a baby out of wedlock. A good education and real job opportunities are the best contraceptives."[36] Here, Besharov both forwards a reductionist explanation of the desires and motivations of "disadvantaged teens" and, like Johnson, acknowledges a social structure that perpetuates disadvantage through unequal distribution of opportunities.[37] Besharov goes on to state that in addition to improving the life chances of poor youth, it would also be worthwhile to make teen parenthood "inconvenient." He observes, "Different welfare policies could have a real impact. The ultimate 'inconvenience,' of course, would be to deny welfare benefits altogether. But there is a less drastic way: impose an unequivocal requirement to finish high school and then to work."[38] He thus portrays reproductive behavior as intimately tied to economic conditions in which raising the "opportunity costs" of teen pregnancy should include both making the avoidance of pregnancy more lucrative and constraining the economic, education, and professional choices of those who become pregnant.

This idea—that engineering economic disincentives for early childbearing would deter teens from becoming parents—permeated 1990s welfare reform discourse, despite the fact that experts questioned the likelihood that such policy measures would be effective. Many legislators in these hearings state that existing policies are structured to "encourage pregnancy and discourage marriage." As Robert C. Granger, senior vice president of Manpower Demonstration Research Corporation, testifies at the *Teen Parents and Welfare Reform* hearing, "Should teen mothers be denied cash benefits? It seems like a logical question to pose, given that many people are believing that cash assistance is encouraging out-of-wedlock births. Our work suggests that a categorical denial of public assistance to certain teens will have many effects. Some women will not become pregnant. Others will abort. Some will have children and work. Some will have children and marry. And many will have children and be much poorer." Granger ultimately recommends against cutting cash assistance to teen parents in the name of protecting their children, but his testimony indicates how the belief became an important frame for debate in the face of a clear lack of evidence to substantiate it.[39]

Similarly emphasizing the importance of this belief, Representative Christopher Shays, in the *Preventing Teen Pregnancy* hearing, insists that economic incentives for teenage childbearing provided by welfare must be part of the policy discussion at hand:

> I believe that we have more out of wed [*sic*] children and more children raising children, because there are financial incentives. I really believe that there are financial incentives. Now the dialog would be to what extent, but it has got to be out on the table. We have got to say to what extent does welfare for a 14-year-old kid, given all of the other outrageously unavailable options, to what extent does that become a better option . . . I want you to tell me to what extent do you think paying a child to have a baby in a sense creates the possibility that they are going to have a baby?[40]

Although answers to his questions largely refute the notion that welfare leads to teen pregnancy, as did answers to similar questions raised in the earlier *Teen Parents and Welfare Reform* hearing, the potential for altering teens' behavior with monetary incentives and disincentives remains an important part of the discourse during this period. This is likely due to both the repeated posing of questions like Shays' and the continued presence of other welfare policy measures deemed effective in shaping teen conduct.

For example, although Rebecca Maynard, professor of education and social policy at the University of Pennsylvania, disputes the belief that welfare incentives encourage teen pregnancy, she maintains that requiring teens to stay at home with a parent and attend school in order to receive welfare is important to curbing their long-term dependence. "Unconditional welfare benefits promote dependency, while welfare tied to education and employment mandates will promote transitional assistance by the truly needy."[41] In Maynard's formulation, even if economic carrots and sticks cannot prevent teen pregnancy, conditional support can help discipline those who are already parenting. According to her, "adolescents are adolescents" and will engage in "risk-taking behavior," such as reproductive sex, regardless of structural forces like welfare incentives and disincentives; however, she suggests, those structures can provide an important disciplinary function once the damage of risk-taking behaviors has occurred. In this way, the problematic status of teenage pregnancy and parenthood is founded in both the personal deficits of teenagers *as teenagers* and the structure of welfare policy.

Likewise, Kristin Moore, executive director and director of research at Child Trends, suggests that cutting welfare benefits will have no effect on the decisions of teenage girls to have babies, partly because teenage pregnancy is an issue of low motivation on the part of impoverished teenage girls. On the contrary, comprehensive sex education, increased funding for family planning, and the creation of "a set of positive, as well as negative, sanctions" within public policy that includes child support enforcement as a disincentive for adolescent boys and men will help lower the rate of teen pregnancies.[42] Here again, the problem is constructed as resulting from a complex combination of personal and structural factors that require a multi-faceted approach. These discussions of teen pregnancy, when compared with teen pregnancy discourse of the 2000s, create a complex linkage of urban development, education policy, and welfare policy to personal motivation.

The disciplinary rules and regulations up for debate within the context of welfare legislation make up the most significant policy approaches to teen pregnancy and parenthood in these 1990s hearings. Largely in reference to ideas about the general lack of apparent future prospects for impoverished youth mentioned above, participants discuss issues that implicate other societal structures and suggest new policy measures as well. When asked by Senator Packwood "what went wrong" besides the purportedly perverse incentives of the welfare system to create this problem, Maynard states that "a large part of this is the community, and the fact that nobody in an inner city area has employment opportunities, whether male or female, and these young women certainly do not."[43] Here, Maynard presents the geographic dimensions of urban economic structure as clearly implicated in the problem of teen pregnancy and, by virtue of providing this information in response to Packwood's question, she suggests that the state plays a role in structuring those geographic realities. These sentiments, along with testimonies about a lack of access to a decent education, suggest policy solutions in both the realms of job creation and education reform.[44]

One of the clearest examples of the construction of teenage pregnancy as a complex problem resulting from multiple structural societal issues and necessitating systemic change comes from Henry Foster Jr., senior adviser to the president and White House liaison to the National Campaign to Prevent Teen Pregnancy. In his testimony at the *Preventing Teen Pregnancy* hearing, he responds to the question of what the federal government can do about teenage pregnancy, suggesting that a national coalition must be formed to address it, "I think that we need a domestic Marshall Plan. That is what I think we need. I think that the best teacher-pupil ratios ought to be in the inner city than elsewhere until some kind of parity is reached . . . But help us set up a strong coalition at the State level, that would involve the Department of Education, the Department of Health, and it should involve the private sector, all sectors, the clergy, the media, volunteer organizations. That is how the coalition will have to look."[45] Foster describes his vision of a "domestic Marshall Plan" in terms of aiding and overhauling the education system to correct geographic (and, implicitly, racial and class) inequalities, and creating a broad coordinated effort among governmental and nongovernmental entities to address the circumstances of "functional illiteracy" and joblessness that prevent fathers from being "good" fathers. His reference to the Marshall Plan, which aimed to rebuild the European and Japanese economies after World War II, shaping them according to U.S. global political and economic agendas, suggests the need for more than education and health reform. It depicts U.S. inner cities as war-torn zones on the brink of collapse and in need of financial assistance, new infrastructure, and better economic philosophy.

As the American studies scholar Alyosha Goldstein argues, the economic logic behind the Marshall Plan formed part of a broader set of understandings of poverty that shaped international development policy in the 1950s and domestic policy in the 1960s. Policymakers and social scientists applied the concept of underdevelopment to poor communities at home and abroad, identifying them as foreign and possessing of personal character flaws that prevented them from full incorporation into capitalist markets.[46] As such, Foster's reference to a "domestic Marshall Plan" both confirms the status of teenage pregnancy as a structural economic issue and names the context of poverty in which teen pregnancy is purportedly rampant as foreign and deficient. In this way, teen pregnancy requires technical intervention because of structural and personal factors, and the United States, as indicated by the state of its inner cities and the rates of adolescent procreation, requires structural adjustment.

Other hearing participants receive Foster's comments with statements of agreement and appreciation. Some participants in these hearings point directly to racial difference as a factor in the occurrence of teen pregnancy in the United States, and by implication, as a marker of material inequality. For example, addressing the reasons that some European countries have lower teenage childbearing rates than the United States, Kristin Moore states that one of the "most important" things to note is the "limited differences" in these countries, going on to claim that, although this is the case, teen pregnancy in the United States is "not just a race problem."[47] She therefore suggests that racial differences and the inequalities that result from them are key factors in high rates of teenage pregnancy in the United States. In these accounts, race and class appear as social realities that have real consequences, helping to determine the number and types of opportunities children confront and conditioning their sexual and reproductive decisions. Although most participants leave unspoken the causes of inequality, or imply that it is more personally than systemically produced, they suggest that its consequences are under the purview of the government to reinforce or alter with public policy and resource allocation.

In contrast to the testimonies in the 1995 and 1996 hearings, participants in the 2001 *Teen Pregnancy Prevention* hearing before the Subcommittee on Human Resources of the House Committee on Ways and Means significantly narrow the terms by which they define teenage pregnancy. This welfare reauthorization hearing maintains a clear focus on teenage sex as the root of all problems associated with teenage pregnancy. While sex figures quite prominently in the earlier hearings, a number of other concerns offset it. In 2001, despite the similar policy context in which the issue arises, questions of the potential or existing economic carrots and sticks of welfare policy as mechanisms for preventing teen pregnancy are almost completely absent. Likewise, there are very few mentions of the racial and class dimensions of teen pregnancy, and the possible attendant structural changes needed to address those. Instead, participants remain interested primarily in preventing and/or regulating teenage sexual behavior, debating policy measures related to funding for various types of sex education and other methods for instructing teens in certain values pertaining to sex and family. As such, this hearing helps initiate the public redefinition of teen pregnancy in accordance with intensifying discursive frameworks of intimate citizenship and neoliberal multiculturalism. This definitional shift illustrates both the ways that intimate citizenship and multiculturalism constitute each other and the crucial role they both play in the ongoing and insidious project of welfare retrenchment via the politics of teen pregnancy.

In the 2001 hearing, according to Subcommittee Chairman Wally Herger, teen pregnancy remains an important problem that is about more "than just welfare."[48] Herger thus references teen pregnancy's indelible link to welfare politics while setting the stage for a departure from previous discourses. Noting that "impressive progress" has recently been made in teenage pregnancy rates, he insists that continued focus on the issue is necessary, due in part to the "important health consequences for young people who are sexually active as we will hear today." Acknowledging that teenage pregnancy rates were declining throughout the 1990s (years before the PRWORA was enacted), Herger describes the purpose of the hearing as, among other things, asking the following questions: "First, why are we making progress against teen pregnancy? And second, what further steps should we consider during next year's reauthorization of the 1996 Welfare Reform Law?"[49] Progress, then, cannot automatically be attributed to the measures enacted in 1996, suggesting that those measures and their effectiveness might be an important topic of discussion during this hearing. The second question he poses, however, forecloses that debate with the phrase "further steps," implying that current aspects of welfare policy that address teen pregnancy are to be left alone or perhaps built on, rather than dismantled or altered. This confused perspective on the role of the 1996 law in preventing teenage pregnancy provides the introduction for a discussion that does, in fact, largely ignore the existing policy, focusing narrowly on the funding it sets forth for abstinence-only sex education and "further steps" to be taken regarding teen sex in general.

In his opening statement, Representative Benjamin Cardin presents a similarly convoluted perspective on the role of the PRWORA in reducing teen pregnancy and ultimately pinpoints the sexual dimensions of the issue as the most crucial for moving forward. He states, "So the question is, what can we do to build upon the success that we have had as we go to the next level of TANF and Welfare Reform?"[50] Although he later acknowledges that there does not seem to be "any real evidence" that the "direct actions" taken in the PRWORA had any effect, and therefore proclaims, "We need to take a look at that, Mr. Chairman. We need to take a look at what we should be doing on welfare reform," his question implies that to "build upon" that success is to ascend to the "next level" of welfare reform. He goes on to list increased awareness about sexually transmitted diseases, increased accessibility and effectiveness of contraception, and local counseling efforts as the primary contributors to the reduction. Locating contributing factors in areas wholly related to decreasing and regulating teen sex, he sets forth these recommendations: "In terms of what this means for the future, I would say that we should continue our focus on personal responsibility. We should do a better job of not only funding local efforts to combat teen pregnancy, but also highlighting successful programs, which should increase access to youth development and after-school programs that give teenagers productive activities to pursue, and we should promote the value of abstinence without undercutting our commitment to providing access to and information about contraception." Leaving "personal responsibility" undefined, Cardin presents it as part of an interconnected set of strategies aimed at shaping the behavior and decisions of a group defined solely by age.

Despite the continued nods to teen pregnancy as a welfare issue, and despite the larger context of welfare reform reauthorization, participants in this hearing rarely point to welfare as a formative part of the problem. Nor do they overtly dispute its role or call for the rolling back of punitive policies. For the most part, they avoid the implicit and explicit racial and class politics that permeated the hearings of the mid-1990s, focusing instead on the dangers of teen sex, defined as the volatile combination of immature, irresponsible, impulsive minds with sexual, reproductive bodies.

The testimony of Joe McIlhaney Jr., president of the Medical Institute for Sexual Health in Austin, Texas, provides a telling example of how the prevention and regulation of teen sex eclipses all other possible factors in these discussions. Devoting his career to helping prevent the problems of "nonmarital pregnancy, sexually transmitted disease, and the emotional damage of inappropriate sexual behavior," he argues that sex itself is the culprit, and that the TANF emphasis on promoting marriage, two-parent families, and abstinence-only sex education must be maintained and bolstered.[51] Drawing a comparison between smoking and sex, McIlhaney urges an unwavering campaign of abstinence for teens: "What we need to also remember about this is that smoking hardly ever hurts a teen while they are a teen—the cancer and emphysema do not usually happen for years. Sexual activity, however, often hurts teens while they are still teens with disease and/or pregnancy. We need to be as comfortable and intentional in urging them to be abstinent from sex as we are in urging their abstinence from cigarettes. And we need to be patient and unrelenting so efforts can mature." McIlhaney utilizes a common theme in advocacy for abstinence-only sex education, claiming that teenagers require a clear, unambiguous message in order to understand that it is necessary to resist their bodily urges. Like smoking, he suggests, sex is unhealthy and should be avoided altogether. Sex, according to him, is not only the root of the problem of teenage pregnancy, but is at the core of a range of other social problems that could be avoided by containing sex within its only redeemable context, marriage. "Sex," he argues, referring presumably to all other types besides marital, "is sexist." Describing various ways that STDs affect women, their fertility, and their babies significantly more than men (who are "hardly bother[ed]" by herpes, for example, and apparently have no concerns about their babies being infected during birth by an infected mother), he goes on to note the ways that women "are the ones who suffer from nonmarital pregnancies" as well.

Rather than the institutions, ideologies, and people who support the structural enforcement of the feminization of poverty and the inequality of access to family planning and health care, McIlhaney frames sex as foundational to sexism. He equates sex with disease and unwanted pregnancy, emphasizing the unequal burden of those things on women and girls. In doing so, McIlhaney draws on the authority of medical science and the cachet of gender equality to present nonmarital sex as a crucial health and social issue—as a secular, liberal concern, "not just a moral and religious issue," and one that requires a unified ideological campaign that will overcome the self-absorption and confusion of adolescence. He proclaims, "We need a cultural transformation regarding sexual activity for the protection of all society."[52] Sex is such a threat to the nation, McIlhaney suggests, that this campaign must also address itself to unmarried people in their 20s as well, because even adults are unable to make responsible decisions when it comes to their bodily desires. In this way, he substantiates the work of the National Campaign to Prevent Teen Pregnancy (later, the National Campaign to Prevent Teen and Unplanned Pregnancy) in which they strive to build a bipartisan consensus around the regulation of sex and reproduction for all unmarried people—especially naïve and unruly teens who occupy the fraught position of both potential innocent victim and potential offender.

Similarly, other participants proposing to address teenage pregnancy with continued and greater funding for abstinence-only sex education uphold virginity as the key to proper adolescence. Gale Grant, director of the Abstinence Education Initiative of the Virginia Department of Health, explains her experience working with teen parents, stating, "I realized that until we deal with teens engaging in sexual activity, we truly cannot have an impact on teen pregnancies. We must deal with the source and the sexual activity, young people engaging in sexual activity that leads to pregnancies and other consequences of that activity."[53] Again, sex is the real issue, not the various circumstances surrounding sex, including the specific sexual behaviors; the use or nonuse of some kind of contraception; the teenager's race, class, school performance; interest in procreating; or ability to care for a child without government assistance. She goes on to promote the apparent success of her Virginia program and its mission, explaining, "We are trying to keep kids

from moving from virginal to non-virginal status in terms of our design."
This work operates on the theory that once a teen engages in sexual activity
(it is unclear what behavior constitutes a shift from virgin to non-virgin), that
teen's likelihood of downward spiral into pregnancy and disease is heightened. As Assistant Secretary of Health and Human Services Bobby Jindal
testifies, the "virginity pledge" has been shown to be successful in delaying
sexual activity, although studies also show that it decreases the likelihood
that the teen will use contraception.[54] Within this framework, teenagers must
be both protected and protected against. In fact, they must be protected from
themselves, making them complex and urgent targets in a moral campaign to
ensure proper intimate citizenship.

Those hearing participants who advocate for comprehensive sex education nevertheless also emphasize the undesirability of teen sex and the need
to address teens' propensity for "risky" behavior.[55] Noting that most of the
American public supports comprehensive sex education that includes promoting abstinence, Representative Benjamin Cardin states, "Two-thirds of
our high school seniors have engaged in sexual activities. That is the facts. We
would all like to see that number lower. We all would like to see that number
lower. We should work to get that number lower."[56] Although supporters of
comprehensive sex education generally believe that abstinence is the best
choice, they acknowledge what they see as the fundamental truth that some
teens are going to have sex. Teenagers cannot be fully controlled and must
therefore be informed. Sarah Brown, director of the National Campaign to
Prevent Teen Pregnancy, notes that "the reality is that many teens in high
school become sexually active, whether we like it or not."[57] The falling teen
pregnancy rates, according to her, are due to teens having less sex *and* more
responsible sex. The reasons for these changes, she maintains, are many, but
revolve primarily around comprehensive sex education and programs that
engage teens in activities other than sex.

If the problem is primarily sexual behavior, then efforts geared toward
engineering proper sexual behavior appear to hold the solution. In addition
to sex education and after-school programs that instill certain values and
occupy teenagers during the hours that their parents are at work, many of
the hearing's participants point to the media as an avenue through which to
alter attitudes toward sex, thereby preventing teen pregnancy. Brown states
that "popular teen culture is sending kids messages that getting pregnant at
a young age is no big deal, that having sex 'early and often' is just fine, that
contraception is not all that important, that refraining from sex is square and

unrealistic, and that parents can't do anything about their children's sexual attitudes and behavior."[58] To confront this influence of teen culture, her organization proposes to use entertainment media to influence the values of teens and their parents. Many other participants in this hearing suggest that combating the proliferation of sex in popular media is a crucial aspect of preventing teen sex and therefore pregnancy.[59] This emphasis on the role of popular media lends itself to privatized approaches, discussed in later chapters, that further promote the economic and cultural politics of neoliberalism.

According to hearing participants, another substantial contributor to the problem of teen pregnancy, in part because it enables teen sex, is "fatherlessness." As Representative Nancy Johnson argues, the lack of "parental oversight" for children with single mothers, particularly when the mother is required to work in order to receive TANF, must be addressed.[60] It is unclear exactly what "fatherlessness" means—whether it refers to fathers who are not known to their children, do not live with their children, do not contribute monetarily to their lives, or some other reality. Nonetheless, it is associated with increased opportunities for teens to have sex, due to lack of supervision, and lack of the requisite love and role modeling that prepares children to avoid the temptation of sex. In some accounts, fatherlessness results in sexual behaviors such as promiscuity in women and rape in men.[61] It is associated with the occurrence of "premature" fatherhood, which then begets more fatherlessness.[62] While these themes were present in the hearings of the mid-1990s, epitomized by the statements of Charles Ballard, director of the Institute for Responsible Fatherhood, and two of the Institute's participants, they were couched in explicitly and implicitly racial terms and were aimed at addressing fathers' ability to provide economically for their children by increasing their education and employment prospects.[63] In 2001, however, very few references to race or class (other than the claim that fatherlessness relates to welfare dependency) frame the discourse of fatherlessness. Instead, participants concern themselves with fatherlessness insofar as it is said to be both the cause and result of teen sex and other unruly teen behaviors.

Overwhelmingly, then, teenage pregnancy is posed in this hearing as a problem essentially about sex. Participants seldom reference generational welfare dependency, inner-city crime, juvenile delinquency, drugs, or educational failure. When these issues do arise, they are presented more often as results of teenage pregnancy, rather than potential contributing factors.[64] Fears about the potential for racial upheaval due to the over-reproduction of poor people of color and about the decline of the American workforce and economy remain primarily as implied corollaries of the now taken-for-granted problematic status of teenage pregnancy. Their role in provoking outrage and urgency in 2001, however, is greatly diminished. Hearing participants relegate these concerns to the background of a discourse in which anxieties surrounding teenage sex take the fore. This focus prevents discussion of the multiple factors legislated and carried out by the state, such as welfare, health care, marriage, child care, labor, and more, that differentially regulate reproduction and parenthood in the United States. As a result, proposed policy approaches for addressing the problem are greatly narrowed as well. In contrast to the mid-1990s hearings, in which sex education was only an aspect of a complex and multifaceted policy approach,[65] the prevention plans proposed in 2001 revolved almost exclusively around funding sex and/or abstinence-based education. Teen pregnancy prevention politics of the early 2000s frames teen pregnancy as an issue of sexuality that requires education about and access to a small spectrum of equally valuable and acceptable consumer-esque choices, including abstinence, contraception, relationship advice, and tools to combat peer pressure.

Debaters on all sides agree that teenagers' unbridled sexuality is volatile and demands regulation, be it through the cultivation of informed individuals, armed with statistics and prophylactics, or through the production of avowed virginal foot soldiers in the war against premarital sex. Sex itself becomes the problem that begets all other problems at hand, which allows for the abandonment of race and class as frameworks for understanding the issue. Rather than being explicitly and implicitly racialized as a problem of poor people of color through the use of racially coded terms like "welfare dependency," "inner-city crime," and "juvenile delinquency," teen pregnancy in 2001 appears as racially nonspecific. Where this might imply a tacit whiteness, as whiteness is the unmarked category and unspoken norm, the legacy of racist and classist representations of pregnant and parenting teens continues to arise, especially in moments when welfare reauthorization—the legislation in question—is directly addressed. With a new focus on sexuality, this political discourse constructs a multicultural model of teen pregnancy. Within this model, bad cultures of sex may have been more prevalent among teens from poor communities of color in the past, but are now equal opportunity problems that plague the generic American family. These bad cultures can theoretically be addressed with a broad-based strategy of strengthening the moral character of entrepreneurial and consuming individuals in their formative years. Indeed, this focus on sex helps consolidate a discourse of neoliberal multiculturalism in which good moral behavior facilitates effective market participation, thereby ensuring individual success and social equality.

Many scholars have examined the emergence in the post–civil rights era of forms of multiculturalism that serve to maintain unequal structures of power and racial exploitation. The critical race theorist David Theo Goldberg and others name these forms "managed multiculturalism," "corporate multiculturalism," and "difference multiculturalism."[66] They point to the ways that these multiculturalisms valorize and fix versions of racial and ethnic difference based on a depoliticized notion of culture, reifying the norms and privileges of whiteness, detaching race from any associations with the forces of political economy, and setting the conditions of possibility for the corporate management of diversity.[67] Building on these analyses, Melamed argues that neoliberal multiculturalism instantiates new forms of racialization that cut across traditional racial categories in ways that justify the distribution of the burdens and spoils of racial capitalism.[68] In her analysis, those who bear the burden of neoliberal policies are racialized as backward and monocultural in opposition to enlightened multicultural citizens. The ethnic studies scholar Jasbir Puar draws on cultural critics Rey Chow and Susan Koshy to discuss the ways that nonwhite subjects become folded into neoliberal multiculturalism through adherence to heteronormativity.[69] In the case of teen pregnancy prevention, teenage sex and reproduction is racialized as naïve and misguided in opposition to heteronormative teenage intimacies, including the delaying of sex until adulthood and marriage. Within the postwelfare multicultural teen pregnancy prevention discourse, this racialization not only does the work of justifying and naturalizing the unequal results of racial capitalism, but at times completely denies the existence of inequality altogether.

Naming various bad cultures of sex as the locus of the problem, postwelfare policy approaches that are markedly less punitive than welfare reform include calls for sex education, family planning, and media campaigns aimed at changing behavior through the cultivation of values, motivation, and self-esteem, not just for welfare recipients, but for teenagers at large. This turn was, of course, accompanied by the silent continuation of more punitive measures for TANF recipients.[70] The multicultural politics of teen pregnancy evolves even further in the legislative debates surrounding teen pregnancy in the years following this hearing, in which teen pregnancy becomes detached completely from issues of welfare and poverty, and appears almost entirely within battles over "family values" and reproductive health.

2001–2010: Pre-Mothers and Abortion Politics

In 2007, Hillary Clinton drew on her mother's birth to teenage parents as an effort to shape her image on the presidential campaign trail. She highlighted her mother's life story as part of the campaign's "ambitious effort to present the candidate the way they want her to be seen: as a pragmatic Midwesterner with a compelling life story of her own, rather than just the famous, and sometimes polarizing, senator and former first lady most of the country already knows she is."[71] In 2009, President Barack Obama relayed the fact of his own birth to a teenage mother as part of an address to a gathering of over five hundred Native American leaders in Washington, D.C. Using his mother's age and his father's departure when he was two years old as way of illustrating that he knows "what it means to be an outsider," Obama labored to convince tribal leaders that his White House would break the pattern of exploitation and marginalization that the federal government had established in regard to Native Americans.[72] In both of these cases, teenage pregnancy and parenthood were evoked as a way of making an extremely privileged and inaccessible person seem more relatable, as well as confirming the myth of the American Dream in which even the child (or grandchild) of a teenager can persevere to become a U.S. senator or the president. By extension, even those who have been systematically excluded for centuries can be drawn into the national fold.

These two strategic uses of teen pregnancy help illustrate the new public image of teen pregnancy in the early twenty-first century and the ways it forwards the neoliberal logics of personal responsibility, multiculturalism, and entrepreneurship. Clinton's campaign counted on the public's lack of historical knowledge about the issue of teen pregnancy, given that the construct of "teenage pregnancy" as a social catastrophe leading to specific and significant hardships emerged no earlier than the 1970s.[73] While adolescent pregnancy certainly existed prior to the 1970s, it was not until increasing numbers of teens began caring for their babies as single parents (rather than either being married or placing their babies for adoption) that the phenomenon of adolescents having children was understood to be problematic in and of itself.[74] As such, her deployment of teenage childbearing shows the ubiquitous public understanding that teenage pregnancy leads and has always led to hardship. Her use of her grandmother's teenage motherhood to indicate something about herself and her own character speaks both to the perceived severity of that hardship—that it could still be felt by a senator grandchild—and to the idea that it could, and can, be overcome. The message is that one can be plagued by teen parenthood, survive it, thrive despite it, and therefore embody the true American experience. Similarly, Obama's teenage mother establishes him as someone who understands adversity, while also marking teenage pregnancy an all-American trait. The fact that neither of them is a teen parent—perpetuating the pathological cycle emphasized in the 1990s—shows that teen pregnancy is no longer to be seen as a one-way ticket to generational poverty, but rather an unfortunate setback resulting from misguided sex.

Rather than incurring the stigma of welfare and crime, these politicians invoke teen parenthood in order to create a point of identification, a sense of normalcy, and the notion that America is the land of equal opportunity. As the 2001 *Teen Pregnancy Prevention* hearing only begins to show, the public identity of teen pregnancy within national political discourse in the 2000s is about inappropriate and irresponsible sex that can occur in any socioeconomic or racial context. Teen pregnancy thus appears generally threatening to the constitution of the American family, which is the sole and rightful unit of social reproduction and well-being. As such, Clinton and Obama can draw on it to gesture toward a "bootstraps" history precisely because they overcame the hard legacy of teen pregnancy to produce their own "intact" families. An analysis of news coverage, legislative debates, and public policy surrounding teen pregnancy during the first decade of the twenty-first century further fleshes out this multicultural politics of teen pregnancy. Sex education, reproductive rights, and family values shape the issue in ways that foreground proper sexual and reproductive conduct as the backbone of American citizenship, and establish race and class as superficial categories that have little bearing on distributions of power, privilege, and opportunity.

In the first decade of the twenty-first century, teenage pregnancy and parenthood were important issues in three main pieces of legislation and surrounding debates: TANF reauthorization (proposed and debated in 2002, 2003, and 2004, but finally enacted in 2005), the Consolidated Appropriations Act of 2010 (CAA), and the health care reform bill of 2010 (PPACA). TANF reauthorization debates, in keeping with the teen pregnancy hearing of 2001, addressed the issue primarily as one of sex

education and the most effective ways of deterring teenagers from engaging in reckless behaviors.[75] The CAA and the PPACA reveal not only a
continued interest in finding the most effective ways to prevent and regulate teen sex in general, but also an explicit linking of teen pregnancy to
abortion politics in which prevention efforts of all varieties are cast within
an agenda of reducing abortions.

Although both the CAA and PPACA include teen pregnancy prevention
measures, neither set of debates entertains teenage pregnancy and parenthood to any great extent. Its rare appearance, however, reveals a telling new
focus. Whereas a rhetoric of protecting children from poverty and their parents' irresponsible and neglectful parenting permeated all sides of the mid-
1990s welfare reform debate, a different kind of menace apparently threatens
children in the following decade. Sex and reproduction endanger children
of all ages. Children in the beginning of the twenty-first century must first
and foremost be molded in a way that helps them avoid or, at the very least,
reduce the negative effects of sex in their lives. Debaters cast the imperative
to shape teens' decisions about sex in terms of preserving their health and
well-being.[76]

Teens are not the only children affected by teen sex, however. As the
Annie E. Casey Foundation claims, "Teen childbearing affects young people
at both ends of childhood."[77] While debates about sex education and teen
pregnancy prevention have often focused on shaping children at the exiting
end of childhood, those at the threshold of childhood—the potential unborn
children of pregnant teenage girls—hold the interest of debaters in 2009 and
2010. Unlike the American fetus as ideal citizen in Berlant's analysis of 1980s
and 1990s cultural politics, however, the fetus of post-welfare teen pregnancy
prevention is a fraught figure whose life is first and foremost to be prevented,
and often ironically and impossibly in the name of its own well-being.[78]

Prevention of the potential children of teenagers has been a primary preoccupation of political discourse related to teen pregnancy since it arose as
a social problem; however, these later discussions revolve almost exclusively
around the issue of prevention. As teen pregnancy becomes all but contained
within abortion politics, the imperative to prevent abortions *and* teen parenthood takes the fore. Discussing an amendment to the CAA that would eliminate funding for Planned Parenthood, Representative Christopher Smith
states, "Mr. Chairman, no child is safe in a Planned Parenthood clinic. That
goes equally for the preborn child who is yearning to be born as well as for
the 15-year-old pregnant girl being told she is entitled to a secret abortion, an

abortion procured with neither her parents' knowledge or consent."[79] Here, the government must protect the children who are "preborn" from both an immoral organization such as Planned Parenthood and the misguided actions of an accidental and underdeveloped pre-mother. Although the term "pre-mother" could refer to the increasingly dominant approach to women's health in which all women who are able to conceive a child are treated as potential child bearers,[80] I use it here to index the assumption that teenage girls are by definition not yet prepared for motherhood. Instead, they are in training for adult womanhood and therefore for motherhood. For the imagined fetus, it would be better never to be conceived at all than to be conceived by such a pre-mother.

While teenage girls are pre-mothers in this sense, there is a widespread sentiment that reducing the number of teenage parents cannot come with the price of increased abortions. This sentiment demands an emphasis on carrying pregnancies to term. Stating that the proposed health care reform involves prenatal care and funding to help pregnant and parenting teens, Representative Marcy Kaptur states, "Mr. Speaker, the best anti-abortion bill we can pass is one that gives women and children a real chance through health insurance coverage that allows fragile life to come to term. This bill does that. It gives hope, to every family, to every woman, to every child yet to be born. It says you have a right to be born . . . No family, no mother, no father will ever have to question again whether they can afford to bring a conceived child to term."[81] In Kaptur's account, teens need to be supported throughout the pregnancy and beyond (should they choose not to place their children for adoption) in order to prevent abortion and facilitate children's health. Kaptur's proposal shows how the contemporary conditions of possibility for reproductive politics are such that an antiabortion stance provides a tool for structural change on behalf of disadvantaged teen parents. The price of using this tool is of course the ongoing naturalization of abortion as an invalid and demonized reproductive choice.

Similarly, teen pregnancy also arises in the discussion of a proposed aspect of the CAA called the Reducing the Need for Abortions Initiative. An effort on the part of antiabortion Democrats to establish common ground within the polarizing abortion debate, the initiative aims to reduce unintended pregnancies and provide support for women to carry such pregnancies to term. As such, it includes funding for teen pregnancy prevention, adoption awareness, parenting skill building, and child care for parents attending college, among other things. Teen pregnancy is therefore again mentioned as part of a larger set of issues within a narrowly defined reproductive politics frame-work. Whether or not teens should become parents is not up for debate; the teen pregnancy prevention efforts passed as part of both the CAA and the PPACA make it clear that they should not. Rather, debaters are concerned with both preventing such pregnancies through the cultivation of certain types of moral individuals and shaping what happens when something goes awry and teens do become pregnant.

In this way, antiabortion and pro-choice debaters are able to agree that if unintended pregnancy can happen to anyone (not just the self-serving wel-fare recipients of 1990s political discourse), support must be made available for teenage girls and women choosing to carry the pregnancy to term. Advo-cating for the Pregnant and Parenting Teens and Women Amendment to be included in the CAA, Senator Robert Casey states, "There is a . . . category [of pregnant women] where a woman finds out she is pregnant and that moment of discovery is not a moment of joy. For her, it is a moment of terror or panic or even shame . . . She could be wealthy, middle income, or poor—but most likely, if that pregnancy is a crisis, she is poor. Whatever her income, she feels very simply all alone."[82] Including teenage girls in the category of "women" here, Casey emphasizes that unintended pregnancies happen, regardless of factors like class (although, he notes, poor people are more likely to consider it a "crisis"). For a teenage girl, it is presumably the timing that is an issue, as she may not feel prepared to support a child "at this point in her life."[83] He goes on to describe the ways that the amendment supports pregnant women and girls with funding for prenatal care, education, and other services in order to create the best outcome for their children.

The idea of making resources available for pregnant teenagers to help facilitate their childbearing runs exactly counter to previous claims about the role of welfare as catalyst in the production of teen parents. As the his-torian Karissa Haugeberg illustrates, efforts in the 1970s by the New Right to curb abortion through support to pregnant and parenting women lost political ground to Republican interests in reducing welfare spending.[84] In 2010, the construction of accidental pregnancy as devoid of racial and class dimensions allows this notion to regain some footing, at the same time that it continues the trend within teen pregnancy prevention politics of nullifying structural inequity.

Indeed, debaters often present income as largely incidental to whether pregnancy will be difficult or require various types of support. Discussing a similar amendment that eventually passed as part of the PPACA, Casey states,

> Why should a woman on a college campus who makes a decision to have a baby be left alone? Why shouldn't we be giving her help? We don't do it now. I know some do it, and I will hear from others that this group does this and this group does that, but unfortunately it is not nearly enough, especially for someone who happens to be a teenager, a woman who is pregnant, or a young woman who is pregnant as a teenager or before the age of 18. Are we doing enough to help that woman who happens to be pregnant get through the challenge of a pregnancy?[85]

Emphasizing again that unintended pregnancies are "faced by pregnant women of all incomes, of all backgrounds, and of all circumstances," Casey suggests that pregnant women ought not to have to go through the "challenge" alone.[86] The notion that pregnancy might just "happen" to anyone at any time appears to be a fundamental justification for the outlaying of support, which comes primarily in the form of services rather than direct monetary assistance. This, again, is in sharp contrast to the 1990s situating of teen pregnancy squarely within the racialized discourse of welfare, and the austere and punitive response.

Rather than the earlier emphasis on withholding government assistance to coerce impoverished teenagers into specific conduct, policies debated and passed in 2009 and 2010 approach teen pregnancy as an issue requiring public expenditure to inform, guide behavior, and enable choice. As referenced in the NPR story with which this chapter began, the CAA provides funds for "competitive contracts and grants to public and private entities to fund medically accurate and age-appropriate programs that reduce teen pregnancy," as well as for "research and demonstration grants to develop, replicate, refine, and test additional models and innovative strategies for preventing teenage pregnancy."[87] The PPACA includes a similar focus on medical accuracy and innovation. It establishes funding for Personal Responsibility Education Programs (PREP) geared toward reducing teen pregnancy.[88] PREPs focus primarily on influencing sexual behavior, but programs must also include at least three "adulthood preparation subjects," such as "healthy relationships," "adolescent development," and "healthy life skills." A portion of PREP funds goes toward "innovative strategies," which must be aimed at "high-risk" populations as well as pregnant women under the age of twenty-one. Abstinence-only sex education funds that were originally part of the PRWORA were also included in the PPACA, as well as some funding for programs supporting pregnant and parenting teens and women.[89]

As these measures illustrate, while punitive welfare policies still exist after the passage of the CAA and the PPACA, the public focus on teen pregnancy has shifted along with these new policies. Concerns about educating teenagers on sex and cultivating the values and skills required to avoid it or properly execute it eclipse any explicit interest in deterring teen pregnancy through the disciplining of teenage welfare recipients. Within this paradigm, teens ought not to be mothers and fathers because they should not have sex and are broadly not prepared to be parents. Although justifications for teen pregnancy prevention efforts are often completely absent, these notions appear to be the guiding logic. Teenage girls are, by definition, pre-mothers. Should they become pregnant, however, the best option for them appears to be adoption. Barring that, they require support and instruction in order to carry out the task of parenthood in an inopportune situation. These pre-mothers are, for the most part, implicitly racially and class nonspecific, and their potential premature motherhood constitutes not a national disaster, but an inconvenience that, if not well handled, jeopardizes the potential for normalcy for the individual and her family.

In the 2008 presidential election, Republican candidate Senator John McCain named Alaska governor Sarah Palin as his running mate after learning of her seventeen-year-old daughter's unplanned, out-of-wedlock pregnancy. Questioning if women voters would back Palin and "embrace her all-too-human story," the *Washington Post* quotes a spokesperson from the Republican National Coalition for Life: "Everybody, especially women as well as men, knows people who have been in this situation before. It makes their family real, which is what we've seen from Day One . . . It will resonate with women voters because they'll say, 'That happened to me. That happened to someone down the street.'"[90] Like the strategies of drawing on histories of teenage pregnancy in the Clinton campaign and Obama's address to tribal leaders, many accounts of the effects of Bristol Palin's pregnancy on her mother's campaign stated that it made her more relatable.[91] As Sarah Palin was lauded for being open about her family circumstances and helping her daughter avoid abortion, she provided a prominent example to the country that teenage pregnancy is not a problem of the impoverished inner city. As long as it is part of a past in which a generational cycle of early childbearing has already been precluded (as in the Clinton and Obama cases), or embedded within a familial context of private wealth and conservative family values, teenage pregnancy can be rendered familiar and domestic.

The issue is not cleansed of its problematic status, however. In keeping with Senator Robert Casey's remarks above, Palin's familial debacle confirms that teen pregnancy is in fact a problem—one that can happen to anyone, bringing hardships that are not the result of income levels, geographic factors, or social inequality. Palin's story suggests, as the NPR story argues, that teen pregnancy may be largely the result of teenagers' bad relationship skills. In a public service announcement against teen pregnancy put out by the Candie's Foundation, Bristol Palin emphasizes her relative privilege and how much more difficult her early childbearing would have been under different circumstances (those of the presumed average American teenage audience). Nonetheless, she presents the real costs of teen pregnancy as having to grow up too fast and not being able to behave and consume like a regular teenager.[92]

In the mid-1990s, teen pregnancy was equated with excessive and misguided public expenditures to poor people of color living in dirty, dangerous, and devastated city centers. In his remarks during the 1996 *Preventing Teen Pregnancy* hearing, Representative Christopher Shays illustrates the former public identity of teenage pregnancy. He states, "When Newt Gingrich talked about orphanages, people jumped on him. But he was putting it not in the same relationship of a Norman Rockwell, two cars in every garage, and two-and-a-half kids, he was talking about crack mothers raising kids."[93] In his formulation, teen pregnancy was a problem of racialized, welfare-seeking, drug-addicted adolescents whose best hope was the denial of government assistance and perhaps even the removal of their children from their care. He suggests that this is not a problem that can be solved with government outlays of money for programs that "we would not want if we were doing it for our own kids," but instead with direct manipulation of people's intimate lives and relationships. Only a few years later, teen pregnancy was largely presented as exactly a problem threatening the "Norman Rockwell, two cars in every garage, two-and-a-half kids" type of home. If teen pregnancy is a problem about individual morality, then policies developed to address it logically provide government funds in the form of competitive grants for "innovative" programs and campaigns that engineer specific values—virginity, marriage, "safe sex," "life skills"—to teach teenagers how to live properly.

The teen pregnancy prevention measures of the PRWORA, most of which are still in effect, are largely geared toward a specific set of poor, racialized teenagers. They serve, along with welfare reform in general, to widen racial and class inequalities, conditioning meager public relief for the most impoverished Americans on specific personal, reproductive, and economic decisions, plainly increasing their vulnerability to labor exploitation and physical harm. At the same time, the racialized public discourse of teen pregnancy that helped occasion these punitive policies also allowed for the acknowledgment of structural inequalities. Without convincing evidence that the PRWORA has reduced teen pregnancy rates, dominant teen pregnancy prevention efforts have departed completely from a focus on welfare dependency.[94] This departure is not due to a public realization that teen pregnancy may be a valid reproductive choice for impoverished young people whose economic and social circumstances, regardless of the timing of childbirth, provide little opportunity for upward mobility. Instead, the lack of discussion of welfare represents the intensifying attribution of personal deficiency to hardships that are structurally produced.

Along these lines, rather than the recognition that the category of "children" encompasses people who are sexual and reproductive, those traits have come to occupy the sole perversion within and the crux of a social problem that had previously been considered far more complex. A focus on the intimate and sexual lives of abstractly equal teenagers fuels a multicultural understanding of teen pregnancy in which a "culture" of sex must be targeted, while racial difference is depoliticized and rendered incidental. This discourse sets the stage for a proliferation of teen pregnancy prevention media aimed at changing this bad culture.

These media campaigns, discussed in the next two chapters, valorize difference in its superficial form as a way of denying the existence of substantive racialized inequality, while promoting a narrow definition of proper moral and economic adolescent citizenship. Therefore, privatized teen pregnancy prevention efforts—conditioned by the changes in political discourse—form a crucial counterpart to welfare reform by popularizing the neoliberal logics of multiculturalism, intimate citizenship, and privatization that underwrite welfare retrenchment.

2

"Taming the Media Monster"

Teen Pregnancy and the Neoliberal Safety (Inter)Net

In December 2012, the Centers for Disease Control and Prevention launched its "Teen Pregnancy and Social Media" webpage, which includes content that organizations working on the issue can copy or use directly. Badges, buttons, content syndication, e-cards, Facebook, podcasts, Twitter, mobile web pages, video presentations, and widgets are all examples of the CDC's strategies for utilizing social media toward teen pregnancy prevention goals.[1] In the early 2000s, social media gained popularity as a venue for health education and social reform efforts, and the National Campaign to Prevent Teen and Unplanned Pregnancy spearheaded many of these reforms in the field of teen pregnancy prevention. These strategies both reflect and shape changing notions of social welfare and citizenship in the contemporary moment.

The National Campaign to Prevent Teen and Unplanned Pregnancy, as the leading national nonprofit advocacy organization focused on teen pregnancy, arose out of and was an important influence on the political discourse analyzed in the previous chapter. An examination of its work in producing materials, commentary, and Internet-based media about sex, age, and reproduction offers further insights into the role of adolescence and teenage pregnancy in the neoliberal discourses of abstract equality and multicultural belonging, and their existence alongside deepening inequality and exclusion. Through their social media productions, the National Campaign and its partners forward a politics of teen pregnancy that mobilizes a new version of the social "safety net." This version eschews the state-arbitrated process of taxation and welfare that redistributes wealth among citizens in favor of a private, market-based model of cyber-linked national subjects who ensure one another's well-being through the dispensation of values and information. Key to this revamped notion of the safety net is the particular construction of teenagers both as volatile, naïve, hypersexual, nascent citizens, and as enigmatic arbiters and consumers of marketable trends.

The National Campaign emerged out of the context of welfare reform as a private solution to problems deemed unsolvable by the state. As such, it forms a crucial counterpart to the punitive work of the Personal Responsibility and Work Opportunity Reconciliation Act (PRWORA), helping to redefine the public image of teenage pregnancy as something no longer tied to poverty or perverse welfare incentives. Instead, the organization portrays teen pregnancy as stemming from inappropriate sex and inadequate personal values, engineering a privatized set of disciplinary tactics and modes of belonging that reformulate the methods through which social well-being is supposedly assured. In the work of the National Campaign and its partners, the welfare of individuals and the nation appears to rest on effective regulation of teenage sexuality, which can be accomplished by operationalizing the apparently already existing linked-in, consumer-oriented, trend-obsessed status of teenagers. Teenagers and their sexuality thus serve as key sites for the pioneering of new market-driven, media-based technologies of national belonging that ultimately serve to uphold and obscure the deepening social inequalities of the post-welfare era.

Privatizing the Safety Net

The National Campaign was founded in the dismantling of the U.S. welfare state. As the looming specter of teen pregnancy helped bring down Aid to Families with Dependent Children (AFDC), it also engendered a nongovernmental response geared in part toward addressing the shortcomings of state social programs. In President Bill Clinton's State of the Union Address on January 23, 1996, he discussed efforts toward welfare reform (a version of which later passed in August of that year), calling on citizens and private groups to support that project, and then announced the creation of the National Campaign:

> Let us be candid about this difficult problem. Passing a [welfare reform] law, even the best possible law, is only a first step . . .
>
> To strengthen the family we must do everything we can to keep the teen pregnancy rate going down . . . Tonight I am pleased to announce that a group of prominent Americans is responding to that challenge by forming

an organization that will support grass-roots community efforts all across our country in a national campaign against teen pregnancy. And I challenge all of us and every American to join their efforts.[2]

The neoliberal critique of the welfare state holds that the private sector is better suited to the task of caring for the disadvantaged and solving social problems than the apparently plodding, out-of-touch, inefficient federal government. The National Campaign, despite providing no material assistance to anyone regarding means of survival, access to health care, child care, or work, theoretically addresses the problems posed by teen pregnancy better than federally mandated social programs. Based on the idea that the private sector, fueled by good will, can effectively streamline and innovate the work of ensuring social welfare, Clinton urges "every American" to contribute to their work. Arguing that nonprofit organizations "do a much better job than the government could" in addressing certain social needs, a Copley News Service editorial states,

> With many government services in decline and welfare reform changing the way we help the less fortunate, the need for volunteers and for support of nonprofit service agencies is greater than ever.
> Already, volunteer organizations and nonprofit groups are shouldering responsibilities that once might have belonged to government programs. For example, in his last State of the Union speech, Clinton spoke out against teenage pregnancy. But instead of a new federal program, a nonprofit organization called the National Campaign to Prevent Teen Pregnancy was formed.[3]

Here, the National Campaign is viewed as a direct response to welfare reform, as it effectively "plugs a hole" in the "safety net." Born out of neoliberal welfare reform, the National Campaign is the post-welfare response to teen pregnancy. It forges a discourse of teen pregnancy that eschews welfare as a frame for debate and thereby forecloses the possibility of revisiting the PRWORA, discussing its failure at meeting its nominal goals, and rolling back its severely regulatory measures. Instead, the National Campaign bears out its neoliberal destiny by emphasizing personal responsibility, abstract equality, and national consensus around the issue, while drawing on market rationality and corporate partnerships.

With its origin story as the impassioned answer to Clinton's call for a coordinated, private response to teen pregnancy, the National Campaign has helped shape notions of proper adolescence, sex, and reproduction since 1996.[4] Its board consists of high-ranking individuals from the various sectors of society that shape its mission and which it aims to affect. The president of the board, Isabel Sawhill, and three other members, Ron Haskins, William Galston, and Hugh Price (member emeritus), are Brookings Institution Senior Fellows. They were influential voices in national political discussions of the 1990s and 2000s surrounding the roles of family structure and welfare policy in the economic and social well-being of the country. Other similarly important participants in such discussion include National Campaign CEO, Sarah Brown, and other board members such as Roland C. Warren (member emeritus, from the National Fatherhood Initiative), former Republican Representative Nancy Johnson, and former Republican Senator Nancy Kassebaum-Baker (member emeritus). The board also contains members from other national think tanks, research organizations, and academic institutions that reflect and shape the organization's emphasis on social scientific study.[5] Another contingent of board members includes National Campaign partners, such as Planned Parenthood Federation of America and Advocates for Youth, who have overlapping goals regarding notions of adolescent and sexual health. The board also includes celebrities and figures from the news media (Whoopi Goldberg [member emeritus], Judy Woodruff, and David Gergen [member emeritus]), as well as media network executives (from MTV Networks, OWN Network, and Warner Bros. Television Group), relating to the organization's mission to use popular media to influence the attitudes and behavior of its target populations.

Broadly, the National Campaign strives to reduce teen and unplanned pregnancy by affecting the values and attitudes of teenagers, young adults, and society. Specifically, the organization encourages parenthood within the context of adult, college-educated, married couples who expressly intend to become parents. In doing so, the National Campaign aims to increase well-being for all families and children.[6] It works toward this goal by producing and disseminating research and materials (to state and local organizations, schools, and parents, for example), influencing national and popular media portrayals (with shows and movies like those discussed in chapter 3), and supporting specific policy measures (funding for teen pregnancy prevention programs, increased access to family planning services, etc.).

The National Campaign presents deviant pregnancy as a chief cause of individual and familial hardship and itself as the primary rational response to it. The organization draws on and continues a tradition of social science that places reproductive behavior at the root of social inequality, forwarding its own social research and advocacy efforts as non-ideological, objective, and science-based, and thus discursively positioning itself as both respectful of and rising above the divisions between Republicans and Democrats. In this view, while Republicans and Democrats have failed to ensure the well-being of the nation's vulnerable through decades of misguided welfare programs and policies, the apparently clearheaded, unbiased, scientifically grounded, collaborative efforts of private, concerned citizens will negotiate political differences toward the greatest good.

The National Campaign's leadership is positioned squarely within the camp of social science that helped generate the rhetorical legitimacy of welfare reform. Part of a longer social scientific tradition of explaining social inequalities by compiling and interpreting data about marginalized groups' reproductive behavior, family structure, and parenting techniques, poverty research of the 1980s and 1990s generally constructed poverty as a problem related to individual deficits resulting in a person's inability to compete in a politically neutral market.[7] National Campaign President Isabel Sawhill, working for the Urban Institute in the 1980s, co-headed a wide scale effort to study Reagan-era workfare initiatives called Changing Domestic Priorities. The decade-long study was part of what Alice O'Connor refers to as "the prevailing culture among mainstream analytic experts," in which they "let the facts speak for themselves, maintaining a veneer of apolitical neutrality, and in this way stradd[le] the hazards of assessing Reagan administration policy while continuing to rely on federal government contracts for support." Claiming to be non-ideological, such research was nonetheless criticized by the Right for being politically biased and the Left for presenting poverty as an individualistic problem.[8] Ultimately, O'Connor argues, it was the individualistic framing of poverty within the context of supposedly objective research that paved the way for the increased pathologization of the "undeserving" poor and undergirded the dismantling of AFDC.

As senior fellow of economic studies at the Brookings Institution, Sawhill has authored and coauthored numerous studies and briefs that continue to support the scaling back of public assistance and the backing of social engineering projects, such as marriage promotion and work incentives. For instance, she and Ron Haskins—who codirects the Brookings Institution's Center on Children and Families with Sawhill, was a Republican welfare reform advisor, and is also a National Campaign board member—coauthored the report "Work and Marriage: The Way to End Welfare and Poverty" in 2003. This report argues that work, marriage, education, and family size are more important "determinants" of poverty than the amount of welfare benefits received, and therefore promoting work, marriage, education, and family planning are better policy solutions to poverty than cash assistance.[9] With Sawhill representing an apparently more liberal point of view and Haskins providing the conservative perspective, the brief appears as both expert and moderate. It proposes a "set of normative expectations for the youngest generation. They would be expected to stay in school at least through high school, delay childbearing until marriage, work full-time to support any children they choose to bear outside marriage, and limit the size of their families to what they could afford to support." They go on to list policy measures to enforce these expectations, including making assistance conditional on work, capping benefits at two children per family, and eliminating marriage and work "disincentives." While these are clearly the same or more extreme versions of policy measures that are incorporated into the PRWORA, the authors present them as solutions that are "far more popular than existing programs."[10]

This policy brief falls in line with a general trend within poverty research, outlined by O'Connor, of using scientific language and quantitative data to present individual behaviors as the causes of class inequality, ignoring economic structure, racial and gender discrimination, and other factors, while rendering market forces stable and neutral. In so doing, it supports the National Campaign's role as an objective, non-ideological, post–welfare reform replacement for the safety net. It helps elide the role of the current workfare policy in relinquishing support from single mothers by suggesting that high school dropout, early childbearing, and out-of-wedlock births continue to occur because the government rewards single motherhood.[11] It also sets forth precisely the formula that the National Campaign names the "success sequence"—high school, then college, then marriage, then children—and forwards as the proper path from adolescence to adulthood, claiming "research makes clear" that teens who follow this sequence are more likely to reach their "life goals."[12] According to Sawhill, Haskins, and the National Campaign, all teenagers can and should follow the "success sequence," thus ensuring the prosperity of all Americans far better than any redistributive policy could.

National Campaign CEO Sarah Brown also comes from the tradition of social scientific support for individual behavior and familial form as the causes of social ills with a revolution of values as the solution. As senior study director at the Institute of Medicine, she headed the 1995 study *Best Intentions: Unintended Pregnancies and the Well-Being of Families*. Its primary claim is that all pregnancies should be intended. This claim is based on a long list of negative outcomes associated with unintended pregnancies, including lower rates of prenatal care, lower birth outcomes, lower rates of health care for the child, greater rates of child abuse, greater rates of maternal health problems and depression, greater likelihood of parental separation, greater economic hardship, greater parental difficulty in achieving goals, and higher rates of abortion. The study also notes that unintended pregnancies, while an issue facing people of all ages and socioeconomic status, tend to occur most among adolescents, unmarried women, and women over the age of forty, "demographic attributes that themselves have important economic and medical consequences for both children and parents."[13] Although the causal relationships between all of these factors remain unclear, the study forwards the goal of building a "national consensus around th[e] norm" that all pregnancies be intended.[14]

Noting that, contrary to the statements of some politicians and pundits, AFDC does not encourage unplanned pregnancy, *Best Intentions* holds that a complex mixture of individual and structural factors is involved in the high rates of unintended pregnancy in the United States. The authors' proposed methods for addressing the problem, however, would indicate that the issue is primarily about the individual behavior of contraceptive use and a few select structural forces that enable that behavior. The study proposes that a "national campaign" to reduce unplanned pregnancy should improve knowledge about contraception and pregnancy, increase access to contraception, "explicitly address the major role that feelings, attitudes and motivation play in using contraception and avoiding unintended pregnancy," create and evaluate programs to reduce unplanned pregnancy, and produce more research about new contraceptives and contraceptive use.[15] Aside from the discussion of access to contraception and the claim that a dearth of educational and job opportunities in poor communities may contribute to a lack of motivation to prevent childbearing, these goals largely sidestep any historical or current economic and political processes that variously condition the circumstances of pregnancy in the United States. The report relies instead on statistical correlations between seemingly discrete, supposedly knowable attributes (efforts to determine the "wantedness" of pregnancies and children, for example, have been heavily criticized)[16] to project an authoritative, apolitical claim. By proposing to address poverty, child abuse, single parenthood, and more through promotion of contraception, *Best Intentions* suggests that unintended pregnancy is the root cause of a variety of social and health problems that can be cured by a large-scale emphasis on the importance of sexual responsibility. The study therefore lays the groundwork for Brown and the National Campaign to present access to contraception as the only materially redistributive aspect of a newly defined safety net that otherwise largely consists of increased access to instruction in proper life goals and morality.

In keeping with the legacy of social science research that ushered in its existence, the National Campaign relies on social scientific methods to legitimate its claims that teenage pregnancy is the rightful target of post-welfare social reform. The organization's self-generated social science aims to prove that teenage pregnancy is inherently undesirable, resulting in numerous social ills, and solvable by values and sex education campaigns. Promoting its interest in "high-quality research" as one of the things that makes it "distinctive," the organization's website is filled with studies, reports, fact sheets, surveys, polling data, maps, and charts.[17] For example, its Putting What Works to Work (PWWTW) initiative, first funded in 2002 through a Centers for Disease Control and Prevention grant, aims to compile research on the best teen pregnancy prevention practices, repackage that research into an easily consumable form, and distribute it to state and local entities. Collaborating with Child Trends and other research organizations, the National Campaign creates reports on effective prevention programming as well as studies of the relationships between teen pregnancy and other factors, such as sexual abuse, sexual "risk," and low school readiness.[18]

In an effort to generate "user-friendly" versions of the PWWTW research, the National Campaign also produces a series of research briefs called "Science Says." Between 2003 and 2010, the organization created over forty "Science Says" briefs on topics ranging from where and when teens have their "sexual debut," to the particulars of the sexual behavior of community college students. One 2010 example, "Science Says 45: Evaluating the Impact of MTV's *16 and Pregnant* on Teen Viewers Attitudes about Teen Pregnancy," summarizes the findings of a study attempting to assess the ways that the television show *16 and Pregnant* affects its teenage audience.[19] The study surveyed 162 Boys and Girls Club members from ages ten to nineteen. It concluded that the episodes have a largely "positive" effect on teens' attitudes about teen pregnancy, meaning that they prompted conversations with parents and others and convinced most viewers that teen pregnancy is both less common and more difficult than they previously thought, rather than "glamorizing" it as many of the show's critics have asserted. The brief encourages parents and teens to watch these shows and discuss them together, directing

readers to the discussion guides created by the National Campaign on MTV
.com and Stay Teen, the National Campaign's teen-oriented website. The
organization therefore draws on the authority of science, in its assumed
detached objectivity, to evaluate its own work in collaborating with MTV on
the production and promotion of *16 and Pregnant*. This research provides
both a salient counterargument to the show's critics and an additional vehicle
with which to promote MTV and the National Campaign.

"Science Says 45" is also a prime example of the ways that the social
scientific study of human attitudes and behaviors often manufactures self-
contained categories and false oppositions that elide complexities. For
instance, it is difficult to ascertain using a questionnaire the complex ways
that a television show can denigrate, caution against, glamorize, and cele-
brate teenage pregnancy all at once in a fashion that may have both felt and
unfelt effects on its audience. The brief reads,

> The teens in this study enjoyed watching and discussing the *16 and Pregnant*
> episodes and thought that the show was realistic. Neither the boys nor the
> girls who watched the show wanted to imitate the teens in the episodes they
> watched. In fact, nearly all teens (93%) who watched the show agreed (53%
> *strongly* agreed) with the statement: "I learned that teen pregnancy is harder
> than I imagine from these episodes." Although some have claimed that the
> show "glamorizes" teen pregnancy, the findings from this evaluation and the
> polling data noted above show that teens do not share this view.[20]

In the questionnaire, research subjects are asked to strongly agree, agree, disagree, or strongly disagree with the statement, "I learned that teen pregnancy
is harder than I imagine from these episodes." Yet this statement does not
directly address the question of whether *16 and Pregnant* presents a "realistic"
portrayal or a "glamorized" portrayal. In fact, the research brief implies that
a realistic portrayal automatically discourages the audience from becoming
teen parents, but does not substantiate this. The question of whether most
teens think that teen pregnancy is more difficult (however they may define
that) after viewing *16 and Pregnant* does not necessarily have a clear and
direct relationship to the portrayal's relative realism or romanticism. In other
words, the glamorization of something does not preclude an emphasis on
the hardships and difficulties it entails. Because the brief does not provide
a full description of the questionnaire and its results, readers cannot ascertain whether the claim that teens do not want to imitate the *16 and Pregnant*
cast is based on the one response that is noted or some more directly related
question. Also unknown within the context of this brief are the methods by

which the study determined the level and nature of "enjoyment" attained by the participants.

Despite these ambiguities, the brief aims to convey a concise message that *16 and Pregnant* is a positive, rational, scientifically proven, effective response to teen pregnancy. Without explicitly claiming to rebut criticism of the National Campaign's work, the brief clearly participates in a wider public debate about the role of *16 and Pregnant* as a teen pregnancy prevention tool. The authors betray this further with this caveat:

Television Shows versus Prevention Programs

Television and other media alone do not cause—and cannot prevent—teen pregnancy. However, entertainment media can reach millions of teens with important messages about teen pregnancy. It is important to note that there is a critical distinction between this evaluation—which attempts to understand teens' views about teen pregnancy as a result of MTV's *16 and Pregnant*—versus an impact evaluation of a prevention program whose sole purpose is to reduce teen pregnancy. While evidence-based teen pregnancy prevention programs are guided by specific behavioral theories and have the explicit goal of changing behavior to reduce risk of teen pregnancy, television shows such as *16 and Pregnant* are created for entertainment with the goal of attracting viewers and keeping them engaged.[21]

This is a somewhat confused disclaimer, implying that teen pregnancy prevention programs have the potential to directly prevent teen pregnancy, whereas television shows do not, despite being able to "reach millions of teens with important messages about teen pregnancy." The brief does not actually describe the crucial differences between the types of evaluations needed to measure these varying programs. Rather, the authors emphasize the distinction between evidence-based programs and TV shows themselves, erecting another false division between the goals of "changing behavior to reduce risk of teen pregnancy" and "attracting viewers and keeping them engaged." This paragraph seems to simultaneously promote and deny the National Campaign's work with corporate entertainment television, suggesting that TV shows cannot prevent teen pregnancy, while also pointing to them as the frontier of such work. In this way, the authors obscure the National Campaign's stake in the efficacy of *16 and Pregnant* to affect teen viewers' attitudes and behavior in particular ways, preserving the veneer of scientific objectivity, and celebrating the show's apparently inadvertent usefulness.[22] In keeping with the social scientific methods and premises that helped bring down AFDC and inspire the creation of the National Campaign itself, the organization produces and disseminates a self-justifying body of research that poses teenagers as the most vulnerable and important beneficiaries of a redefined, information-based, mass-mediated, cyber-linked, value-laden system for ensuring social well-being.

It is not surprising that the National Campaign would be interested in providing justification for its role in *16 and Pregnant,* given the show's controversial status and the organization's attempt to appear neutral, bipartisan, and practical concerning the diversity of beliefs and opinions about teen sex. Part and parcel of forwarding its scientific authority is the way in which the National Campaign actively presents itself as the site of sensible negotiation between liberal and conservative concerns pertaining to reproductive politics. Op-ed pieces in the *Washington Post* by Sarah Brown exemplify the ways the National Campaign attempts to be seen as a vehicle for concerned citizens to reach consensus about social and sexual health outside of the established political divisions that bog down the government. Brown repeatedly confirms "conservative" family values, while proposing to use "liberal" policy measures to advance them, effectively forwarding a sharply narrowed reproductive health and social welfare debate in which contraception and sexual responsibility eclipse all other possible terrain, such as wealth redistribution; access to jobs, health care, nutritious food, child care services; and the ability to care for one's children.

On March 26, 2011, Brown argues in "Is Contraception a Code Word?" that rather than being opposed to contraception, Republicans are actually opposed to the "crude culture" in the United States, in which people have casual sex, sex outside of marriage, and out-of-wedlock births. She writes that Republicans are worried about the "discouraging state of the American family and intimate relationships at present—hook-up culture, high levels of divorce and extra-marital affairs, violence against women, date rape, sexting, online child pornography and . . . well the list goes on."[23] In stringing together these drastically different phenomena as though they are related equally detestable social ills, she suggests that Republicans use the term "contraception" as a code word for sexually deviant culture, missing the importance of contraception to married people's lives and its role in reducing abortion. In another *Washington Post* essay published on January 26, 2012, "Abortion-Contraception Arguments Are Really about Teen Sex," she suggests that politicians and religious leaders who oppose contraception and abortion are actually opposed to teenage sex, or "'bad' sexual behavior."[24] After all, she posits, if we imagine that the majority of abortions and contraception use occurred within the context of marriage, it is doubtful that such a protest against these things would exist. With this "relevant thought experiment," she aims to prove that unruly sex is the problem. In other words, deviant sexual behavior and pregnancy are the legitimate targets of stigma and regulation, but reproductive services should not be blamed for them.

Simultaneously, in much National Campaign rhetoric, abortion actually deserves stigmatization along with deviant sex. In "Is Contraception a Code Word?" she asks national leaders, "Aren't you, in truth, more worried about things like the fact that 60 percent of women ages 20 to 24 who gave birth in the U.S. last year were unmarried? Or that seven in 10 pregnancies to single women in their 20s are unplanned? Or that about one-third of women in the U.S. will have an abortion by age 45?"[25] These are the issues, she argues, that require everyone's attention. In this way, she assumes widespread support for anything that will effectively reduce abortions and out-of-wedlock pregnancies, forwarding contraception as, at best, a method married people use to space their children, and at worst, an unfortunate but important tool in the battle against the universally disdained behaviors of abortion and deviant pregnancy.

This framing of reproductive rights contains a similar logic to the proposed Reducing the Need for Abortions and Supporting Parents Act, introduced first in 2006 by Democratic Representatives Tim Ryan and Rosa DeLauro, in which increased teen pregnancy prevention, access to contraception, and services for poor mothers are presented as a means toward achieving the bipartisan goal of reducing abortions. It aims to "provide for programs that reduce the number of unplanned pregnancies, reduce the need for abortion, help women bear healthy children, and support new parents."[26] The assumption present in this proposed legislation and the National Campaign's rhetoric—that abortion is inherently undesirable and should be prevented— eschews its status as both a right and the valid action of a legitimate citizen. It creates a false opposition between contraception and abortion, portraying them as inversely related, rather than two services among many that, when available, help a person make whatever reproductive decision is appropriate for her.

This discourse also obscures the drastically different circumstances in which women make decisions about their reproductive lives. Poor women, whose access to abortion is severely limited due to the Hyde Amendment (which prohibits federal funding for abortion services, effectively preventing Medicaid from covering abortion), often carry pregnancies to term that they would have terminated if able.[27] Although perhaps increased access to contraception could prevent pregnancies that would otherwise be aborted or carried to term by women whose access to abortion is severely limited, abortion for many women is already an inaccessible option and their likelihood of avoiding it would not be increased with access to contraception. This framing constructs a moral hierarchy of reproductive choices and ignores questions of social inequality that lay bare the need for federal funds to enforce reproductive rights, including abortion. Although the bill provides for increased access to "family planning services" for low-income women, pregnant girls and women are largely presented within this antiabortion discourse as abstractly equal and interchangeable individuals in a reproductive landscape in which abortion is a wholly undesirable, but supposedly available, last resort. Here, again, contraception emerges as the only material good to which all citizens have a legitimate right in the broader effort to ensure social well-being.

When a version of the Reducing the Need for Abortion bill was reintroduced in 2009, the National Campaign came out with a statement supporting it. Noting the organization's belief that "reducing conflict and respecting a range of deeply held opinions is essential to making progress on the important issues of reducing both teen and unintended/unplanned pregnancies," the National Campaign reminds readers that it does not have an official stance on abortion.[28] Rather, it supports the bill's efforts to build "common ground" in its goal of reducing deviant pregnancy. Based on the apparent consensus that "virtually all of us see value in lessening the need for abortion," the organization's stance forecloses any opportunity to address the role that unequal access to abortion plays in denying women a reproductive right. At the same time, the statement presents particular types of pregnancy as universally undesirable.

In another *Washington Post* essay, "Why Aren't Faith Leaders Top Advocates for Birth Control?" (March 4, 2011), Sarah Brown argues again that antiabortion advocates should support birth control because it prevents abortions, which is the greater of two evils (the lesser being casual, nonmarital, and teen sex).[29] Appealing this time to the authority of science as that which transcends the subjective commitments of politics, she argues that rather than being a form of abortion, as some conservatives suggest, contraception is technically an alternative to abortion (preventing pregnancy, rather than terminating it) and should therefore be highly valued by antiabortion advocates. To summarize the series of misconceptions about contraception and their results, she writes, "So, here we are: birth control and abortion are the same, contraception doesn't even work, and we'd rather have pregnant teens than a cost effective initiative to prevent teen pregnancy in the first place. How, for heaven's sake, does all this square with the CDC's recent declaration that modern contraception is among the top ten public health advancements of the entire 20th century—on par with antibiotics, clean water and modern sanitation?"[30] Brown thus sidesteps the various reasons for why religious leaders oppose contraception despite its role in preventing abortions—having to do with religious doctrine, competing definitions about the beginning of a fetus' life, and the scientific ambiguity as to the actual function of certain forms of birth control. Instead, she again validates the status of abortion as universally disdained by presenting the potential for unruly sexual behavior as the unfortunate price of fewer abortions and, by implication, fewer deviant pregnancies. Taken together, these positions exhibit a stance in which unruly sex (both enabled and mitigated by contraception) is the price of fewer out-of-wedlock pregnancies and abortions, despite being a legitimate target of concern and social action.

The National Campaign employs a similar consensus-building strategy within sex education debates. In her testimony before the Senate Finance Committee Hearing on Building Strong Families in 2002, Isabel Sawhill discusses potential measures in TANF reauthorization that could help "build stronger families." In an effort to bridge the gap between advocates of comprehensive sex education and supporters of abstinence-only education, she notes that the National Campaign supports an "abstinence first message," in which teens are encouraged not to have sex (because "abstinence is the first and best choice for young people"), but are given information about contraception as well.[31] Because the efficacy of abstinence-only programs has not yet been proved, she argues, the federal government can "signal its support of abstinence as a value," but should not dictate the content of sex education curriculum. In a similar strategy of appealing to conservative family values, Sawhill cites statistics that show women who have a child out-of-wedlock have reduced future prospects for marriage.[32] Since marriage is taken to be the rightful goal of a government interested in reducing poverty and promoting "strong" families, according to Sawhill, policy should engage in comprehensive teen pregnancy prevention services that publicize this negative outcome of out-of-wedlock pregnancy.

In these ways, the National Campaign proposes to meet conservative goals through liberal policy, forwarding teen pregnancy prevention through comprehensive sex education as marriage promotion, and access to contraception as abortion reduction. By presenting its stance as the product of consensus building and scientific rigor, the organization's pro-contraception, antiabortion, pro-marriage viewpoint appears moderate and normal, while also affording it an air of transcendence above the "muddied" debates that it claims ordinarily govern reproductive politics.[33] In these ways, the National Campaign cultivates its status as the purveyor of a new and improved safety net, one that ensures individual and national well-being by benevolently and expertly providing the means through which teens can effectively manage their sexuality. In doing so, it overshadows the harsh regulation of impoverished teens and adults that results simultaneously from workfare and the demonization of certain forms of pregnancy and childbearing. The organization embarks on this mission by drawing on the widely touted efficacy and efficiency of market models and profit-making strategies in order to take advantage of some of the supposed defining aspects of adolescence.

Harnessing the "Cool Factor"

The National Campaign's use of media reveals strategies that draw on and promote certain characteristics of adolescence as it is defined in popular U.S. culture, such as distractibility, rebelliousness, preoccupation with trends, and an unwavering love of screens. These characteristics are compatible with the market models, corporate partnerships, and low overhead costs that typify the organization's media-based tactics. From its inception, the National Campaign has named popular media a crucial factor in the problem of teenage pregnancy and the manipulation of it a primary method for influencing the attitudes and behavior of young people.[34] With heads of major media corporations on its board, such as Bruce Rosenblum, president of Business Operations for Disney/ABC Television Group, and member emerita Judy McGrath, former chairman and CEO of MTV Networks, the National Campaign's approach to working with networks on shows and films like those analyzed in the next chapter is in line with the producers' profit-making goals. The organization recognizes TV's ability to generate a "cool factor" that a nonprofit could not.[35] As such, they claim not to change storylines, but instead to provide writers with information about the apparent causes and consequences of teenage sex and pregnancy. In this way, it is possible for teenage pregnancy prevention to become commensurate with the high levels of sex, drugs, and other content that help create a sense of intrigue, rebellion,

or "coolness" and draw adolescent viewers. Working with media conglom-
erates, piggybacking on their already established access to and cachet with
the target population, makes the National Campaign's efforts highly visible,
controversial, and fraught with conflicting meanings.

Approaching the Internet in much the same way, the National Campaign
works diligently to harness the power of social media. During a 2009 conference put on by the National Campaign titled "Taming the Media Monster," Laura Lloyd, assistant director of digital media, discusses the National
Campaign's efforts toward utilizing social media as a sex education tool.[36] She
explains the broader organizational strategy of enveloping "conversations
that are already happening," such as those generated by YouTube-based
celebrity personalities who already have a large following, in order to influence a broader audience.[37] In this way, teenage and unplanned pregnancy are
framed as problems related to attitudes and behaviors that can be effectively
altered through the forces of the free market, which sets the standards of
what products adolescents and young adults are willing to purchase and what
messages they will internalize.

A 2000 print ad and poster campaign titled "Sex Has Consequences"
exhibits the extent to which the National Campaign utilizes market logic,
while challenging the conventional definitions of "sex education" and "raising awareness" and mobilizing a particular construction of adolescence. In
collaboration with the international advertising agency Ogilvy and Mather,
whose former chairperson and CEO, Charlotte Beers, is a National Campaign
board member, the organization produced images of skinny, scantily clad,
sad-faced girls of various ethnic backgrounds wearing heavy eyeliner with the
words "CHEAP," "NOBODY," "DIRTY," or "REJECT" written in red letters
across them. In much finer print are the phrases, "Condoms are CHEAP. If
we'd used one, I wouldn't have to tell my parents I'm pregnant," "Now that I'm
home with the baby, NOBODY calls me anymore," "I want to be out with my
friends. Instead, I'm changing DIRTY diapers," and "I wanted to have sex so
my boyfriend wouldn't REJECT me. Now I have a baby. And no boyfriends."[38]
Sparking significant controversy for the ways that these ads appear to present
negative messages about teenagers, primarily girls, and their sexuality, the
National Campaign held that their goal was to get teens' attention, specifically
the attention of "the ones that aren't listening, the ones that are still giving us
the highest rates [of teen pregnancy] in the industrialized world."[39] In addition
to being posted in health clinics and schools, these images appeared in *Teen
People, The Source, Cosmo Girl* and other teen print publications, as well as

on websites such as Ricki.com and Oxygen.com, were sold on the National Campaign website in hard copy, and were available as e-postcards.[40]

This campaign drew on the resources and techniques of the advertising industry in order to provoke interest, appeal to emotions, and ultimately sell the idea that "sex has [*depressing, degrading, and miserable*] consequences." The goal was to get teens to "listen" and change their sexual behavior by any means necessary. The implication is that those teens who are "still giving us the high rates" are particularly attention deficient and need to be addressed in terms that will both draw them in and communicate a message they will understand. Implicit in this analysis of teen pregnancy is a multicultural logic in which the depiction of teenage mothers of multiple ethnic backgrounds attests to the universality of the problem (that of the fundamentally distractible abstract teenager), the pathological nature of too-early sex and pregnancy, and the inherently inclusive and equalizing force of proper heteronormative participation in U.S. society.

Because the posters were founded on the idea that teenagers will not pay attention to the average public service announcement, requiring a provocative veneer disguising an educational message, the meanings the posters convey are multiple and conflicting. Critics called on the National Campaign to defend these posters, just as some called on the organization to defend its work with *16 and Pregnant* and other shows, because the content both denigrates and glamorizes sexualized, reproductive teenagers precisely as methods for conveying a disciplinary, officially nonjudgmental, antisex, antipregnancy message. These methods take teenage pregnancy prevention far outside the realms of conventional sex education, abstinence training, welfare disincentives, or family planning provision, making it instead a business of selling ideas, promoting trends, and delicately balancing risqué representations with conservative moral messages. Following a logic that constructs teens as best disciplined via the market, these efforts constantly call into being, promote, and rely on that which they aim to prevent and contain, appealing to the purported hedonistic, self-absorbed nature of adolescence. Specifically, they provoke interest in sexual abandon, while cautioning against it as that which prevents other forms of indulgence. In using these controversial methods in the "Sex Has Consequences" posters, the organization garnered national news coverage for its name and its cause, while Ogilvy and Mather likely raised its profile by doing pro bono work for a cause backed by numerous powerful politicians and businesspeople.

In similar fashion, one of the National Campaign's partners, the Candie's

Foundation, enmeshes the goals of nonprofit advocacy and corporate profit-making even further in an effort to sell teen sexiness while quashing teen sex. Founded in 2001 by Iconix Brand Group, Inc. CEO Neil Cole, the Candie's Foundation is a teenage pregnancy "awareness-raising" organization aimed at "shap[ing] the way youth in America think about the devastating consequences of teen pregnancy and parenthood."[41] The foundation carries the namesake of Candie's, Inc., Cole's fashion brand specializing in shoes, clothing, and accessories for women and teenage girls. It effectively functions as a secondary source of promotion for the fashion brand's products. Defining its primary work as the creation of video and print public service announcements to be used by community-based organizations, the Candie's Foundation similarly employs the strategies of the advertising industry.[42] Aiming to "use celebrities that teens can relate to, in a style that speaks to teens on their own terms," the foundation utilizes precisely the celebrities who are employed as spokespeople for Candie's, Inc. products.

For example, Jenny McCarthy, subject of the infamous 1997 Candie's, Inc. shoe advertisement in which she is seated on a toilet wearing nothing but her underwear around her ankles and pumps, as well as other more recent Candie's, Inc. ads, is featured in the video "Welcome to Reality."[43] In this video, she interrupts a teenage couple making out in a car, just as the boy is convincing the girl to have sex. She presents them with the crying baby that will implicitly inevitably result from their behavior, at which point the boy exits the vehicle and the girl is shown holding the baby, looking up into the camera with an expression of panic. This video forwards Jenny McCarthy's status as an authority on female desirability, while defining the appropriate limits of a girl's sexuality. The "reality" of smart girlhood sexuality is that one should look sexy, but not have sex. Or, as one Candie's Foundation slogan puts it, "Be Sexy: It Doesn't Mean You Have to Have Sex."[44]

Media created by the Candie's Foundation literally advertises Candie's, Inc. products, promoting sexiness as a consumer good while warning against the nefarious effects of sex. As such, it presents sex as something that ultimately prevents sexiness by ruining one's freedom to properly consume sexy goods.[45] Another video, "Back Talk Baby," portrays a teen mom, all dressed up in Candie's, Inc. gear for a night out on the town, who is stopped by her baby on her way out the door. The baby admonishes her in a fatherly voice about his dirty diaper before celebrity teen mom Bristol Palin appears, saying, "And you thought your parents were controlling? Don't let a teen pregnancy get in the way of your freedom. Pause before you play."[46] In this way, the Candie's Foundation promotes the Candie's, Inc. fashion label by creating more visibility for its spokespeople and products, while also forwarding a message of abstinence and personal responsibility in the name of teenage frivolity, freedom, and consumerism. This video also foreshadows New York City Mayor Michael Bloomberg's use of imaginary future babies of teen mothers to lecture them on the negative consequences of their sexual and reproductive behavior in his 2013 teen pregnancy prevention poster and text message campaign.

The Candie's Foundation promotes this logic in complex interlinked, cross-marketed, multimedia formats. In a 2012 radio contest held by Z100 New York, a Clear Channel Media and Entertainment station, teens were instructed to view the Candie's Foundation video "Consider Your Options," in order to enter to win a concert at their high school with up-and-coming popular music acts Hot Chelle Rae and Karmin. The video, fifty-five seconds long, uses kinetic typography, a method of animation seen frequently in advertising, involving text in motion. The text moves in time with music, the motion simulates camera techniques, and the words mix with animated pictures, all of which are meant to enhance the emotive power and meaning of the text. "Consider Your Options" employs all of these techniques, consisting of pink and white words and girl paper doll shapes moving on a black background to the sounds of dramatic piano and violin music and babies crying. The text of the video reads as follows:

85 girls get pregnant each hour
2,000 girls a day
Almost 750,000 girls a year
That's more than the entire population of Alaska
It only takes one time
It only takes 1st time
Only time
In love time
One time = the rest of your life!
Think it can't be you?
Think again
3 out of 10 girls becomes [sic] pregnant!
Consider your options
[Underneath that sentence these words appear one at a time]
waiting, condoms, abstinence, birth control, condoms, abstinence,
    birth control, waiting, think about your future
the candie's foundation
[facebook and twitter symbols pictured][47]

Presenting these various options (condoms, waiting, abstinence, birth control) as discrete, uncomplicated, interchangeable choices in a broader project of avoiding the obvious mistake of pregnancy, the video employs a popular paradigm of reproductive politics. Drawing on a larger discussion by the historian Rickie Solinger and others, the American studies scholar Laura Briggs writes that such a politics "only makes sense in the context of consumerism, with individuals picking and choosing between variously enticing but essentially equivalent things (what we might call the *Juno* narrative)."[48] This video is an example of such politics, while providing nothing in the way of information about how to use and access resources or accomplish the potential goals of waiting or abstinence. It uses the veneer of objectivity and authority afforded to the fast-paced presentation of statistics and stand-alone, boldface text to construct the ominous specter of teenage pregnancy as the imminent result of poor consumer decision making.

By baiting teenagers into watching this video with the possibility of a free concert, the Candie's Foundation and Z100 epitomize a new, convoluted, market-driven, self-serving variety of teen pregnancy prevention. They promote their own brands, relying on and raising the recognition of celebrities Hot Chelle Rae and Karmin, while delivering a highly contested message of personal responsibility in which the lyrics to these pop artists' songs, which openly advocate for unfettered sex, debauchery, and narcissism, simultaneously undercut and serve as the vehicle for the official goals of the contest. The concert itself, held at Bethpage High on Long Island, New York, included teen pregnancy "facts" discussed between musical acts by "Erica America," a Z100 radio personality. As Evan Dahlquist of the Candie's Foundation says, "We are trying to get across our message about teen pregnancy prevention in a way that kids will listen . . . This concert is much better than those educational pamphlets you pick up in the nurse's office."[49] This statement reveals the extent to which teen pregnancy prevention discourse has narrowed since 1996. Whereas teen pregnancy was previously viewed as problem related to poverty, access to education and jobs, health care, and the structure of welfare policy, Dahlquist sees two possible types of intervention in the current moment: pamphlets in the nurse's office, or corporate-sponsored events incentivized by celebrity and saturnalia. In this comparison, "pamphlets" appear as an outdated and ineffective vehicle for boring information. The idea that health professionals, such as nurses, would be the appropriate authorities on sexual health is equally passé and misguided. Rather than the importance of access to health care, toward which the pamphlets option at least gestures, the preferred teenage pregnancy prevention strategy relies on cutting-edge media technology and chic to get teens, again, to "listen," which they are apparently notoriously unwilling to do. That this method targets a certain group of teens—those who have both the requisite Internet access and interest in the latest pop music sensation—is obscured by the larger set of generalizations made about teenagers and their obsession with marketable "coolness."

Together, these examples illustrate a particularly neoliberal response to "holes in the safety net" left by welfare reform. Engaging in mutually beneficial partnerships with corporations, utilizing the techniques of the advertising industry, harnessing the popularity of celebrities, and relying on the skill of television writers, these private organizations produce a public image of teen pregnancy as a personal, sex-related problem solved through innovative, market-driven campaigns that arm teens with key information. This approach is based on the assumption that all teenagers are basically equal, attention deficient, and driven by mass-mediated trends, an interest in manufactured rebellion, and an aversion to anything difficult. As there is no need, in this understanding, for government assistance that helps to create equal access to health care, shelter, and nutrition, national teen pregnancy prevention efforts capitalize on young girls' purported inherent consumerism to instruct them on the undesirability of pregnancy. This complex formula of profit making and social reform grows out of and results in a multicultural politics of teen pregnancy prevention in which popular media-based campaigns target affluent and impoverished teens alike, working to create a widespread cultural consensus in which sexual responsibility is viewed as the path to normalcy and prosperity, regardless of race and class. Rather than striving to discipline welfare recipients, these efforts aim to change the concept of welfare.

The Biopolitical Media Monster

Mobilizing the construction of adolescence outlined above, the National Campaign and its partners have located new social media technologies as the frontier of their work. Based in the reality that social media interfaces, such as Facebook and Twitter, increasingly shape the daily lives and identities of the majority of Americans, a growing number of nonprofit and governmental organizations utilize them for certain aspects of their missions.[50] In developing social media–based tactics of teen pregnancy prevention, the

National Campaign and its partners rely on the notion that teenagers typify a general trend toward a perpetually interlinked, screen-based society in which individuals publicly and semipublicly define themselves by selecting preprogrammed characteristics and consuming and sharing online activities, media, and information. An answer to the call for "innovative" approaches to teen pregnancy prevention present in the post-welfare political debate, these strategies make up a set of biopolitical technologies that help construct a kind of cyber safety net based on the notion that social well-being is secured through appropriate sexual behavior, which is in turn secured through dissemination of key information and proper values to teenagers.

Michel Foucault's theory of biopolitics holds that the modern state simultaneously operates on both the individual level by disciplining behavior and the level of the population by regulating the national body based on notions of desirability and undesirability.[51] These efforts to cultivate the optimal citizenry follow a eugenic logic, encouraging and cultivating the lives and reproduction of some, while discouraging, neglecting, or preventing others. Modern state power, particularly in the era of neoliberalism, is diffuse, flowing through public as well as private institutions that are sanctioned and supported by the dominant political logic and help to produce particular types of citizen-subjects. Efforts to prevent teen pregnancy via new media technologies—such as social media websites, smartphone applications, and web-based video games—instruct audiences on proper behavior and values, enlist participation in desired activities, and compile data about target populations. As such, teenage sexuality forms a primary site for the biopolitical operations of the redefined safety net, which draws on the perceived neutrality and universality of Internet-based technologies to produce desired national subjects.

The National Campaign's teen-oriented website Stay Teen (stayteen.org) is an important hub within the massive web of teen pregnancy prevention media created and proliferated by the organization. Linked on the corporate website, thenationalcampaign.org, Stay Teen also has a YouTube channel, Facebook page, and Twitter feed. The website itself employs a number of elements characteristic of social media, such as low-budget videos, interactive games, opinion polls, opportunities for users to leave comments on various content, and journal-style essays, making it appear as a venue for user-led, networked sociality in which teenagers perform their identities and values. These public performances derive from the simultaneously personalized and massifying qualities of social media. As Robert Gehl argues, Web 2.0

sites—including Google, Facebook, Wikipedia, and more—function to structure users' experiences and emotions in certain uniform ways, while offering degrees of personalization that allow for users to indicate preferences and experience intimacy. They are designed to both circumscribe the actions, identities, and lives of their users while also extracting value in the form of creative labor and user data.[52] Stay Teen, along with other social media–based projects aimed at preventing teen pregnancy, relies on precisely these characteristics to generate and promote norms, as well as compile content by and information about their users in an effort to optimize their work.

In an apparent attempt to speak to teens on their own terms, the website presents writing by teenagers about issues related to sex and relationships, videos featuring "real" teens, and results from polls of ostensible teens. It also strives to generate its "cool factor" by enticing participation with games and prizes.[53] The website's mission reads:

> The goal of Stay Teen is to encourage you to enjoy your teen years and avoid the responsibilities that come with too-early pregnancy and parenting. The more you know about issues like sex, waiting, and contraception, the better prepared you will be to make informed choices about the future. We're not telling you how to live your life . . . we just want to give you some food for thought and the latest facts. It's up to you to make your own smart decisions.[54]

Although the website is heavily disciplinary, it is strategically framed as "not telling you how to live your life." As discussed above, the governing logic of the organization's tactics targeting teenagers holds that market forces—those that supposedly naturally produce YouTube's viral videos and promote MTV's teen mom cast members to fame—dictate the vernacular of adolescence and determine the popularity and effectiveness of a product or message with teens. The social media aspects of Stay Teen are particularly well suited to the task of simultaneously manipulating the website's structure and content to forward its values—framing, developing, and harnessing certain kinds of user participation—while claiming unadulterated, voluntary teenage participation.

The "Fun and Games" page, for example, includes interactive elements that instruct and discipline while also compiling data about the website's users. This section includes polls and browser-based games. The polls elicit responses to questions like "Would you talk to your parents about sex?" "Can guys and girls be 'just' friends?" "Are guys more likely to cheat than girls?" and "Did you learn a lot from your school's sex ed program?"[55] The poll questions are overtly heteronormative (like all National Campaign–created materials), and once the user provides an answer, the results are provided along with instructional commentary in line with National Campaign values. There is no assurance that responders to the polls are universally teenagers and the lack of accountability for the accuracy of the polling results allows for the possibility that they may be manipulated. For example, the results of "Would you consider dating someone if you knew that they believed in abstinence until marriage?" showed 70 percent of responders choosing "Yes, if I liked them, I'd respect their decision." The commentary below the results reads:

> In your grandparent's day and maybe even in your parents [sic] it wasn't uncommon for people to wait until after they'd tied the knot to have sex. This generation is a different story. Sex is very much a part of teen culture. If you don't believe it, read the lyrics to Katy Perry's "Teenage Dream". It's in our TV shows, music, and magazines. It'd be easy to look at this generation's obsession with sex and assume that everyone is having it, but what about those teens who still want to wait?
>
> The temptation to have sex, especially as a teen, is no doubt great. Believe it or not, there are teen couples who don't even kiss in order to avoid the temptation. Some might call this extreme, while others might see it as romantic. It's easy if you both agree, but what if you like someone who has different beliefs about sex before marriage than you do? Would you respect their beliefs or drop them like a bad habit? Let us know what you think![56]

The results of this poll and accompanying commentary are meant to convince teenagers that the "crude culture" of sex does not fully dictate individual teens' attitudes about their own sexual behavior. The commentary suggests that abstinence both was traditionally normal (before this apparently more sex-obsessed generation of popular media) and still is, despite what Katy Perry may suggest. So normal, in fact, that "some" teens do not even kiss in their relationships and this is just as likely to be considered "romantic" as "extreme." This poll defines normalcy, creating the impression of consensus among actual teens about the acceptability of abstinence, and advocating "respect" for people who abstain as opposed to "drop[ping] them like a bad habit." By addressing users directly and commanding them to contribute to the discussion, the poll and its commentary enlist users to publicly partici-pate in that definition of normalcy.

In response to the injunction to "Let us know what you think!" the com-ments section under the polling results includes numerous endorsements of waiting until marriage to have sex and respecting a person's desire to wait. Of the first fifty comments listed, nineteen proclaim that the users themselves are abstaining from sex until marriage, the vast majority exhibit some kind of reverence for abstinence, while only seven either say they would not date someone who wanted to abstain or admitted to having had premarital sex.[57] The fact that there is no reliable identifying information for commenters allows for both the anonymity that such a public discussion would require in order to garner participation and, again, a lack of accountability or assurance that the information is not being manipulated by the website administrators or others. Nevertheless, the polling results and comments are presented as "What other teens are saying," without any qualifiers to this effect. Visitors to the website are thus asked to believe in and perform a shared and mutually enforced valuing of abstinence.

The Stay Teen games are similarly designed to recruit users into disciplinary activities that cultivate particular values. Previously viewed as useless, time-wasting activities, video games are now often "perceived by corporate managers and state administrators as formal and informal means of training populations in the practices of digital work and governability."[58] Stay Teen's games represent the increasingly popular use of this training technology in nonprofit advocacy, specifically as it relates to teen sexual health. The website has five games, each conveying the National Campaign's information about sex, teen pregnancy, "healthy" relationships, and sexually transmitted infections. In this way, the organization both enlists participation by engineering this typical teenage recreational activity as an educational tool and generates data about usage that purportedly helps it better reach its target population.

Debuting in May 2012, *Crush!* is a platform-style video game that contains messages about sex and peer pressure.[59] The goal is to help the character on each level avoid being crushed by peer pressure to have sex. Players drop various ladders, platforms, and bridges, flip over springboards, and unlock doors to facilitate characters' movement through an obstacle course, helping them collect "power-ups," such as headphones, running shoes, and cell phones that allow them to block out, outrun, or talk through the peer pressure. Meanwhile, peers on either side of the screen slowly push the walls of the game in toward the center, threatening to crush characters who do not reach the end of the obstacle course fast enough. Players must also help characters avoid "power-downs," such as alcohol and drugs, rumors, and the "heat of the moment," which will thrust them into a vulnerable state in which they are likely to succumb to pressure. Once the game is won, a message appears informing the player that "sex is a big deal" and in order to avoid succumbing

to pressure, a person must know the "facts, have a plan, and take control."
Players are then directed to Stay Teen for more information.

With its variously raced characters (presumably white, Asian, and black),
it is an example of the multicultural politics of teen pregnancy prevention, in
which racial difference is deployed in a way that assumes a basic interchange-
ability between teenagers of different racial and ethnic backgrounds. The
gameplay is simple and the educational value consists of one lesson: avoiding
peer pressure to have sex is tricky, but necessary. While each player may have
a unique experience playing the game (advancing levels at different times,
choosing certain paths and tools over others), the lesson remains constant. In
the world of *Crush!*, regardless of race, class, gender, or any other factor, the
problem and solution are basically the same for every teen.

The game thus recruits players into a course that instructs them on good
and bad behaviors, relying on an assumed distinction between peer pressure
and trendiness, as the widespread success of the game actually depends on
the pressure one might feel to play *Crush!* after a friend shares it on Facebook. Sexual responsibility is figured in *Crush!* by the possession and proper
utilization of certain trendy material goods—running shoes, cell phones,
portable music players—that secure the desired moral fortitude necessary to
survive adolescence (and not be literally crushed to oblivion). Succumbing
to peer pressure, the path toward sex and demise, derives from a weakness of
character or moral vice emblematized by alcohol, drugs, and sexual arousal.
This formulation continues the post-welfare teen pregnancy prevention work
of promoting certain forms of teenage consumerism as natural and desirable,
and in opposition to deviant sex and pregnancy. In presenting a multicultural
cast of characters, it also organizes the boundaries of good versus bad personhood around a set of character traits and consumer behaviors that appear
equally accessible to all.

In addition to its intended disciplinary functions, the game also offers
more opportunities for the National Campaign to extract labor from users
in the form of publicity and usage data. Sexual health education browser
games can bypass the constraints of public policy and school bureaucracies,
utilizing the private infrastructure created by Internet-based corporations to
communicate directly with teenagers. During his presentation at the organization's 2009 "Taming the Media Monster" conference, Dan Melton, founder
and CEO of npT Labs (a now-defunct company that consulted with nonprofits to enhance their online social networking capabilities), explains the
potential power of sexual health education video games. In his presentation,

he describes the current generation of teenagers as the "MyTwitFace" genera-tion, indicating their always socially networked status via sites like MySpace, Twitter, and Facebook.[60] Establishing that this generation, while not inter-ested in perusing a sexual health clinic's Facebook page, is willing to play an interactive sexual health education game, he describes the multiple benefits of this approach:

> [W]e're developing a system in my company to help organizations develop question sets and deliver 'em through an interactive game on Facebook that are [sic] tailored to your geographies. And what's really interesting and what I love about the MyTwitFace generation is that they give us their demographic information so I know who is accessing your service by demographic, by location; by age; by race; by gender; by the content on their actual site; by what they look at online; what other games they have and how many friends they have. Who are those friends? What are [sic] their demographic informa-tion? What do they do on Facebook?[61]

This information, available to Melton's company via a sexual health Facebook game, allows npT Labs and its partners to enter into the private lives of its target population. The demographic information Melton is able to compile theoretically helps organizations to construct an image of their clientele based on a given set of variables meant to signal the types of services and information those individuals need and the best ways of delivering it to them.

This technology, Melton suggests, can revolutionize sexual health care by creating low-cost methods of individualized service provision. In addition to providing "all the data on all the plays, all the shares, all the demographic information associated with every single player when they play it" as well as "pre-imposed surveys on a percentage of people who play it," his company creates a "tailored intervention" for each player based on that demographic information. Melton admits that this kind of program is extremely difficult to evaluate due to the individualization he describes and the unknowable pres-ence of uncontrolled advertisements with sexual content in them that can accompany the game. Nonetheless, he states, "You can pay fifty, a hundred dollars a month and still have access to things like this [system] and deploy 'em at your local level and get evaluation data out of it as well."[62] An online sexual health education game, he implies, can mimic the personalized and informative experience a teen might have in an actual sexual health clinic in their "geography," but at a fraction of the price.

This approach is in keeping with the tenet of neoliberal social policy that suggests that local control facilitates the accommodation of local particularities. Whereas, in the case of welfare reform, the valorization of local control helped to dismantle federal mandates, here it is used as part of an argument for further privatization, reduction of overhead costs, and the detachment of sexual health education from the provision of health services. This method of promoting sexual health takes advantage of the ways that Facebook directs participants to define themselves through the structure of the interface (choosing from preset gender options, filling in birth date, providing a representative photograph, compiling friends, etc.). It thus relies on and helps cultivate a model of social welfare in which citizens become demographic profiles that are linked to virtual resources by the private sector.

Constructed as obsessed with marketable trends and new media technologies, teenagers are theoretically the perfect population for this new privatized model. During the question-and-answer period after Melton's talk, he was asked what tips he has for organizations working with teens through social media. His response reveals a continued focus on "coolness" as a crucial but difficult landscape through which nonprofits must navigate. He states,

> Uh, it was cool in the eighties, but it's not cool now, so just don't type it. Don't ... don't put it in there. Anytime you're gonna have word [sic] that you think is cool, uh, don't use it; just don't do it ... Like so focus group first I mean, right, I mean this is, you need to have like thirteen to seventeen year olds like telling you what's cool ... let them say it themselves ... is the biggest piece of advice.[63]

Teenagers are presented in this discourse as a mysterious monolith reachable only through a shared language governed by consumer preferences. As the National Campaign's work would indicate, popular culture and cyberspace purvey that language most effectively. Melton and the National Campaign thus propose that sexual health education video games attract teens; deliver pertinent, individualized information; and enhance sexual health organizations' knowledge about their enigmatic target population.

While Melton's promises at "Taming the Media Monster" describe the potential of and intentions behind this technology to mobilize a demographic calculus toward individualized sexual health messages, the Stay Teen games may not be so evolved. *Crush!* and its counterparts can easily be shared on a variety of social networking sites, including Facebook, MySpace, StumbleUpon, Tumblr, Bebo, and Twitter, but it is unclear whether the act of sharing these games results in the same deluge of information from users' profiles that Melton describes into the hands of the National Campaign. However, this function does facilitate rapid and direct publicity for Stay Teen via users' friend networks. The games also elicit information from users in the comments section of the website, where hundreds of presumably teenage players discuss the games' effectiveness in communicating sexual health information, their level of difficulty, and the amount of fun derived from them. The games are designed to entice teenagers based on the presumed cachet and entertainment value of video games, providing them with simplistic sexual health messages, which they will hopefully disseminate widely via the lightning speed of the Internet. No public infrastructure of any kind is necessary for this technology, which will reach only those teens who concern themselves with and have access to online leisure time.[64] Rather than providing information about or advocating for confidential reproductive health services for teens, such as medical exams, contraception, abortion, or counseling of any kind (let alone actually providing the services themselves), these social media–based strategies aim to cultivate and mobilize teenage citizens to perform sexual responsibility in the online public.

One social media–based teen pregnancy prevention strategy is designed to both cultivate public performances of sexual responsibility and enter directly into intimate moments as a kind of virtual chastity belt or reminder to use condoms.[65] The Candie's Foundation's *Cry Baby* app, an iPhone application developed by the digital marketing firm York & Chapel, is dubbed a "turn off for when you are feeling turned on . . ."[66] As the application loads, a picture of a pink pacifier with the words "Cry.Baby." appear on the screen. Next, a set of teen pregnancy statistics inform the user that "Teen pregnancy can take away your freedom," as the user is encouraged to "share this App!" with "friends and family." Then, four differently raced (black, white, Asian, and Latino) babies appear on the screen. The user chooses one of the babies, initiating an eighteen-second video of that baby crying. Last, appear the words "Pause before you Play. The Candie's Foundation." Users can thus personalize their cry-baby experience, participating in a multicultural politics that depoliticizes and dehistoricizes racial difference by presenting it as a consumer preference.

Rather than an experience to *remember,* like *Crush!,* when trying to avoid "the heat of the moment," the *Cry Baby* app is meant to be used *in* that moment. The Candie's Foundation description reads, "Get an insta-dose of parenthood with the 'Cry Baby' app, brought to you by The Candie's Foundation. This revolutionary new app keeps teens one crying click away from getting caught in the moment. Help teens protect themselves against pregnancy. Spread the message and download the app today!" Similar to Jenny

McCarthy's role in "Welcome to Reality," the *Cry Baby* app explicitly aims to intervene into an intimate moment to discourage sex by instilling fear and anxiety about its consequences (rather than directly advocating abstinence or providing condoms). As the description on the iTunes website reads, "Find out how much you can handle—if just 30 seconds of crying makes you want to tear your hair out, that's nothing compared to taking care of a real-life baby 24 hours a day!"[67] While "Pause [to listen to this baby crying] before you Play" may sound like an even less realistic request than asking teens to stop to put on a condom, teens are ostensibly meant to stop making out, find their phones, play the app, get "turned off," and decide not to have sex. More likely, the makers hope that promoting the app—thus getting teens to download it and share it with their friends—will create a community of people who recreationally play their crying babies as an indirect affirmation that teen pregnancy is bad. The app will thus further the cause of teen pregnancy prevention by reminding teens how inconvenient and socially unacceptable getting pregnant would be.

The National Campaign, Candie's Foundation, and others forward this kind of cyber-biopolitics aimed at producing proper teenage subjects through the management of teen sexuality.[68] Regardless of their ability to affect actual teens' sexual behavior in the desired ways, these methods reveal the key role of privatized teen pregnancy prevention in the broader framework of neoliberal social politics through their cultivation and mobilization of a multicultural, consumer-based model of heteronormative sexual and reproductive behavior as the path to successful U.S. citizenship. In this context, adolescent sexuality is constructed as a particularly fragile and fraught site for the production of proper citizens that demands a delicate balance between, on the one hand, operating within and producing provocative trends and dangerous desires, and, on the other hand, instructing, managing, and cultivating values and behaviors based on notions of responsibility, self-control, and virtue. This moral frame of citizenship, constructed through the enlistment of Internet and smartphone users, is seen as more urgent for and applicable to adolescents than any other age group.

Adolescence versus the "Odyssey Years"

In 2007, the National Campaign expanded its mission beyond the prevention of teenage pregnancy to include the prevention of unplanned pregnancy in general.[69] Among the multifarious "resources" that the organization produces for download or purchase by state and local entities (which include fact sheets, lists of tips, brochures, videos, and more aimed at teens, parents, religious groups, educators, Latinos, males, etc.) many express the organization's conflation of teen pregnancy and unplanned pregnancy. For example, "Aunt Sarah's List: Things We *All* Need to Say to Teens and Young Adults," apparently written by National Campaign CEO, Sarah Brown, instructs readers on how to explain to teens and young adults that families are not something to be "stumbled into." "We," it reads, are always focusing on "less important things," like "what's for dinner, March Madness brackets, and what movie to see this weekend," but we should devote at least some time and attention to thinking about "when to become a parent, with whom, and under what circumstances." She then presents her list of things that all teens and young adults should think about before becoming parents:

1. Babies need adult parents.
2. "If it happens, it happens," is no way to start a family. And "I just never really thought about it" isn't either.
3. Babies don't cement relationships; they often put great stress on them. Be sure you are in a solid relationship before you begin a family.
4. Sex has meaning, risks, and consequences. It's not a casual activity. Take it seriously.
5. Babies don't give unconditional love; they demand it from the adults around them.
6. Children do best when they are raised by parents who are committed to each other and to years of devoted parenting.
7. *To boys and men:* Making babies doesn't make you a man. Being a devoted partner and father may.
8. *To girls and women:* Sex won't make him yours and a baby won't make him stay.
9. Personal responsibility and parental responsibility mean it's not just about "me" the adult—it's also about what's in the best interests of children, the community, and future generations.[70]

Sarah Brown is positioned here as the ultimate authority on the proper way to budget attention, have sex, become a parent, and navigate a romantic relationship. Her list of insights constructs sex and pregnancy outside the context of a "solid," "committed," and long-term relationship (presumably marriage, as National Campaign discourse often presents "cohabiting, unmarried parents" as less than ideal)[71] as reckless, irresponsible, and damaging to babies, children, and future generations. This list reveals that while teenagers are by definition not ready to be parents, adulthood does not necessarily confer readiness. Rather, young adults must be properly situated and their pregnancies must be planned and guided by the correct intentions.

While teen pregnancy maintains its status as an unambiguously undesirable phenomenon, the contours of its problematic image are transforming. As teen pregnancy becomes separated from its connections (however tenuous or robust) to structural inequality, national economic demise, and apocalyptic visions of urban decline, its undesirability is tied ever more exclusively to the inappropriate sex and reproduction that it evidences. Unmarried sex and reproduction, however, are realities that extend well into adulthood. National Campaign board member and Brookings Institution Senior Fellow William A. Galston argues in his essay, "The Changing Twenties," that while people in their teens and people in their thirties experience the same things they did a generation ago, people in their twenties, or in what some have called "the odyssey years," do not.[72] They are now more likely to live on and off with their parents, rely on parents for health care, go back and forth between jobs and educational pursuits, get married later, and cohabit with significant others, and they are less likely to consistently think of themselves as adults. Although Galston does not provide direct evidence of this, he implies that all of these changes contribute to an increased likelihood that people in their twenties will participate in unmarried sex and reproduction while being less prepared to enter parenthood. He suggests that twentysomethings experience an "extended adolescence,"[73] an argument similar to the one made at the dawning of the category of adolescence, when teenagers were considered to be in an extended period of childhood.[74] As such, he claims, people in their twenties are the rightful targets of efforts by the "National Campaign and others in the field."[75]

Even so, important differences exist in the constructions of adolescence versus the odyssey years. As we have seen, teens are consistently constructed within teen pregnancy prevention discourse as impulsive and risky, not fully aware enough of themselves and the world to avoid dangerous temptations. As such, they not only require guidance in the form of good parenting and instruction from other adults but they also need responsible popular media portrayals and widely marketable, innovative sexual health campaigns. In contrast, as indicated by the National Campaign website Bedsider.org—the "Birth Control Support Network" geared toward twentysomethings—young adults simply require neatly packaged information on how to have non-procreative sex. With this information, their path toward preparedness for parenthood, in which they float back and forth between dependence and independence, education and career, and singlehood and monogamy, can be fully realized. While twentysomethings are assumed to be sexually active, teens who have sex are often constructed as lacking self-control, responsibility, confidence, knowledge, and resources. Teens are the more pressing and vulnerable subjects in the war against unprepared parenthood, as their engagement in sexual behavior in general is immediately viewed as deviant, reckless, and dangerous. They are also the more accessible and malleable of the two age groups. As Galston points out, most twentysomethings "are living outside of institutions and, therefore, without the structure and norms those institutions provide."[76] Campaigns to engineer adolescent behavior are thus more straightforward, common, and acceptable.

This is evident in "Aunt Sarah's" lesson for both "men and boys" on how to become a "man." The project of instructing a "man" on becoming a "man" is confused from the outset. The firm linguistic status of men in their twenties *as men* indicates a long-standing reality of the construct of adulthood beginning after adolescence, making people in their twenties a somewhat more difficult disciplinary target. For example, in 2006, the Bush administration made a controversial effort to promote federal funding for abstinence-only programs for people ages nineteen to twenty-nine. Resistance to this policy, deemed an "ideological campaign" that "has nothing to do with public health" by Advocates for Youth president James Wagoner, was expressed even by those, such as Sarah Brown, who accept abstinence-only approaches as a legitimate teen pregnancy prevention tool.[77] She states, "The notion that the federal government is supporting millions of dollars [sic] worth of messages to people who are grown adults about how to conduct their sex life [sic] is a very divisive policy . . . I think the program should talk about the problem with out-of-wedlock childbearing—not about your sex life . . . If you use contraception effectively and consistently, you will not be in the pool of out-of-wedlock births." According to this reasoning, while teens could benefit from having information about contraception withheld from them during conversations about sex, people in their twenties are actually the rightful users of birth control. Brown's logic maintains that teens are appropriately discouraged from having sex, whereas young adults already automatically have a "sex life," which ought to be none of the federal government's concern. Since over ninety percent of "adults ages 20–29 have had sexual intercourse," she suggests, it is an absurd strategy to encourage them to abstain.[78] Rather, the National Campaign holds, "grown adults" merely require access to information about contraception (and perhaps a little relationship advice from Aunt Sarah) to prevent transgressive citizenship.

These examples reveal the continued status of adolescence as a category uniquely suited to neoliberal citizenship regulation. Within the neoliberal politics of personal responsibility, multiculturalism, and privatization, age categories can signal race, gender, and class neutrality in ways that other social demarcations cannot. Teenagers' social and legal status as children makes their potential interest and engagement in sex deeply disturbing to the institutions and discourses of citizenship that hold children to be asexual, vulnerable, unable to give consent, and in need of protection. On the other hand, adolescence is seen as a precarious period of transition, in which concerns about popularity, conformity, and rebellion against authority meld with hormonal mayhem and tendencies toward risky behavior. Within the framework of neoliberal intimate citizenship, adolescence appears as a fragile period of sexual- and consumer-citizen formation, one that presents a dire need for direct and indirect modes of regulation and intervention. Operating on the assumption that all teenagers are equally trend-obsessed and engrossed in social media, the market-based models of teen pregnancy prevention that I have been describing claim to effectively navigate the difficult terrain of shaping teenagers' attitudes and behavior, thereby increasing social and national well-being through the management of teen sexuality.

In 2008, the National Campaign generated a report titled *Managing the Media Monster: The Influence of Media (From Television to Text Messages) on Teen Sexual Behavior and Attitudes,* available for download on its website. In conjunction with this report, the website presented a "Quick Link" to the document "Tips for Working with the Media."[79] This document, geared toward state and local agencies working on teen pregnancy prevention, delineates strategies for utilizing media and constructing easily consumable messages. Instructing advocates to "capitalize on existing opportunities," "simplify your message," and "personalize, personalize, personalize," the document encapsulates some of the founding principles of the post-welfare safety net. The new biopolitics of teen pregnancy is a coordinated effort to instill values and alter behavior via the flexible personal media technologies that already permeate the lives of teenagers and most people of all ages in the United States.

This new safety net, rather than a set of publicly funded services meant to ease the burden of social inequality and enable the equal participation of all citizens in the dominant standard of living, is built on the notion that individuals are wholly culpable for their circumstances, which arise out of unencumbered choices. While the National Campaign at times advocates for increased access to reproductive services, its funds and efforts are largely wrapped up in its intersecting and mutually enforcing projects of packaging social scientific data and manipulating popular media in the service of changing the culture of sex and reproduction in the United States. In this framework, what rescues individuals from a life of hardship is not government assistance but the best, most attractively packaged information. The private sector, rather than the state, is the logical venue for the work of circulating such information. Where an earlier discourse of teenage pregnancy constructed the deviant teenage welfare mom of color, which helped to dismantle the already tenuous welfare state, teenage pregnancy now serves to enforce a collective amnesia around welfare reform, erasing questions of race, class, and public accountability from discussions about reproduction, sexuality, and age. This discourse and the media-based biopolitical regime that disseminates it work to usher a form of U.S. citizenship in which abstractly equal adolescent citizens—whose ties to the state and other citizens can and should be mediated through privatized, seemingly transparent and unvested technologies—can achieve proper American adulthood only through the effective navigation of their sexual and reproductive lives.

3

Televised Teen Pregnancy Prevention

Multicultural Sex Edutainment

Throughout the first decade and a half of the 2000s, there was a swell of popular media addressing teen pregnancy.[1] This was in large part due to the National Campaign to Prevent Teen and Unplanned Pregnancy's Entertainment Media program, described as an effort to reach teens through their interest in and consumption of specific forms of popular culture. On its website, the National Campaign explains, "We do this by cultivating relationships and partnerships with media leaders, educating them about our issues, supporting their efforts to include our issues, and collaborating with them to produce fresh, engaging, and relevant content."[2] In comparison to this surge in teen pregnancy–related media, popular culture renderings of teen pregnancy during the 1980s and 1990s were not as prevalent.[3] In the era leading up to welfare reform, the news media and political discourse surrounding pathological communities of poverty, analyzed in chapter 1, generated the primary public discourse about teen pregnancy. In contrast, popular culture in the post-welfare era disseminates the most prominent public discourse surrounding teen pregnancy. As critics argue about the effects that this media has on actual teen pregnancy rates, it becomes clear that some of the most widely viewed television shows and movies about the topic—even those that explicitly aim to prevent teen pregnancy—generate complex and contradictory meanings.[4] The question of whether these texts promote certain sexual, reproductive, and contraceptive behaviors over others in U.S. teens has provoked multifarious responses.

Rather than evaluating the effects of shows like *16 and Pregnant* (2009–) and *The Secret Life of the American Teenager* (2008–2013) on teen sexual and reproductive behavior, I am concerned with the representations and regulatory technologies that these texts forward and how they further the post-welfare discourses and strategies surrounding teen pregnancy set forth by public policy and political discourse. As such, I center my analysis on texts that explicitly claim a prevention agenda, focus entirely on teen pregnancy and motherhood, and result from partnerships between the producing television channel and the National Campaign to Prevent Teen and Unplanned Pregnancy.

As the previous chapter makes clear, the National Campaign is a private, nonprofit advocacy organization (originally the National Campaign to Prevent Teen Pregnancy), "inspired" by the Clinton White House and founded in 1996. It receives a portion of its funding from the Department of Health and Human Services along with private funds.[5] The organization plays a prominent role in advocacy and policy debate about teen pregnancy at the congressional level. The National Campaign is one of the foremost national voices in teen pregnancy politics and represents the leading logic by which a variety of interested parties construct the issue, including policymakers, social scientists of prominent conservative and liberal think tanks, national reproductive health organizations, and media corporations. It offers a publicly supported while simultaneously privatized approach to teen pregnancy prevention in the post-welfare era. Its partnerships with television corporations represent the enlistment of profit-driven industry into the prevention project. A direct response to the call within welfare reform for "innovative" approaches to teen pregnancy prevention, these collaborations produce texts that participate in and further neoliberal multiculturalism and the discourse of intimate citizenship.

In this chapter, I examine three such texts: the MTV show *16 and Pregnant*, the Lifetime movie *The Pregnancy Pact* (2010), and the ABC Family series *The Secret Life of the American Teenager*. These mass-mediated programs project the post-welfare politics of teen pregnancy directly onto the personal screens of millions of viewers across racial and class lines. Teen pregnancy prevention on television portrays adolescent pregnancy as something that can happen to anyone, regardless of race, class, and geography. In the framework of neoliberal multiculturalism, teen pregnancy stems from problematic sexual behavior and familial relationships, resulting in stifled physical, emotional, and consumer development for the individuals involved. The apparent solution is thus to raise awareness about the dangers of sex and the hardships of too-early pregnancy, instructing parents on how to effectively regulate their children's sex lives and persuading teens not to reproduce by emphasizing the importance of achieving bodily, economic, and familial normality.

While the welfare reform legislation of 1996 represents the defining biopolitical approach to teen pregnancy of that decade, with its focus on dictating the household, familial, and labor arrangements of impoverished teen moms of color, these texts are part of the dominant biopolitical approach to the reformulated social problem in these first decades of the twenty-first century. They institute a new regime of teen pregnancy prevention, instructing American teenagers in the forms of comportment, sexual conduct, and consumption that make up proper adolescent citizenship. This new biopolitics of teen pregnancy both coexists with and serves to obscure the more punitive work of welfare reform. As welfare reform pushes poor "noncompliant" families off the rolls and into deeper poverty, materially enforcing their expendability, mass-mediated teen pregnancy prevention efforts ignore the existence of these families altogether. Rather than targeting the purportedly wayward teens of impoverished inner cities, these efforts focus on disciplining teenagers at large, presenting a moral frame of economic success and multicultural equality. In this way, they help to confirm, enforce, and obscure the disposability of the nation's deeply impoverished, furthering the neoliberal project of welfare retrenchment.

Teenage Frivolity Sacrificed: A Multicultural Politics

MTV's reality series *16 and Pregnant* has been both listed as one of the "most dangerous shows your kids are watching"—because it is thought by some to glamorize teen pregnancy—and credited with informing and dissuading teens from sex and pregnancy.[6] While the direct effects of the show on teenagers' decisions regarding sexuality and reproduction are difficult to determine, the series is clearly helping to shape the dominant construction of adolescent pregnancy. The episodes illustrate the transforming racialization of teen pregnancy and parenthood, where images of the generational poverty of black and Latina single-parent households give way to a multicultural teen motherhood. In these episodes, race and class appear incidental to a teenager's circumstances, while morality determines her personal success.

Scholars of neoliberal multiculturalism argue that it presents superficial forms of difference as inherently valuable in order ultimately to reify white, middle-class norms.[7] By presenting a somewhat diverse cast—*mostly* white and *mostly* middle-class—in which there is no explicit discussion of racial and class differences and the social inequalities they represent and engender, *16 and Pregnant* naturalizes the norms of the white, heteronormative, middle-class, nuclear family. In her discussion of the relationships between multiculturalism and biopower, Rey Chow points to the replacement of biological definitions of race with a putatively more tolerant cultural framework of difference. Drawing on the philosopher Etienne Balibar, she argues that the resulting proliferation of biopolitical processes that classify and define cultural groups are compatible with and extend racial discourse. She writes, "Humane, genteel, philanthropic, ever-expanding, ever-eager for a bigger and brighter future, this liberalist alibi is itself generating endless discourses of further differentiation *and* discrimination even as it serves as enlightened correction/civilized prohibition against physical and brutal violence . . ."[8] In keeping with Melamed's formulation of neoliberal multiculturalism, Chow points to the ways that apparently benevolent discourses of cultural difference produce new hierarchies of value.[9] The multicultural discourse present in *16 and Pregnant* promotes heteronormative whiteness as a means to individual success for each member of the show's multiracial cast and presents deviation from those norms as naïve, misguided, and morally bankrupt.

Chow, Melamed, and others argue that multiculturalism provides liberalism and neoliberal capitalism an alibi for racial exploitation and violence.[10] I contend that the texts analyzed here do more than naturalize the unequal outcomes of racial capital. In presenting teen pregnancy as an unfortunate problem of morality, disconnected from its former associations with material hardship, they occlude the existence of substantive inequality within the United States altogether. Instead of material hardship, these texts portray both the causes and costs of teen pregnancy as primarily personal and interpersonal. The negative consequences appear as the inability to achieve normalcy and a grimly tenuous grasp on happiness. As Sarah Ahmed illustrates, the cultural machinery that defines and promotes happiness associates it with particular social ideals, familial forms, and types of personhood, which, in the case of teen pregnancy prevention, makes it a crucial mechanism for biopolitical governance and multicultural racialization.[11] *16 and Pregnant* constructs the enactments and rewards of proper adolescent citizenship wholly within intimate and affective terms, thus helping to set the cultural conditions in which the privatized dispensation of instruction on proper intimate and moral behavior appears to ensure public well-being.

16 and Pregnant has a viewership of over two million and, at the time of this writing, has run for five seasons.[12] Scholars of reality TV point to the ways that the genre is particularly suited to the cultivation of personal and intimate citizenship in the face of a scaled-back public welfare apparatus.[13] *16 and Pregnant* performs this work by utilizing "real" pregnant and parenting teenagers to instruct young people in the characteristics of proper and improper adolescent sexual behavior, consumption, and recreation, elucidating the path to suitable adulthood. The show's critique of teen parenthood draws on and revises welfare reform rhetoric of cycles of broken families and too-early pregnancy, eschewing any analysis or recognition of social inequality, and eliding the complexity of structural forces by which people's reproductive behaviors are produced, enabled, regulated, and prevented. This multicultural politics of teen pregnancy is in stark contrast to the heavily racialized and class-based depictions of teenage pregnancy in the 1990s, in which concerns about national economic and social decline at the hands of teen mothers of color on welfare provided some of the most salient imagery in the drive to end welfare.

The National Campaign partnered with MTV, owned by media conglomerate Viacom, to create *16 and Pregnant* and its spin-off series *Teen Mom* and *Teen Mom 2*.[14] These programs are part of the organization's long-standing goal of using media as a "force for good," showing that "sex has consequences," and presenting "teens making the case to each other that postponing sexual involvement is their best choice for many reasons."[15] Meanwhile, the shows' unscripted, heavily edited format; use of nonactors; and emphasis on apparently unpredictable real-life drama follows a current template of successful MTV programming. *16 and Pregnant* is thus a product of a complex intersection of public, private, philanthropic, and profit-driven interests aimed at influencing its young audience.

The makers of *16 and Pregnant* may have multiple, sometimes conflicting aims, producing various intentional and unintentional representations of sex, teen motherhood, and proper adolescence. Nonetheless, its explicit cautioning against teen sex, premarital sex, unprotected sex, and pregnancy in the episode narrations, intermittent public service announcements, and "Finale Specials" with "Dr. Drew" Pinsky display a clear prevention agenda. In these episodes, teen pregnancy and parenthood are problematic for reasons entirely separate from poverty. There is barely any mention or depiction of welfare or urban decay in the entire series. In the few instances in which public assistance of some type comes up in the show, it makes only a passing appearance.[16] In the absence of any discussions about substantial welfare use, these teenage parents appear to draw on themselves and their relatives for their material needs. The show presents financial hardship primarily through teen parents who are unable to purchase key luxury items or to live separately from their parents or grandparents.

Similarly, the previous connections between teen pregnancy and urban blight are left unsubstantiated within the context of the show. Out of forty-seven teen mothers portrayed in the first four seasons of the show, a handful are depicted as struggling with these issues in some way, but often only temporarily and with no racialized geographical dimension.[17] Most of the cases in which someone commits a crime appear to be isolated incidents, most perpetrators are apparently white, and even those perpetrators that are portrayed as having long-term problems rarely fit clearly with the previous imagery of city centers overrun with drug trafficking, murder, and welfare fraud.

Rather than being a one-way ticket to lifelong poverty and dependence in a crime-ridden inner-city setting, teen pregnancy appears to be an unnecessary curtailment of normative adolescence and all its sanctioned frivolity. Teens who become parents can no longer participate in the carefree, narcissistic consumption, social life, and recreation that are apparently integral to a proper teenage life. Many of them lament that they are missing their prom, or cannot fit into their desired prom or homecoming dress. For example, in the "Unseen Moments Special" episode of season two, Dr. Drew says, "It's hard for a woman of any age to accept the way her body changes when she's pregnant, but it's *really* hard for a teenager, especially when she wants to be a part of *normal* teenage life," as the show cuts to a sequence of clips in which Megan "agonizes," in Dr. Drew's words, over finding a homecoming dress to fit her pregnant body.[18] Next, Kayla is shown trying on a dress one week after her baby is born and being unsatisfied with it. The show then skips to three weeks later when she is wearing the dress she eventually chose and Dr. Drew says, "At least for one night, Kayla could still be a teenager. Well, almost," as a shot of her baby flashes on the screen.[19] In this way, the show identifies an apparently definitive experience of all women's pregnancies—struggling with bodily changes—while opposing that experience to "normal" adolescence. Teenage motherhood thus appears to both exacerbate the automatic burdens of motherhood and counteract the joys of being a teen.

The show also emphasizes the monetary, bodily, and time constraints that reproduction puts on other appropriate teen activities. Some teen moms emphasize their own ability to "grow up" in an instant, while their baby's fathers continue to spend money on unnecessary things as normal teens do.[20] Most episodes emphasize the teen mom's favorite extracurricular activities (e.g., Farrah and Leah are cheerleaders, Jenelle likes going to the beach, Brooke races cars, Lizzie plays in a marching band, Jordan is a model, Kayla does gymnastics, Izabella is on the drill team, Kianna does softball, Lindsey does cage fighting, etc.) and the ways that being a teen mom infringes on those.[21] As Mackenzie tries on her midriff-bearing cheerleading outfit while pregnant, she says she is determined to be wearing it "with a six-pack and no stretch marks" soon after the baby is born.[22] Her mom looks on in disbelief and her sister sarcastically says, "Good luck with that," to which Mackenzie rolls her eyes and bows her head to look at her belly as somber music begins to play. Likewise, the episodes repeatedly stress the havoc that teenage pregnancy and motherhood wreak on a girl's social life. For instance, when Katie wants to go to prom, she not only has trouble finding a dress, but her experience at the dance is also unsatisfying, as people stare at her, her feet get sore, and she gets tired quickly.[23] She is physically inappropriate for both the attire and strenuous activity of dancing, and she must cope with social discomfort.

Whereas the dominant 1990s critique of teenage pregnancy drew on racialized discourses of poverty and welfare, 16 and Pregnant's multicultural critique attributes undesirable characteristics to adolescent childbearing in any racial and class context, ultimately signaling the inherent superiority, inclusivity, and universality of heteronormative reproduction. Twelve of the sixteen pregnant teenagers followed in the first two seasons appear unambiguously white and the majority are middle class. Their pregnancies are presented as unsettling and burdensome in a way that affects all teenage girls with the same basic consequences—by ruining their lighthearted innocence and disrupting the course of their lives. This is well illustrated by a close look at Kayla's episode in season two. Kayla lives in rural Alabama. She and her boyfriend JR appear to be white and middle class. Although a major source of drama throughout the series is the apparent irresponsibility of teenage fathers, JR has a high school diploma and a steady (while perhaps low-paying) job as a mechanic. He is portrayed as committed to Kayla and their baby Rylan. Kayla and JR each live with their parents who are married to each other and accommodating of the pregnancy (although Kayla's mom does talk about being sad about the news at first). Both Kayla's and JR's parents appear to provide emotional and material support to them.

Nonetheless, Kayla's life is not free of turmoil. One major source of conflict in the episode is that JR wants to marry Kayla and move in to a house (which appears spacious and has "brand new cabinets and appliances in it") that his parents own, but Kayla is not ready to move away from her mother. Kayla is also portrayed as somewhat distraught over having to sacrifice apparently crucial high school experiences and go to community college instead of the university she had planned on attending with her friends. As Kayla puts it to JR, "you got to have your senior year, but I had to miss out on a lot of stuff, like me moving off with all my friends and going to college."[24] Although her mother tries to reassure her that the community college is a "wonderful" school, and that she will still be able to pursue the career as a nurse that she had planned and make new friends, the episode depicts Kayla crying over these changes in her life. Kayla has no apparent cause for concern over providing for the material needs of herself and her baby, she says repeatedly that she "love[s] being a mom," and she is fully able to complete high school and go to college to pursue the career she had planned (her mother and JR's mother have agreed to provide child care). Despite these realities, the show presents Kayla's story as a cautionary tale against teenage pregnancy.

While the episodes of *16 and Pregnant* produce many different and contradictory meanings, the authoritative prevention message of Kayla's episode and most others is that teenage girls should not get pregnant if they want to continue participating in *normal* teenage activities. Such activities include playing sports, looking thin and fashionable, attending a regular high school, buying trendy nonessential goods, and moving away to college to live in a dormitory with friends. The social science and political discourse that defined teen pregnancy as a social problem in the 1990s held it to be a dire symptom of a larger culture of poverty that accepted early childbearing as the norm due to welfare incentives and the decline of family values.[25] On the contrary, Kayla and many of the other *16 and Pregnant* teen moms are portrayed as enduring social ostracism due to the precisely nonnormative status of their actions. In one of the animated illustrations that punctuate certain moments throughout the episodes, Kayla is depicted as back at school pulling bottles out of her locker while her schoolmates stand by discussing a party, cheer practice, and going to the game. They then walk away, leaving her standing alone and dejected (her head hanging) next to a wall of lockers.[26] Kayla does not live in a pathological community in which babies are commonly having babies to get a welfare check, while deadbeat dads are shirking their parental responsibilities. Rather, she lives in an apparently normal setting in which the consensus about what constitutes proper adolescence makes teen pregnancy alienating.

Not only is she growing apart from her friends because of becoming a teen mom, she is also no longer able to participate in beauty pageants, a previous pastime of hers. She is shown calling a local pageant director to ask why girls with children are not allowed to participate and being told, "This is for kids who just don't have children." In another segment, an animation depicts her standing in a line of pageant contestants while her belly grows and knocks them all over like dominoes. This is similar to an illustration that shows her pregnant belly growing until it breaks the school desk in which she is sitting. As the education policy scholar Wanda Pillow points out, pregnant teenagers do not "'fit' literally and figuratively into educational research, theories, policies, and practices."[27] The exclusion of pregnant and mothering teens from their desired extracurricular activities and social circles, as well as from the educational politics and practices that Pillow discusses, is reflected and reinforced in Kayla's episode as a way of demonstrating the universal wrongfulness of teen motherhood.

Social exclusion, relationship turmoil, and decreased freedom of recreation and consumption are shown affecting almost all the teen moms of *16 and Pregnant* (perhaps with the exceptions of Catelynn, Lori, and Ashley, who place their babies for adoption). In the final segment of Kayla's episode, she states, "When I had unprotected sex, I really wish I had thought it through more, because even though I had all the love and support in the world, the emotional struggle that you have to go through along with being pregnant is really, really hard and I just wanna slow down my life a little bit."[28] As some of Kayla's final words, these help solidify the notion that the problem with teenage motherhood is not that it might lead to poverty, crime, or generational welfare dependency, but that it interferes with the natural and logical course of life. As such, no structural factors, such as social policy, racial inequality, economic structure, reproductive politics, or health policy, appear to be in play. Rather, teenage motherhood is universally a personal failure that comes with personal sacrifices.

A defining aspect of the "epidemic" of teen pregnancy that helped drive social reformers to overhaul welfare in 1996 was its purported self-perpetuation.[29] Babies were having babies who would have babies as babies, and so on, due to a lack of proper role models and the perverse incentives of Aid to Families with Dependent Children (AFDC). The intersecting racialized tropes of the culture of poverty, generational welfare dependency, and teenage pregnancy painted a harrowing portrait of U.S. economic and social decline at the hands of misguided, inner-city adolescents of color, whose actions were part of a cascading snowball of degeneracy. The cycle of teen pregnancy needed to be broken, and welfare reform, with its monetary carrots and sticks, was an important strategy for doing so.[30] Although many of today's teen parents can in fact draw on public assistance, *16 and Pregnant* portrays the perils of early pregnancy as having nothing to do with cyclical dependency on the government. In fact, while there are some instances of relative poverty and some discussions of cycles, these things hardly coexist. Instead, the new cycle of teen pregnancy results from and perpetuates inadequate familial relationships.

Most cast members appear far removed from the stereotypical teen mom of 1990s discourse, but Catelynn comes close. Although she and her boyfriend, Tyler, are white (something true of a large portion of actual teen parents, but obscured by the racialized discourse of the late twentieth century), they describe their lives as "unstable," an apparent euphemism for growing up in relatively impoverished households with emotionally unsupportive parents.[31] Catelynn's mother has substance abuse issues and gave birth to her when she was nineteen. Tyler's dad has been "in and out of prison" throughout his life. In this way, Catelynn and Tyler's situation bears the most resemblance to the cycle of teen pregnancy with which Republicans and Democrats mutually concerned themselves in the 1990s. As the story goes, the child of a teen mom grows up in an impoverished, dysfunctional home, becomes pregnant at sixteen as a result of that dysfunction, and dooms her own child to the same fate. Catelynn's episode, however, forecloses that possibility by depicting the difficult process that she and Tyler go through to place their daughter for adoption, giving her a "better life." In this way, they redeem themselves and, in accordance with Melamed's formulation of multiculturalism as the spirit of neoliberal capitalism, provide compelling evidence that equilibrating markets—in this case, the market for adoptable babies—constitute the avenue toward inclusion into proper American citizenship.[32]

As Catelynn and Tyler choose adoptive parents for their child, rather than continuing the purported pathological cycle, their actions consolidate the heteronormative ideal. Per Catelynn and Tyler's preferences, the adoptive mother will be a stay-at-home mom with a husband who is "a provider." The couple they choose explains that they met at church and that Brandon, the adoptive dad, works as a financial planner, while his wife, Theresa, has a job at a private Christian school that she presumably plans to quit when the baby arrives. This married, white, Christian, middle-class (their large brick house with white pillars and lush, manicured lawn is pictured) couple is attributed by Catelynn and Tyler the ability to give a child a "stable household" and a "better life," and to make her "so happy."[33] Although they name emotional stability as their primary hope for their daughter's adoptive household, the episode does little in the way of explicitly describing what emotional stability might look like. Instead, as Catelynn and Tyler thumb through Brandon and Theresa's portfolio from the adoption agency, visual imagery of Brandon and Theresa's apparent material wealth—their house, dress, and disposable time and income channeled toward recreation—is accompanied by Catelynn and Tyler's exclamations about these things and how "perfect" they would be as parents. In this way, an "emotionally stable household" is equated with being a white, middle-class, nuclear family with traditional gender roles.

In her discussion of how happiness is constructed through the valorization of heteronormative family formations, Sarah Ahmed elaborates a theory of the sociality of happiness. She argues that happiness is understood to be a shared orientation toward the reproduction of social relations. She writes, "Parents can live with the failure of happiness to deliver its promise by placing their hopes for happiness in their children."[34] Catelynn and Tyler's emotional turmoil in placing their child for adoption is portrayed in precisely this light. They offer their baby the apparent happiness of being placed in a white, wealthy, heteronormative home, thus justifying their own pain. As such, they not only secure and take pleasure in their child's future happiness—making her happiness, in Ahmed's words, a "shared object"—but also, in the logic of the show, they open themselves up to a future happiness based in the potential consolidation of the heteronormative ideal through properly timed marriage and parenthood.[35]

In keeping with the show's biopolitical goal of cultivating in its audience specific types of moral subjectivities, Catelynn and Tyler's decision to give their daughter to this couple is unambiguously promoted and celebrated by the moral and psychological authority of the series, Dr. Drew. In the "Life after Labor" special for each season, Dr. Drew speaks with the teen moms about their sex lives, struggles in their relationships, and other hardships attributed to being a teen mom. He probes and gives advice about contraception, healthy romantic partnerships, and parenting. In speaking with Tyler and Catelynn, he repeatedly refers to their "strength and courage" in making the choice that was "natural" to them and "right" for their daughter.[36] Out of the six pregnant teenagers of the first season, Catelynn is the only one to receive this kind of praise and admiration from Dr. Drew. Her choice of adoption is presented as the best and most logical choice that a pregnant teenager can make, not just because of her unstable household, but also because it leaves open the option of postponing parenthood until she and Tyler are "ready."[37] Catelynn and Tyler can presumably form a proper family, regardless of their apparent disadvantages, if they just time their parenthood appropriately.

Catelynn and Tyler's story thus helps *16 and Pregnant* negate the consequences of social inequality, in fact recoding socioeconomic class into the affective terms of "instability" and "happiness," while also dismantling the links between teen parenthood and poverty. After Catelynn explains to Dr. Drew why she is not currently living in her mother's household with "drunks, loud music, and partying," he commends her on her ability to recognize that she could and should "break the cycle." Rather than leading her to become a teen mom, Catelynn's apparent lower socioeconomic status and familial instability seem to have spurred her on in her decision not to parent her child, presenting an opportunity for a celebration of the universal accessibility of white, middle-class ideals.[38]

Laura Briggs outlines a longer history in U.S. policy and social reform of a discourse that poses adoption as a way to break cycles of pathology in poor racialized communities.[39] She argues that in the wake of welfare reform and other neoliberal policy developments, adoption is promoted and structurally enforced as "an ideal solution to the problem of caring for impoverished children."[40] Catelynn and Tyler's story in *16 and Pregnant* provides an important illustration of this. The entire series is engaged in the project of constructing the children of teen parents as adoptable. Briggs argues that Madonna and child images figured "hunger" and "need," fueling a transition from solidarity to rescue in the emergence of international adoption.[41] Similarly, regular shots in *16 and Pregnant* showing teen parents leaving their babies in the bed or on the couch to cry alone figure the need to intervene in their supposed bad parenting. In keeping with a broader adoption discourse that constructs white, middle-class parents as automatically best for children, *16 and Pregnant* obscures the structural inequalities that condition Catelynn and Tyler's apparent inadequacy for parenthood in relation to the rightfulness of the adoptive parents, naturalizing their difference through appeals to happiness, stability, and preparedness.

The trope of the "cycle," however, rather than disappearing in the absence of substantiating evidence in the series, becomes redefined in accordance with the broader shift in the problematics of teen pregnancy. The show presents this newer version of the cycle of teen pregnancy not as the result of class status or welfare policy but as purely intimate and familial. As Dr. Drew interviews each teen mom, he utilizes the term "cycle" liberally and sometimes in the absence of any apparent cycle of poverty, dependency, or teen pregnancy. For example, Dr. Drew prompts Kailyn to talk about her "rocky" relationship with her mother (who is never identified as a teen mom herself). When Kailyn says she is afraid that Joe, her son's father, might leave her because "everyone just leaves," referring presumably to her father (whom she only met for the first time during filming of her episode) and her mother, Dr. Drew says she can "hang in" with her son, adding that she has the ability to "change that cycle."[42] In this case, he uses the term "cycle" to refer to one generation's behavior. Similarly, although Lindsey's mother has not been established as a teen mom, nor does Lindsey appear to be part of a pattern of generational poverty or welfare dependency, Dr. Drew asks her how she plans to talk to her child in order to prevent "the cycle from going on."[43] According to these interviews, adolescent pregnancy is so transferrable to future generations that one instance of it already constitutes a cycle that must be stopped.

At times when he does use the term "cycle" to discuss what could be considered a generational pattern of behavior, it is nonetheless stripped of its associations with theories about poverty and welfare. Dr. Drew says to Samantha, there is a "cycle of teen pregnancy we see here in your family system," and he wonders how she plans to help her daughter break that cycle, when Samantha's parents tried and failed to do so with her. Samantha answers that she will talk to her daughter and give her birth control, and, when prompted by Dr. Drew, says that she will try to get her to delay sex. Samantha is the daughter of apparently middle-class Latino parents. Neither her mother nor Samantha appears to need public assistance, and there is no explicit broader familial or cultural acceptance of adolescent pregnancy as normal portrayed in the episode. In this segment, as in much of the series, teen pregnancy appears problematic solely because it is a "hard" (in Samantha's words) consequence of early and irresponsible sex. Its purported cyclical nature remains tied to parents' ineffectiveness at regulating their children's sexuality. Rather than justifying the burdens felt by those who bear the brunt of capitalist exploitation, as theorists of neoliberal multiculturalism have argued, this multicultural politics of teen pregnancy denies any such burdens altogether, suggesting that generational moral lapses, such as teen pregnancy, are problematic even when they are devoid of material consequences.

Many of Dr. Drew's discussions likewise emphasize how the teen mother in question failed to heed her parents' sound advice about avoiding pregnancy. After talking with Felicia (whose mother had her as a teen) about disappointing her mother by getting pregnant at sixteen, he addresses Felicia's boyfriend, saying, "You come from a broken family, too."[44] The boyfriend explains that his mother raised him, and he did not have a father growing up. In this way, Dr. Drew implicitly equates teen parenthood with growing up in a "broken family." Without elaborating on his reasons for these inquiries into Felicia's and her boyfriend's familial backgrounds, Dr. Drew leaves the audience to refer to his discussion with Brooke, one segment earlier, about the "heritage" of teen pregnancy in her family, and how she ignored her mother's warnings about teen motherhood. The audience can thus assume that Felicia and Brooke (Latina and white, respectively) became teen moms due to an inherent characteristic of their family structure, despite explicit warnings growing up, and regardless of their race, class, or cultural context. Dr. Drew's references to cycles thus repurpose a large body of social science research and political discourse about poor, racialized communities, toward a multicultural critique of "broken families" in which they apparently (no matter how hard they try not to) propagate inappropriate sex and bad morals.

In a telling segment of his interview with Alex, Dr. Drew asks her if she thinks that placing her daughter for adoption would have given the child a better life. After Alex answers with "I don't know," Dr. Drew says the child "wouldn't have to deal with" Alex's boyfriend (who has a drug problem). He also points out that Alex could have had an open adoption. Alex says "And I couldn't have handled that," to which Dr. Drew says, "Yeah, but *you* couldn't have handled that. Was that the right thing for the child?" To which Alex answers "No." After asking her if she ever considers placing her daughter for adoption still and she says no, he asks her what she fears most for her daughter. Alex says she is afraid that her daughter will end up in the same situation she is in, to which Dr. Drew nods, adding, "The cycle continuing."[45] Even though, like Lindsey and Kailynn, Alex's mother has not been identified as a former teen mom, Dr. Drew's line of questioning and Alex's answers suggest that the cycle is underway. Dr. Drew implies that Alex's child is likely to become a teen parent, but would probably not be facing that fate had Alex given the baby to the adult, married couple that offered to adopt her. Here again, teen pregnancy and parenthood are equated with self-perpetuating unhappiness, selfishness, and immorality, while adoption into a heteronormative household is part of the social goal of securing happiness and moral good.

The term "cycle" still deploys the stigma associated with denigrating images of poor people of color, but its application to any kind of familial context that has begotten a pregnant teenager serves to distance the public image of teen pregnancy from its former social, economic, and political implications. The cycles that require breaking on *16 and Pregnant* threaten personal and familial happy futures first and foremost, affecting abstract social goods such as stability and rightfulness. This is a marked shift in the discourse of teen pregnancy from the warnings of national economic demise that accompanied discussions of it in the 1990s. If the PRWORA of 1996 could be said to define the biopolitics of teen pregnancy in the 1990s and early 2000s, *16 and Pregnant* initiates a new stage of the biopolitics of teen pregnancy in recent years.

Although many of the regulatory measures of the PRWORA still affect the lives of teen parents on cash assistance, some of the most publicly apparent discourse around teen pregnancy emanates from and surrounds *16 and Pregnant* and its spin-offs. These episodes appear to be aimed primarily at disciplining the sex lives of teenagers, while generating profit. They present teen pregnancy as a product of personal behavior, and a producer of personal drama and sacrifice. Although some claim the show is not effective in its efforts, or may even be achieving the opposite, *16 and Pregnant* is at least, in part, a prevention strategy. Teen mom after teen mom is quoted saying something similar to "I love my child. I don't regret my child, but I wish I had waited. I wish I hadn't gotten pregnant as a teenager, because I had to grow up so fast." It becomes clear that the goal is to prevent certain lives from beginning, because those lives and the conditions they are thought to create are considered undesirable for individual bodies and the social body. Although sometimes muddled and contradicted, Dr. Drew's urges to make "smart" sexual decisions provide the official message of the show and the backbone of the newest multicultural model of responsible and moral adolescent citizenship.

"Good Girls" Gone Bad: Whiteness in Distress

The National Campaign has also been involved in the production of numerous scripted films and television series that deal with teen pregnancy. Rather than enlisting "real" teens to talk directly to their teen audience, these texts portray the lives of fictional pregnant and parenting teens to illustrate the problematic consequences of teenage pregnancy. One such text is the Lifetime original movie *The Pregnancy Pact,* which premiered with a viewership of over three million adults ages eighteen to forty-nine and continues to air regularly.[46] Another is the ABC Family series *The Secret Life of the American Teenager,* which was cable's foremost program in its timeslot for viewers ages twelve to thirty-four in 2012.[47] These programs overwhelmingly present teen pregnancy as a problem that threatens white, middle-class America, resulting from an almost inexplicable failure of young girls to understand and internalize core family values, an entrepreneurial spirit, and/or merely the barest information about sex.[48]

Within this production of whiteness in distress, even in the context of a fully white cast (as in the case of *The Pregnancy Pact*) these texts promote the logics of neoliberal multiculturalism outlined previously. They participate in the apparently benign and compassionate forms of differentiation Chow identifies as a key aspect of multicultural biopolitics by identifying and describing the cultural context in which teen pregnancy occurs.[49] An example of neoliberal multiculturalism's new forms of racialization that occur across traditional phenotypical race categories, these texts portray white teen pregnancy as backward, morally problematic, and culturally bankrupt.[50] They thus solidify the notion that race and ethnicity are incidental to the achievement of goodness and success. Providing a supposedly universally accessible, practical, and moral guide to proper American citizenship, they construct an apparently rational middle ground between two supposed extremes—sexual liberation and conservative family values—coupled with an emphasis on the liberating and inclusive power of markets. The National Campaign regularly uses this strategy to create the appearance of a commonsense approach to teen pregnancy that gets beyond the entanglements of partisan politics. The result is a pedagogical approach that combines the liberal notion of education and information as empowering and the conservative valuing of abstinence until marriage in an effort to maximize individual teenagers' potential for achieving heteronormative, entrepreneurial citizenship. Similar to *16 and Pregnant,* these texts promote white, middle-class norms while naturalizing the policies and cultural logics of neoliberalism.

The Pregnancy Pact was created by Lifetime Networks, a media company that, according to its website, "celebrates, entertains and supports women" in its content and has a "legacy of unifying both parties to participate in bipartisan activities in Washington, D.C." as part of its advocacy mission.[51] An effort that reflects the company's mission of engaging female audiences across the mainstream political spectrum, the film illustrates the new dominant image of teen pregnancy as a problem that increasingly crops up in white, middle-class America.[52] It begins with the message: "This film is the story of a fictional 'pregnancy pact' set against actual news reports from June 2008, and although some of the locations and public figures are real, any resemblance to actual persons is purely coincidental."[53] Next, the words "Inspired by a True Story" appear on the screen. This confused set of messages garners the film legitimacy in its didactic claims about the true nature of the problem of teen pregnancy, while affording it the liberties it ultimately takes in depicting the events that "inspired" it.[54] News clips flash on the screen from actual events in Gloucester, MA, where seventeen girls became pregnant at one school at the same time. Beginning with news anchor Anderson Cooper and footage of Gloucester's actual mayor explaining the multiple pregnancies that occurred there, footage of these events appears both at the start of the movie and at crucial moments throughout the film, furthering the sheen of authenticity.

The plot unfolds in a small New England town. After the initial news clips, there is a montage of small-town scenes—depicting Main Street, shiny pick-up trucks, clean streets, green grass, a sculpture, and boats in the water—to establish the quaint setting. The main characters are white, many are churchgoing Christians, and they appear to be materially comfortable. The film portrays the unfortunate choices that one girl (Sarah Dougan) makes as she falls victim to her own ignorance and her friends' pressures. Sarah participates in an agreement with her high school friends to each become pregnant. Some of her friends come from backgrounds perhaps more typical of the teen pregnancy discourse of the 1980s and 1990s. For instance, Karissa's mother was a teen mom and is upset to find out her daughter is pregnant because she can "barely feed" Karissa as it is, while Rose lives with her grandmother and is depicted smoking cigarettes and watching television late in her pregnancy. In contrast, Sarah is the daughter of local restaurant owner and head of the Family Values Council Lorraine and temporarily unemployed Michael. She is a typical "good girl," trusted fully by her mother and identified as "such a bright girl" by the video blogger and former pregnant teen Sidney Bloom, who has come to Gloucester to do a story on the upsurge of pregnancies in the town.

The film presents Sarah as having the requisite emotional maturity, self-respect, and parental guidance to avoid sex and pregnancy. When Lorraine justifies to Michael why she let Sarah go over to her boyfriend Jesse's house without ensuring that his parents were home, she states, "She's got respect for herself. I trust her." Always appearing neat and clean, in modest clothes, Sarah's somewhat meek demeanor and glowing, white, un–made-up face indicates her innocence and general unlikelihood as a candidate for mis-behavior. Moreover, Sarah's mother, the film's primary advocate for an abstinence-only approach, has talked to her repeatedly about "valuing her-self," and not "giving it away." Although her father is struggling with his lack of employment, Sarah's family is not "broken," and both of her parents appear to be loving, concerned about her well-being, and cognizant of the appar-ently important differences between adolescence and adulthood. Justifying her strict curfew and rules, Lorraine says to Sarah, "Growing up is not a race. Rushing won't get you there any faster." The film thus conveys that no amount of participating in traditionally adult activities will turn a teenager into an adult, confirming and naturalizing the division between child and adult.

Not only is Sarah an unlikely candidate for mischief but her boyfriend fails to fit the mold of typical teen parent as well. He is the star pitcher for the high school baseball team and his parents are wealthy Christians. Again, justifying her leniency with Sarah and Jesse, Lorraine says to Michael, "Jesse's a good kid. Goes to church. Good morals." Rather than appearing aloof, manip-ulating, or predatory in any way, Jesse is portrayed as a sincere and loving boyfriend who wants to marry Sarah after graduating from high school and attending college. Sarah and Jesse perfectly embody the childhood innocence of "puppy love," as his dad calls it, with no inklings of poverty, welfare depen-dency, or even a dearth of instruction in morality. In other words, none of the former indicators of bad citizenship (such as "broken families," crime, drugs, etc.) help to explain the deviant reproduction that unfolds in the film.

Only a slight disruption in the traditional gendered distribution of power in each household betrays any incompatibility between these families and the heteronormative ideal. Michael, for example, appears slightly emascu-lated as he discusses his lack of work and Lorraine informs him that there is always work to do around the restaurant and that "pride" will not "pay the mortgage." His role as father and head of household is also undermined as Lorraine summarily dismisses his concerns about Sarah and Jesse. Jesse's father is depicted texting during a conversation with Lorraine, as though he is generally detached or distracted with business, and says that Jesse's mother is away visiting her sister. These scenes imply that Sarah's overbearing mother and disempowered father might be factors in her fall, while Jesse's home lacks the appropriate supervision to prevent them from having sex there. The question as to exactly why Sarah ends up pregnant drives both the narrative and Sydney's investigatory blogging. The film slowly reveals the cultural and moral deficiencies that led to Sarah's enigmatic and misguided actions.

Sydney provides both the primary voice of the politically liberal, comprehensive sex education stance (also represented by the school nurse, who resigns in protest over the policy prohibiting dissemination of contraceptives at school), and the vehicle through which the audience comes to understand that Sarah's extreme naïveté and lack of entrepreneurial spirit led her to become pregnant. Sydney not only has a video blog about "teen issues" that has been focusing on teen pregnancy, but she is also a former Gloucester resident and former pregnant teen. In this way, she is another example of a white, middle-class pregnant teenager, but her pregnancy, as we gradually discover, ended in her baby's adoption, unbeknownst to the baby's father, her ex-boyfriend and current assistant principal at Gloucester High School. Sydney lied to the father, who wanted to marry her and raise the child, about having an abortion, and lied to the adoption agency about not knowing who the father was in order to prevent him from protesting. Despite these behaviors, the film presents her decision to place her baby for adoption as the rational choice because, unlike the deluded girls of the pact, she knew she was not ready to be a parent. As such, Sarah's decision to get pregnant intentionally at fifteen years old appears perplexing and irrational when viewed through Sydney's perspective.

As clips of Sydney's video blog, citing teen pregnancy statistics and asking purportedly trenchant questions about the issue, punctuate the film's plot developments, she is presented as the film's moral authority. She repeatedly admonishes the adult townspeople for their complacency about their teen pregnancy problem. To her ex-boyfriend, the assistant principal who advises her to wrap up her story and go back to New York, Sydney passionately states, "I'm giving them a chance to tell their story. Is anyone actually talking to them?" To her blog's audience she asks, outraged, "Why isn't this in the news every day?" In other words, Sydney appears as the only person who understands the gravity of the situation, while local and national authority figures ignore or mischaracterize the crisis in their midst. After a *Time* magazine story breaks about the pregnancy pact and news crews swarm the town, Sydney tells her viewers that everyone is focusing on whether there was a pact or not, which is "the wrong issue. Teen birth rates are up everywhere, not just here. The real question that we should be asking is why are so many young girls choosing to get pregnant and have babies?" In this way, the film establishes the sheer ridiculousness of girls like Sarah *choosing* to get pregnant, meaning something must be terribly amiss in the formerly quaint and reliable rural bastions of true American values where this is occurring.

Teen pregnancy is thus portrayed as an equal-opportunity cultural pathology that will crop up wherever vigilance against it is not properly kept. While *The Pregnancy Pact* does not portray racial diversity, it participates in a key aspect of neoliberal multiculturalism by presenting whiteness as threatened by the lesser personhoods that both generate and result from these intimate transgressions.

Through Sydney, the film gradually reveals that the town cannot solve teen pregnancy using the two established opposing proposals—more access to contraception or more emphasis on abstinence. This is most evident in the scenes that portray Sarah's thought process leading up to her pregnancy. Although Sarah at first seems confused and scared about her promise to her friends, cowering apart from the rest of the group as they watch Karissa go to the nurse for a pregnancy test, she later decides pregnancy is a good way to ensure that Jesse will not leave her behind for college when he graduates before her. First, Jesse tells her that he plans to marry her eventually, by which she is both surprised and elated. Later, she listens intently as her friends talk about how their babies' fathers do in fact plan to be involved in their lives despite the common conception that teen dads tend to abandon their responsibilities. Sarah is then pictured sitting on Jesse's bed, talking to him about what their wedding will be like. A shirtless Jesse shushes her in order to kiss her, lay her down, and, presumably, have sex with her. Sarah says, "I love you. We are going to be so happy." This last scene reveals that Sarah is wrapped up in a fantasy of how sex will lead to marriage, while Jesse is apparently interested in sex in and of itself. Further revealing the moral message of the film, Sarah's father says to her mother, implying that she is too lenient, Jesse may be a good kid, but "he's still a seventeen-year-old boy. They're not much for keeping their pants on, if you know what I mean." The film thus naturalizes a popular narrative about teenage sex in which girls are easily fooled into confusing a boy's uncontrollable sex drive for love and commitment.

The pregnant girls make their naïveté glaringly obvious in their visions of future motherhood. They walk the school halls talking about how they hope to all have baby girls. One says, "Oh my god, that would be so cool— having a little girl to hang out with and be my best friend. We'd get little matching outfits and I'd paint her fingernails." At another point, they explain that their children will all be in the same class and be best friends. They say that they will "dress them up" and "cook them dinner" and "never yell at them." For these reasons, Sydney characterizes them in her blog as living in a "fantasy land," and believing that teen motherhood looks like a "Huggies commercial." She asks why they do not know about the hardships they are going to face and says, "I don't understand why they aren't thinking about these things and why hasn't anyone else made them think about these things. Given them a reality check." Later, in a confrontation with Lorraine, Sidney demands to know why Sarah "is walking around with her head in the clouds." Presenting both the purportedly wholly personal nature of the problem of teen pregnancy and the moral bankruptcy that it apparently engenders, the film portrays Sarah and her friends as extremely ignorant about motherhood and healthy relationships, as they knowingly deceive the boys with whom they plan to procreate.

The delusional and unfortunate nature of Sarah's aspirations become clear through the various responses of everyone around her to her pregnancy. Jesse, not yet realizing that Sarah intended to get pregnant, laments that he has "ruined" their lives and should have "pulled out" or used a condom every time, to which Sarah responds, "You didn't ruin anything. Everything's perfect." When the pact is later revealed, Sarah tells him he must forgive her for the sake of the baby. Jesse exclaims, "No! I don't want a baby, OK? Not with anyone, but especially not with a liar like you! I really thought we'd be together forever. I really did. But you ruined it. It is all ruined because of you. So just leave me alone, OK? Leave me alone." Rather than ensure a lifelong partnership with Jesse, Sarah prevented it. At the end of the film, Jesse happily walks past Sarah, who is in a late stage of pregnancy, to meet up with a different, presumably not-pregnant, girl. Much like the narratives presented in *16 and Pregnant,* teen pregnancy appears in *The Pregnancy Pact* as the precise opposite of heteronormative domestic bliss and thus a crucial tool of racialization within the logic of multiculturalism. Rather than pathologizing an established social group, defined by race, ethnicity, or class, this discourse of teen pregnancy as cultural deficiency constructs it as a problem that creeps up where there are invisible cracks in the intertwining structures of heteronormativity and entrepreneurialism.

Sarah's parents' shock and dismay help present Sarah's pregnancy as a mysterious disaster. Lorraine, who has maintained throughout the film that teen pregnancy is a "private matter," simply does not understand how Sarah has become "that kind of girl—the kind of girl who gets into trouble." In her opinion, Sarah and her parents will now have to "face the humiliation" that will inevitably be the result in their social context. Having completely disregarded both Jesse's aspirations to leave Gloucester and go to college, and her parents' commands not to have sex, Sarah's actions appear totally irrational and confused. This is further emphasized by Karissa's realization that the pact was not a good idea. She says, "I hate this. People were right, you know—we were so dumb," and goes on to recount how unhappy Rose, who has given birth by this point, is as a teen mom. As the pregnant girls begin to understand the gravity of their mistake, teen pregnancy appears to be the result of a cruel hoax the girls unwittingly played on each other. As with Dr. Drew's tautological discourse of cycles, the cause of deviant pregnancy in this film revolves around sex and morality, but is ultimately strangely inscrutable.

A conversation between Sarah and Sydney further reveals this inscrutability, but points to a fundamental lack of entrepreneurial spirit as the main reason for Sarah's downfall. When Sydney is still the only person who knows about the pact, she asks Sarah why she and her friends wanted to get pregnant. Sarah responds that it is really no "mystery. Everyone wants a baby." Sydney points out that not everyone wants one when she is fifteen, and Sarah says that all she really needs to be happy is Jesse and her baby. Sydney responds in disbelief, "Really? You're such a bright girl. Is that really your only dream for yourself? . . . I just don't understand. I mean, if you're gonna make a pact with your friends, yeah, but why not make a pact to go to college, go to Europe, start a rock band, plant a tree?" Sarah accuses Sydney of being "judgmental" right before a phone call cuts their conversation short and they learn that Rose had her baby. This moment is accompanied by a foreboding, low-pitched piano chord in a minor key. Part of the problem with these girls, this scene illustrates, is their lack of imagination and ambition. Sydney's flabbergasted response to Sarah's dreams of happiness indicates that knowingly choosing teen parenthood over the other options would seem to be impossible. Unlike Sydney, who, as a pregnant teen, aspired to be an online journalist rather than a parent, these girls lack the ability to envision themselves as anything else and thus to take advantage of the opportunities afforded by a presumably free and equal society. In keeping with the logic of neoliberal multiculturalism, in which markets provide the avenue toward success and equality, Sarah and her friends' improper conduct at this key period of intimate citizenship sentences them to lives of physical and emotional discomfort.

The film casts doubt on the liberal agenda of providing contraceptives—summed up by the high school principal, who points out that girls who are trying to get pregnant will not use contraception anyway—and the conservative abstinence-only approach. Sarah had sex despite her parents' "single, unambiguous message," because she wanted to be "close" to her boyfriend, but she also wanted a baby, making the issue of information about and access to birth control a moot point.[55] The film constructs teen pregnancy as a problem that stems from a mysterious breakdown in communication between adults and teenagers about the relationship between intimate behavior and economic success. Somehow, Sarah and her friends missed crucial instruction about the equal opportunity to wealth and success afforded by free markets, U.S. neoliberal governance, and proper intimate behavior. Talking to Sydney, one pregnant girl comments that "in the old days, girls our age always had kids, so it can't be that bad," citing that Mary, the mother of Jesus Christ, was only fourteen years old. Sydney responds that in the "old days," those girls were all married and they did not need "two incomes just to survive." Adhering to an antiquated view of proper womanhood, these girls are ignorant of the opportunities and the hardships afforded them by modern life. Not only have they been deprived of basic information about the American Dream—anyone can achieve material success and self-fulfillment with the right amount of ambition, entrepreneurship, and perseverance—but no one has explained to them that the price of acquiring the American Dream is delayed marriage and parenthood. Their small pocket of American culture is thus pathologically traditional and deficient.

Throughout the film, Sydney's video blog, in which she is often shown speaking directly into the camera, citing general information about teen pregnancy, and advising teens on how and why to avoid it, functions in a similar way to Dr. Drew in *16 and Pregnant*. She says, "The truth is, when you get pregnant that young, there are no good options. Adoption, abortion, keeping it. They're not gonna turn out exactly like you think. They're gonna be painful and your life will be completely changed forever." Brandishing expert status, resulting in this case from her own pregnancy as well as her career reporting on the issue, she explicitly instructs her audience (both fictional and real) about reality, seeming to move beyond the petty politics about reproductive rights and religious morality to tell the "truth." Within the logic of the film, teen pregnancy is "painful" and should therefore be avoided.

In accordance with racializing discourses that portray the enlightened accommodation of difference as the multicultural ideal, *The Pregnancy Pact* portrays the solution to the encroaching problem of teen pregnancy as a rational, natural, and balanced response between two extremes. Lorraine, abstinence-only advocate and mother of a pregnant teen, addresses the Family Values Council, persuading them to keep her as their president despite her personal scandals (aside from her daughter's pregnancy, her husband, perhaps redeeming his injured manhood, spent a night in jail for attacking a press crew trying to report on the pregnancy pact). She states that although she still thinks abstinence is the "healthiest choice for our kids . . . we need to be more honest with ourselves. A fifteen-year-old girl is too young to be a mother. Now, birth control may not be a choice that I would accept in my home, but we can't stand in the way of schools offering contraceptives for the families that want them." The experience of having her daughter ignore her discussions of abstinence and intentionally get pregnant has persuaded her that birth control should be available through the school. Although it is not clear how "families" (like hers) that do not want their teenagers to use contraceptives would be able to prevent them from getting it at the school, Lorraine's conclusion is apparently received by the council as perfectly logical.

This rational compromise is further illustrated by the next scene, in which Sydney explains to Sarah that the Family Values Council did not vote Lorraine out of her role as president. Sydney claims that the council retained Lorraine as president because of her ability to persuade a "knee-jerk liberal" like Sydney that "that there's a lot more to" dealing with teen pregnancy than "just hand[ing] out enough condoms." In the end, both Lorraine and Sydney learn that their previous views of the problem were one-sided and overly simplistic. The film illustrates that an emphasis on abstinence and information about contraception are both important for teen pregnancy prevention, but it is even more crucial to instill in young girls the proper desires for achievement leading to heteronormative adulthood. Without this, sex and reproduction will apparently win out over the most comprehensive and morality-infused sex education.

This politics of teen pregnancy is consolidated in the sole reference to welfare in the entire film. Sarah's out-of-work father protests against Lorraine's suggestion to ask Jesse's wealthy father for help paying for the baby, exclaiming, "[We] might as well put our hand out for welfare." In this scene, public assistance appears as an always already unacceptable recourse with which to cope with teen pregnancy. At the same time, the real dissolution of the white middle class becomes palpable. Rather than turn to the stigmatized social supports of a previous era's typical teen mom, afflicted communities must shore up their family values, engage in bipartisan compromise, and forward the American bootstrap ethic. In this way, discourses about teen pregnancy's attack on whiteness register social anxieties about the reality of a shrinking middle class and an increasing poor population.

While deep impoverishment of the racialized poor is completely ignored in this discourse, teen pregnancy becomes a scapegoat for the circumstances in which low wages, high unemployment, increased flexibilization of labor, and the lack of a material safety net thrust middle-class families into the ranks of the poor. The right combination of morality, birth control, and entrepreneurial spirit appears to provide protection from these naturalized social trends. Thus, in this brief moment in *The Pregnancy Pact*, the racialization of teen pregnancy performs the kind of "rationalizing power" that Melamed identifies as a key function of official antiracisms and, in particular, neoliberal multiculturalism.[56] However, with the relative absence of portrayals of any material consequences to teen pregnancy or any significant class inequality in most post-welfare teen pregnancy prevention discourse, the costs of moral and cultural deficiencies are largely presented in terms of physical pain and unhappiness.

As Sarah and Sydney visit Rose in the hospital after giving birth, they arrive to Rose saying pathetically, "It hurts." Karissa responds, "Tell the nurse to give you another shot of morphine." Iris, another pregnant teen, turns to Sarah and Sydney saying, "She had to have, like, thirty-seven stitches," to which Sydney replies, "She must have tore really bad." Sarah, showing her ignorance once again, says, "Tore? Tore what?" "Down there, stupid," says Karissa. Similarly, when Rose attempts to breastfeed her baby, her grandmother looks on and says, "With all the sores you got, the baby probably don't like the taste of blood," to which Rose says, "But my boobs are full! They hurt!" Showing no sympathy, her grandmother says, "Welcome to motherhood. Why don't you try the breast pump?" Rather than rationalizing inequality, teen pregnancy's multicultural discourse more often denies it altogether, portraying the burdens of backwardness as bodily and affective.

Many more scripted popular culture texts of this period depict the face of teenage pregnancy as a white, middle- or upper-class girl. While such texts often portray pregnancies that do not result in teen motherhood—as each character either places her baby for adoption, has a miscarriage, or, however rarely, has an abortion—perhaps the foremost example of teen pregnancy that results in teen motherhood is *The Secret Life of the American Teenager*.[57] The series ran on ABC Family, owned by the Walt Disney Company, and aired a parental advisory notice before each episode due its sexual content. The show begins with fifteen-year-old Amy Juergens finding out she is pregnant after having sex only once at band camp the summer before her first year of high school. She lives in a middle-class household with her younger sister and two parents—although it later turns out that her father is having an affair, because her mother has lost interest in talking to and having sex with him. Her defining characteristic before becoming pregnant is that she plays the French horn, and her mother refers to her as "the good girl" in comparison to her sister.[58] The multicultural cast of teenage characters includes Ricky, a suave white foster child who seduces Amy; Adrian, a promiscuous Latina who is in love with Ricky; Grace, a blonde cheerleader and chaste Christian; Jack, Grace's sexually frustrated blonde boyfriend who cheats on her with Adrian; Ben, a geeky, nice white guy who loves Amy even though she's pregnant with someone else's baby; Lauren, Amy's calm and rational black friend; Madison, Amy's sweet and naïve white friend; and Henry and Alice, Ben's Asian American friends who date each other and obsess over their computers. While these teens and their parents come to represent some standard perspectives on abstinence and birth control, the first season of *The Secret Life* all but sidesteps questions of sex education and access to contraception, jettisoning any connections to social and political concerns, and rendering teen pregnancy completely personal and familial.

The show displays its explanation for Amy's pregnancy most overtly in the penultimate episode of the first season, "One Night at Band Camp."[59] In this episode, shots of Amy in labor, lying in her hospital bed, are intercut with flashbacks of her short journey toward sex and pregnancy eight months and two weeks earlier at band camp. In this way, Ricky's skillful seduction is juxtaposed with Amy's excruciating labor pains to convey a clear causal relationship and associate teenage sex with unnecessary suffering. The episode begins with a shot of horn players marching under a banner that reads "Welcome to Best of the Best 2008 Band Camp." The camera cuts to Ricky and two other boys sitting on the bleachers as the musicians march by. Ricky, holding his drumsticks, nudges one of his friends with a knowing grin. Amy is one of the marchers and looks over at Ricky as she passes. He smiles and waves and she gets out of step with her band members and runs into a tuba player. Ricky smiles again and then the picture fades out before his face reappears, much more somber this time, as he stands gazing at Amy in her hospital bed. It is already clear from these opening shots that teen pregnancy results, as in *The Pregnancy Pact,* from sex-driven boys manipulating naïve and likely unsexual girls. As Amy describes it to Lauren and Madison in the first episode, "It was not that great . . . I'm not even sure it was sex, OK guys? . . . I didn't exactly realize what was happening until, like, after two seconds and then it was just over and it wasn't fun and definitely not like what you see in the movies. You know, all romantic and stuff."[60]

The scenes leading up to the seduction further display Amy's innocence and Ricky's ill intentions. Back at band camp, Ricky approaches Amy as she thumbs through her French horn music in the cafeteria. They discuss how she will be starting at Ricky's high school in the fall, and he asks her if she wants to hang out after the concert that night, in which she will be the featured soloist. During this exchange, Amy's inner monologue (saying things like, "Oh my god! I think he likes me!") conveys to the audience how nervous and excited she is to be talking to a cute, older boy, and how oblivious she is to his desires, even as he is approached by another girl—obviously a former conquest—whom he pretends not to remember.

Ricky's moral bankruptcy combines with Amy's labor pains and continued naïveté to portray the inherently brutal and perverse nature of teen pregnancy. During the labor, Amy appears as a bitter, reluctant, and ignorant participant in the birth of her child. She is rude to Ricky, who has changed his smarmy and irresponsible ways since attending counseling and gaining a sense of responsibility in the face of teen fatherhood. Her mother says, "I really don't think this is the time to be resentful." To which Amy sarcastically responds, "When would be a good time? I'm thinking the rest of my life." Amy apparently sees herself as a victim of Ricky's recklessness, her future needlessly sacrificed. After sending Ricky on an errand for a hamburger, she says to her mother, teary-eyed, "I'm hungry and I'm tired and I don't want to do this." Her mother responds, "Well, I don't really think that you have much choice." Illustrating the apparently inevitable and painful force of labor set in motion by a single sex act, another contraction begins and she exclaims, "Oh no, here it comes again!" After the contraction, noting that she is looking forward to her epidural, she says, "This stinks." Amy is not only descending down a path of physical turmoil she did not anticipate when she had sex and feels she does not deserve but is also apparently still very childish and ignorant. Complaining desperately to her mother about her predicament, she says, "I just don't see how this is gonna work. I mean, how do we even know I have a birth canal?" When her mother looks at her with exasperation, she exclaims, "What?! I don't know anything about anything other than the French horn!" and the show cuts to her playing her horn at band camp. In this way, the audience learns that not much has changed since she fell for Ricky's wiles. She is still a child who understands very little about how the world works.

The show thus suggests it is some cruel act of nature that children can physically have sex and get pregnant but cannot possibly prepare themselves mentally for the result. As such, teens form the perfect vehicle for a multicultural politics that naturalizes cultural deficiency as a justification for misfortune. Teenagers of all races are apparently inherently culturally deficient, unable to control their bodies and unable to comprehend consequences, which take the form of physical and emotional pain rather than economic degradation. Since teenagers are naturally pathological in this manner, parents and other adults must compensate in particular ways or risk exacerbating the problem.

Unlike in *The Pregnancy Pact,* teen pregnancy in *The Secret Life* results in part from Ricky's pathological sexual behavior that stems explicitly from bad parenting. At band camp again, Ricky unveils more calculated wooing techniques—flattering Amy about her looks and her musicianship, and touching her leg. Later, he tells her she is "special" and that he hopes "this can be the start of something big" (of course, the audience knows that "something big" really is beginning, despite Ricky's short-term intentions). In addition to the cues about his insincerity present in this episode, previous episodes establish Ricky as a "troubled" foster child who is not to be trusted.[61] A victim of sexual abuse at the hands of his birth father, Ricky sees a counselor, who tries to dissuade him from his compulsively seductive ways. In addition to Amy, he manages to garner the affections of Grace and Lauren (both in danger of losing their virginity to him) and have regular sex with Adrian, all in the first season. He is thus established as a sexual predator, the regrettable result of bad parenting (his birth mother and birth father also had drug problems) and sexual deviance. In this way, teen pregnancy enters the white middle class by way of predatory bad boys preying on innocent girls.[62] This narrative about the special dangers and needs of foster children likely stems from a National Campaign initiative to address the particular occurrence of teen pregnancy amongst teens in foster care.[63]

The final scenes of "One Night at Band Camp" drive home the show's commentary about teen sex and pregnancy as a personal problem with personal consequences. On the night of Amy's deflowering, while sitting on the couch with Ricky in the cafeteria that they had broken into after hours, she tells him it is time for her to go back to her cabin. Her voiceover says, "Why did I say that? He's being so nice. I'm an idiot," again displaying her naïveté.[64] Ricky says, "All right. If you want—I just thought we were both enjoying this." He then persuades her to stay by reasoning that if they feel the same way about each other, what is the harm in hanging out for a few more minutes? Amy says, "Yeah, what's a few more minutes?" and then the picture fades to white before a shot appears of Amy in her hospital bed, saying "Crap!" She touches her belly and says, "Not you. Me." That few more minutes, the audience is asked to assume, was all it took to propel Amy into this painful and unreasonable situation, generating collateral damage in the form of a fetus that is even more fragile and innocent.

Unlike Sarah in *The Pregnancy Pact,* Amy is not delusional about the joys of teenage motherhood, but about her prospects for having an impressively older and good-looking boyfriend. Both girls fail to receive the proper education from the knowing adults in their lives before it is too late. Both girls also come from ostensibly heteronormative nuclear families that, on closer inspection, do not measure up to the ideal. While Sarah's father is unemployed and struggling with his pride and familial authority, Amy's father finds the emotional and physical attention he does not get from his wife outside of his marriage. It appears that the breakdown of white, middle-class, patriarchal marriage is in part to blame for teenage pregnancy, because it prevents each parent from fulfilling his or her rightful role in the upbringing of proper young women.

Without question, specific types of parental participation are required to end teen pregnancy, as *The Secret Life* makes clear. When "One Night at Band Camp" ends, Shailene Woodley, the actor who plays Amy, appears on the screen, dressed in her character's clothes and seated on Amy's dining room table. She delivers a public service announcement that appears during and after many episodes: "The first time too many teens have the sex talk with their parents is when they're telling them that they're pregnant." As she speaks, the words "national campaign to prevent teen and unplanned pregnancy stayteen.org" appear on the screen. She continues, "Parents, if your teens have a question about sex, don't assume they're doing it. And teens, if your parents aren't talking to you about sex, don't assume they don't care. Teenage pregnancy is 100% preventable. Start talking. For more information, please visit stayteen.org or abcfamily.com." The PSA is implicitly aimed at girls, as they are the ones who would be telling their parents they are pregnant. The message suggests that teen pregnancy can be completely eliminated by the right kinds and amounts of discussions between parents and their daughters, which would convince teenage girls not have sex. The claim that it is 100 percent preventable betrays an emphasis on abstinence over forms of contraception, all of which have an effectiveness of slightly less than 100 percent. The website Stay Teen, examined at length in chapter 2, is created and maintained by the National Campaign and is devoted to informing teens on how to avoid sex and pregnancy.

In this way, like *16 and Pregnant*'s use of Dr. Drew and *The Pregnancy Pact*'s teen issues blog, *The Secret Life* participates explicitly in a new dominant bio-political approach to teen pregnancy. Rather than altering the material world that teenagers live in, making it easier or more difficult to become pregnant through changes in access to contraception, public assistance, education, jobs, and so on, this prevention strategy utilizes popular entertainment as a forum to teach teenagers how to avoid the unnecessary emotional and physical pain that comes with inappropriate sex. The replacement of welfare-drawing black and Latina teen moms with white, middle-class pregnant teens helps convey the multicultural politics of teen pregnancy—that it is an equal-opportunity personal disaster. It also conveys the moral message that necessarily results from that revelation—that in a society governed by open access to freedom, prosperity, and happiness through proper moral and economic behavior, every American has both the opportunity and duty to reach these ideals. In other words, in a post-racial, multicultural context, there is neither systemic racism nor white privilege. In fact, there appears to be no significant social inequality at all. Rather, there are individuals who are more or less equipped to achieve success in the form of happiness, physical comfort, and normalcy.

Together, these texts help to consolidate a new discourse of teen pregnancy in the post-welfare era. They construct teen pregnancy as a problem that exists independently of racial and class differences, threatening the comfort and happiness of would-be normal Americans. In so doing, and in keeping with multiple iterations of multicultural politics that have had both antiracist and normative effects, they may help debunk long-standing racist stereotypes surrounding adolescent pregnancy, but they also have many more implications.[65] In the 1990s, teen pregnancy helped to usher in the severe regulation of welfare recipients and poor people at large through welfare reform. It did so as a vehicle that combined concerns about the structure of welfare programs with an emphasis on personal responsibility. Welfare reform debate was riddled with discussions of changing the "culture of welfare," raising "self-worth" through work experience, and cultivating "hope" and "self-sufficiency" by taking away a "perverse system of incentives" to have babies and draw on taxpayers' money.[66] While these sentiments clearly constructed poverty as the result of bad decision making and irresponsible behavior by using racialized stereotypes of welfare queens and teen moms to demonize poor people, they also necessarily implicated societal structures in personal, sexual, and reproductive choices through their indictment of the welfare system. Out of this context came punitive legislation that continues to curtail the choices of impoverished people, while teen pregnancy takes on a new identity toward different ends.

Today's public discourse of teen pregnancy foregrounds the emphasis welfare reform put on personal responsibility, thereby eliding the role that legislation and other social structures continue to play in regulating reproductive behavior. The popular culture texts analyzed here promote an apparently apolitical citizenship, explicitly teaching proper sex, reproduction, consumption, and recreation as the desired modes of adolescent participation in U.S. society. They attempt to convince their audience that teen pregnancy is universally unpleasant—portraying the physical discomfort of pregnancy and labor, the social turmoil that results from being pregnant in high school, and the stress of caring for a crying newborn. Counting on the commonly held conception of teenagers as universally averse to hard work and unnecessary trials of character, these programs emphasize the irritating, excruciating, and disgusting aspects of parenthood—things that are a part of parenting for most people of any age—in hopes of deterring them. This is part of the goal of "helping young women make more informed choices for themselves," as Sydney puts it in her video blog. Rather than justifying and naturalizing the economic burdens of racial capitalism, then, the neoliberal multicultural politics of post-welfare televised teen pregnancy prevention portrays almost no such burdens at all. These texts suggest that if teenage girls were properly educated in some important truths—that unprotected sex leads to pregnancy, which leads to physical pain, unhappiness, and failure to achieve entrepreneurial success—they would not choose to do it and would instead reap the personal, emotional, physical, and consumer benefits of multicultural enlightenment and normalcy.

Multiple policies and institutions differentially affect the choices of teens and teen parents—legislation and programs related to health insurance, abortion and contraception, sex education, welfare, immigration, and more—based on race, class, gender, sexuality, and other categories of social difference. However, these televised texts are part of a broader trend of portraying personal decision making as separate from social structures. They underwrite the delinking of social welfare from the formal state apparatus both institutionally and in public consciousness. They are part of a larger channeling of private funding and private industry into the business of cultivating a narrow definition of citizenship focused on intimate relationships, and ignoring unequal access to resources and support for reproductive choices. This new biopolitics of teen pregnancy attempts to directly discipline a broader swath of the population than punitive welfare policy. At the same time, its embeddedness in profit-generating industries results in perhaps a more convoluted message. In the previous chapter, I showed how the market logic of such media-based tactics lends itself to multiple conflicting meanings about the social desirability of teen sex. Perhaps most important, though, this new approach results in the wholesale depoliticizing of reproductive issues, removing them from questions of access to health care, public assistance, child care, sustainable jobs, adequate housing, and so on, posing reproductive behavior as the effect of unencumbered choices based entirely on personal morals, values, and responsibility. Ultimately, this new popular discourse of teen pregnancy effectively eclipses the deepened social inequalities and heightened differential regulation that the older discourse of teen pregnancy helped to initiate. As such, and in accordance with the teen pregnancy advocacy work examined in the chapter 2, it furthers neoliberal cultural politics by promoting versions of citizenship and social well-being defined through properly cultivated morality and entrepreneurial spirit rather than publicly ensured material and bodily health and safety.

4

Pathologizing and Path Breaking

Teen Pregnancy and Young Parents in New Mexico

In a 2002 *Albuquerque Journal* article, Linda Phillips Lehrer, a community liaison for New Mexico Teen Pregnancy Coalition (NMTPC), discusses the high rates of teen pregnancy, particularly among Hispanic teens, in New Mexico. "'Adults must do a better job of reaching the youths who are most likely to wind up pregnant[—]those who have behavioral problems, are reared in dysfunctional families, live in poverty and are failing school,' Lehrer said. 'This is really key to New Mexico's (teen) birth rate,' she said . . . 'One of the major solutions to teen pregnancy is parents being more parental. Parents need to be sexuality educators for their kids.'"[1] Her peculiar way of naming poverty as an important factor in the occurrence of teen pregnancy, while leaving it out of any recommendations for prevention, is a common characteristic of the dominant discourse around teen pregnancy in the state.

Every year, when state teen pregnancy rates are calculated and released, representatives from NMTPC and other interested groups have given their analyses of the causes of and solutions to New Mexico's always higher (and sometimes highest) rate among the fifty states.[2] As the personal and multicultural discourses of teen pregnancy that this book documents have solidified on the national level, the high rates of teen pregnancies and births in New Mexico have remained the subject of an arguably more complex struggle over the contours, rights, and responsibilities of citizenship within the state. The state's ongoing struggles around colonialism, racism, land appropriation, poverty, and environmental degradation have made the promotion of neoliberal multiculturalism a challenging task for social reformers. In New Mexico, racialized discourses of cultural pathology, like that espoused by Lehrer above, compete with and exist alongside narratives of neoliberal multiculturalism. At the same time, the activism of young parents of color, rooted in analyses of structural social inequality, challenges the normative prevention frameworks, racist portrayals, and punitive policies that affect pregnant and parenting teens.

A close look at the particular context of New Mexico reveals that teen pregnancy is a crucial cultural battleground in the ascendancy of neoliberalism. It illustrates a powerful alternative feminist reproductive justice framework for approaching the issue of teenage reproduction that affirms adolescent girls' rights to health care, education, and reproductive choices. Given the visibility and salience of this feminist organizing, the continued funding and audience for dominant national discourses of personal sexual responsibility only confirms the widespread acceptance of such logic. This localized study points to the role of neoliberal multiculturalism as a defense of racial capitalism, as well as to the cracks and fissures in that rationalizing power. In the face of explicit racism on the one hand and transformative grassroots rights-based advocacy on the other, neoliberal multiculturalism appears at least partially exposed as an inadequate framework for explaining and promoting public well-being. Nonetheless, teen pregnancy in New Mexico political discourse serves primarily as a vehicle for the continued racialization and stigmatization of poor people of color, and a continued lack of public investment and redistributive programs to address inequalities.

Colonialism, Racialized Poverty, and Reproduction in New Mexico

In order to understand current reproductive politics in New Mexico and their intersections with questions of race, class, and citizenship, it is crucial to review some of the formative historical and ongoing processes that have led to high rates of both poverty and the purportedly deviant familial configurations that are often associated with poverty. While there may not be a direct causal relationship between this history and the present-day politics of teen pregnancy, a brief look at the historical development of racial politics and poverty in New Mexico reveals the continued centrality of discourses about reproductive behavior to the maintenance of inequalities within the state. The colonial history of what is now the state of New Mexico is layered and complex. The territory was originally colonized by the Spanish, then became part of Mexico, and was later colonized by Anglo-Americans and annexed as a territory by the United States After an unusually long push for statehood fraught with racial tensions, New Mexico became a state in 1912. Since then, the forces of tourism, uranium, environmentalism, and immigration, as well as ongoing struggles over land and water rights, have informed reproductive politics in the state.

As many scholars illustrate, gendered, sexual, and reproductive discipline and regulation have been constitutive of colonial power.[3] This is evident in the various iterations of colonialism in New Mexico. Native American groups living in, as well as coming and going from what is now New Mexico prior to European contact, included Pueblo, Apache, Comanche, Navajo, and Ute Indians.[4] Initial Spanish explorations of the area occurred in the 1500s and resulted in Spanish settlement at the turn of the seventeenth century. Native Americans endured the violent consequences of Spanish colonization to varying degrees throughout the following two and a half centuries. During this time, ties of servitude, economic exchange, and blood developed between Native Americans, peasants of mixed Spanish and indigenous Mexican (referring to what is now Mexico) descent, and colonists of Spanish descent.[5] As the historian James Brooks argues, the relationships between and among the various groups living in the area prior to U.S. colonization were structured in part through forms of slavery and kinship that resulted from the "exchangeability of women and children."[6] The historian Ned Blackhawk also notes, "Captives were overwhelmingly women and children whose sexual and reproductive behavior became essential to the colony."[7] In this way, gender and reproduction structured relations of subordination, conflict, and cooperation between the internally stratified groups of colonizers and colonized.

As Anglo-Americans began settling in New Mexico, both Native American and Mexican American populations—those of mixed Spanish and indigenous heritage—were the target of reforms. Increasingly throughout the 1800s, the prevailing racial logics that justified slavery and Manifest Destiny, which presented the assumed inferiority of non-European groups as hereditary, began to inform New Mexican politics and culture. With the long history of intermixing between Spanish colonists and indigenous New Mexicans, this ideological shift resulted in a society hierarchized by perceived ethnic heritage, as well as a campaign to present the elite Mexican American population in New Mexico as purely Spanish.[8] These discourses of Spanish purity were key to the ultimate success of New Mexican politicians aiming to achieve statehood and thus allowed for both the incorporation of New Mexican bodies into the national citizenry and the maintenance of relations of colonialism and inequality for most Native and Mexican Americans.

In contemporary New Mexico, such discourses continue to shape and describe divisions between a relatively powerful "Hispano" elite, and the poorer, discursively browner, Mexican American and Latino people in New Mexico—a group that includes an expanding immigrant population. As Pablo Mitchell illustrates in his study of race and colonialism in territorial New Mexico, technologies of discipline that targeted bodily comportment, sexuality, and gender performance were central to constructions of racial difference.[9] These histories of Spanish and U.S. colonialism in New Mexico foreshadow the racial dimensions and ongoing settler-colonial relations of the contemporary politics of teen pregnancy in the state, in which reproductive behaviors continue to characterize perceived racial difference, while an institutional focus on "Hispanic" teens brackets Native American and African American teens out of public discourse.

Accompanying these racial ideologies and technologies of sexual and reproductive discipline were new forms land management, which divested both Native American and Latino people of their livelihoods and set the stage for centuries of struggle over land and resource ownership. The historian Maria Montoya describes the processes by which land use rights held by Native and Mexican Americans have been rendered invalid through the U.S. legal system, along with the Mexican land grants that bestowed usufructuary rights on groups of rural New Mexicans after the United States-Mexican War. She argues that the concept of "landlessness" was used to racialize impoverished Native and Mexican Americans and fueled the processes by which these groups were dispossessed of land they were considered incapable of properly utilizing. "Indeed," she writes, "it was important to conflate landlessness with ethnicity as Americans fulfilled their Manifest Destiny to occupy, liberalize, and democratize the open spaces of the American West."[10] Once conflated with ethnicity, misuse of the land becomes an inheritable trait, which results from either genetic or cultural generational incapacities. Battles over property and land use rights continue to rage, perpetuating discourses of cultural pathology against poor communities of color.[11] Racialized poverty and dispossession in New Mexico, then, cause and result from denigrating discourses in which deviant genetics, reproduction, parenting, and/or cultural practices purportedly pass from one generation to the next.

The military industrial complex and other polluting industries have also contributed to poverty and degradation throughout rural and urban New Mexico. These industries have generated racialized conflicts in which the survival of impoverished communities of color becomes contingent on the contamination of their land and resources, causing dire generational health effects. The uranium industry in New Mexico, for example, made up of uranium mining; nuclear weapons engineering, testing, and storage; and nuclear waste storage, has occurred mostly in and around marginalized communities who form a core part of the low-wage labor force in these businesses.[12] Largely white, mainstream environmentalist movements have emerged in response to various forms of environmental degradation in New Mexico, as the anthropologist Joseph Masco and the geographer Jake Kosek have examined in their research on nuclear and forestry politics, respectively. These movements have often served to further racialize and marginalize the communities that rely on such industries for their livelihoods.[13] In these ways, Native American and Latino people in New Mexico have incurred the intergenerational effects of intertwining material and discursive denigration. Although these processes do not directly determine reproductive behavior or politics, they contribute to a political, cultural, economic, and physical environment that exerts ongoing stress on the reproductive lives of racialized communities in New Mexico.

All of these processes—the construction and deployment of racial difference, the divestment of land and resources from impoverished communities, and the pollution and destruction of healthy landscapes—hinge on and contribute to the ongoing interstitial status of New Mexico as both foreign and belonging to the nation. In his study of poverty and community action, Alyosha Goldstein explains that even after statehood was attained, New Mexico continued to be understood as a foreign and primitive part of the nation, resulting in part from the increasing association in the mid-twentieth century of poverty with racialized underdeveloped nations. The American studies scholar Lena McQuade argues that this interstitiality has been constructed partly through the notion of New Mexicans' "troubled reproduction." New Mexico has a long history of generating "troubling" reproductive health outcomes, such as high infant mortality rates. In accordance, its inhabitants have been routinely portrayed as "troubled" reproducers for the nation. McQuade traces the "symbolic and material relationships between reproductive outcomes and national belonging," uncovering the ways that the reproductive lives of Native and Mexican Americans in New Mexico have been shaped by neglect and stigma.[14] Current approaches to teenage pregnancy in New Mexico revise and reiterate such stigmas and structural neglect, contributing to the status quo of racialized poverty within the state.

At the same time, this marginalization has historically engendered grassroots organizing and radical activism to challenge the status quo. Some examples include indigenous resistance to Spanish colonization, a long history of Hispano activism against the Anglo and U.S. government occupation of land in northern New Mexico, and Native and Mexican American reproductive health workers organizing in response to both the rise of institutionalized public health and white women's takeover of reproductive health professions.[15] These counter-hegemonic projects have historically disrupted the processes of dispossession that characterize New Mexico's history. Within the contemporary politics of teen pregnancy in New Mexico, grassroots activism on the part of women of color, young parents, and queer families plays a crucial role in contesting the pathologizing discourses and structural forces that condition inequalities in New Mexico.

Players, Policies, and Programs: Teen Pregnancy in Twenty-First-Century New Mexico

The contemporary politics of teen pregnancy in New Mexico serves as a site of contestation for definitions of race, citizenship, and public well-being. Debates about the issue are characterized by a set of intricately intertwined differing frameworks, including prevention agendas aimed at curbing sex and reproduction among teens, promotion of services targeting teen parents and youth considered "at risk" for a variety of interrelated so-called problems, and activism geared toward increasing the resources available to pregnant and parenting young people. One of the most visible players within the politics of teen pregnancy in New Mexico has been the New Mexico Teen Pregnancy Coalition (NMTPC), founded in 1989 and based in Albuquerque.[16] Before the organization closed its doors in August 2014—after losing $130,000 in funding from the state—almost two-thirds of its funding came from federal and state government grants and the rest from private donors.[17] Although it predated the National Campaign to Prevent Teen and Unplanned Pregnancy, NMTPC served as one of the main conduits for National Campaign materials and discourses into New Mexico. For example, the banner at the top of the NMTPC website, ahead of even the name, "New Mexico Teen Pregnancy Coalition," contained a large red block with the words "Find Out Now" in white and a link to the National Campaign corporate website. The NMTPC website also contained numerous other links to National Campaign documents and media, reiterating the National Campaign's emphases on disseminating "the best and latest information, training, and research on teen pregnancy," and foregrounding the role of social networking sites (Facebook and Twitter, specifically) in communicating information about sex and pregnancy to teens.[18]

Despite this obvious relationship, NMTPC's focus on the particular circumstances of teen pregnancy in New Mexico resulted in a greater stress on "improving outcomes for teen parents" (a part of the organization's explicit mission) and a more concentrated centering of its work on impoverished and Latino communities.[19] Before its closure, its most recent program initiatives included the New Mexico Young Fathers Project (supported by the Children, Youth, and Families Department [CYFD] of New Mexico), which aimed to "promote social and family stability by improving the quality of father/child relationships in young families and by preventing repeat pregnancies." NMTPC also developed and coordinated the Plain Talk / *Hablando Claro* program, geared toward teaching parents and community members how to talk to youth about sex, and a Teen Outreach Program that combined educational activities and community service to steer youth away from "negative youth behaviors."[20] Despite breaking with the national multicultural politics of teen pregnancy by explicitly targeting impoverished Latino youth, all of these programs continued the long-standing, national trend of attempting to engineer personal and intimate behaviors in communities considered problematic to normative notions of Americanness.

NMTPC also collaborated with the New Mexico Department of Health Family Planning Program (NM DOH FPP) on a state-run Teen Pregnancy Prevention Program. NM DOH FPP, located in Santa Fe, administers Title X family planning clinics throughout New Mexico,[21] and aims to "promote health and reproductive responsibility" by providing clinic-based family planning services, community outreach, and education.[22] The Teen Pregnancy Prevention Program includes comprehensive sex education, both in and outside of schools, training for those doing teen pregnancy prevention, service learning for youth, and education for parents. Funding for the Teen Pregnancy Prevention Program comes in part from the Personal Responsibility Education Program (PREP) funds that form part of the federal approach to teen pregnancy in the 2010 Affordable Care Act.[23] The NM DOH FPP website cites the National Campaign numerous times in a discussion of teen pregnancy statistics in New Mexico and links to the National Campaign's teen-oriented website, Stay Teen, directing youth to take a quiz in honor of the National Day to Prevent Teen Pregnancy (May 1, annually).[24]

Aside from these explicit linkages to the national politics of teen pregnancy, in the early 2010s, the NM DOH FPP Teen Pregnancy Prevention Program website also displayed a telling graphic. Next to the description of the program there was a black-and-white rectangular image depicting an apparently not-pregnant teen on one side and an apparently pregnant teen on the other. At the top are the words "What's worse? Telling him to wait or telling him you're late," and at the bottom, "Sex has consequences."[25] The prominent placement of this graphic on the website suggests that it represented the NM DOH FPP philosophy about teen pregnancy, defining teen pregnancy as a personal behavior problem in which teenage girls make the wrong choice in allowing their boyfriends to have sex with them. As such, it falls in line with the broader intimate and multicultural politics of teen pregnancy at the national level.

While the work of NMTPC and NM DOH FPP most resembles the current national agenda, other New Mexico–based groups, such as NM GRADS and YWU, have attempted to shift public discourse in a different direction. NM GRADS, founded in 1989 with a main office in Socorro, is now a statewide school-based program for increasing the graduation rates of teen parents in New Mexico. The organization's mission is to "Facilitate parenting teens' graduation rates and economic independence; Promote healthy multi-generational families; [and] Reduce risk-taking behavior."[26] Throughout most of the organization's history, it has been represented as a social service provider aimed at mitigating the damage done by teen pregnancy. For example, articles in the *Albuquerque Journal* have frequently mentioned NM GRADS in the context of portraying the disturbing nature of high teen pregnancy rates within New Mexico and localities throughout the state.[27] NM GRADS, along with New Futures High School in Albuquerque (the Albuquerque Public Schools' "school of choice" for pregnant and parenting teens), is generally listed among the entities that help to give teen parents a "second chance."[28] NM GRADS has been described as teaching teen parents how to "balance education and parenting," implicitly presented as naturally incompatible roles.[29] Representations of NM GRADS and New Futures illustrate how public debate often frames attempts to provide material assistance to pregnant and parenting teens as rehabilitating teens, rather than as ensuring their basic rights. Recently, however, NM GRADS has emerged as an active public advocate for the educational rights of teen parents, taking part in a broader project of redirecting the discourse and policy around teen pregnancy in New Mexico, and intentionally amending the educational landscape to make it more compatible with parenting.[30]

Spearheading these efforts is Young Women United (YWU), an Albuquerque-based grassroots organization founded in 1999 and run by and for young women of color. YWU bases its work in an analysis of systemic racial, class, gender, and sexual inequalities in New Mexico and has aimed to "change the relations of power in Albuquerque."[31] In the early 2010s, the organization began leading a campaign to alter public debate around adolescent reproduction and change the structures that deny rights and opportunities to young parents.[32] In years prior, YWU has had an explicit teen pregnancy prevention agenda as part of efforts to advocate for comprehensive sex education.[33] However, in the 2010s, YWU has eschewed the fundamentally judgmental prevention framework, which critics argue has had no meaningful effect on teen behavior aside from further isolating and marginalizing teen parents, in favor of one that stresses the need for young people to be able to make "real decisions about their bodies and lives."[34] Within this framework, teens in rural and urban New Mexico need access to affordable, safe, and confidential reproductive health services in order to make unencumbered choices that may or may not involve the decision to parent. Beyond that, though, as YWU, NM GRADS, and their partners have argued, pregnant and parenting students need policies in place that help them graduate from high school, thereby increasing their prospects for jobs, housing, health care, and more.[35]

In April 2013, New Mexico Governor Susana Martinez announced that she signed into law the bill that YWU and NM GRADS promoted to serve those ends.[36] HB300, *School Excused Absences for Pregnancy,* mandates all New Mexico public school districts and charter schools to a enact a policy allowing for a minimum of ten days of excused absence for the birth of a child and four days of excused absence throughout the year for prenatal care and parenting.[37] This victory was the product of a large-scale mobilization of pregnant and parenting teens, as well as strategic work with both Democrat and Republican state legislators. This agenda addresses some of the shortcomings within the structure of public education for dealing with pregnant and parenting teens. It also works to replace images of irresponsible, deviant teen parents with those of responsible, hard-working young people. At the same time, it makes only a small dent in the structures of inequality that leave many New Mexican families in conditions of poverty.

Aside from HB300, there has been very little state policy directly aimed at improving the conditions in New Mexico that make being a pregnant or parenting teen difficult. Prior to the January 1, 2014, implementation of expanded Medicaid in New Mexico under the PPACA, New Mexico's Medicaid program included a Family Planning Waiver that covered services for up to twelve months for "women of child-bearing age," or ages eighteen to fifty, whose household incomes were up to or below 185 percent of the poverty level (or $2,391.13 per month for a family of 2).[38] While this program made family planning services available to many otherwise uninsured women, it did not help the plight of sexually active, pregnant, or parenting teenagers under the age of eighteen who did not otherwise qualify for Medicaid and did not have access to private insurance. Prior to Medicaid expansion, New-MexiKids and NewMexiTeens, the Children's Health Insurance Programs in New Mexico, provided health insurance to minors whose parents earned up to 185 percent of the poverty level.[39] There is no hard data on how many pregnant and parenting teens in New Mexico were uninsured at this time, but estimates based on data from live births to teens ages fifteen to nineteen in New Mexico between 2009 and 2011 suggest that about 24 percent of teens were uninsured before conception, 9 percent during pregnancy, and 4.5 percent at the birth.[40] People in this category likely included undocumented immigrants or noncitizens who did not meet immigration eligibility criteria, as well as teens who were disconnected from information about subsidized insurance and/or access to the application process.[41]

Due to the lack of coverage for undocumented immigrants under the PPACA and the ongoing barriers to access for disconnected teens, these groups undoubtedly continue to make up the ranks of the uninsured in New Mexico, despite Medicaid expansion in 2014. For these uninsured teens, reproductive health care is available at the Title X family planning clinics administered by NM DOH FPP throughout the state.[42] Beyond these health insurance and health care programs, as well as some early childhood education programs for impoverished children, many of the proposed policies for allocating material assistance specifically to pregnant and parenting teens in recent years have not succeeded in the legislature.[43]

New Mexico's TANF program, NM Works, adheres to all of the federal regulations for TANF public assistance programs, including time limits, work and school requirements, the mandate for minor parents to live with a parent or guardian, child support enforcement, and sanctions for noncompliance.[44] Providing minimal monetary support conditioned on extreme regulation of parents' professional and personal choices, NM Works generally constrains rather than enables the choices of adolescent parents. The Personal Responsibility and Work Opportunity Reconciliation

Act (PRWORA), the federal policy that enacted TANF in 1996, dictates that states spend Maintenance of Effort (MOE) funds at a rate of 80 percent of the state's 1994 Aid to Families with Dependent Children (AFDC) expenditures. These funds must be spent on programs that support TANF goals, two of which include curbing out-of-wedlock pregnancies and promoting two-parent families.[45] As such, the state of New Mexico has allotted MOE funds (otherwise known as "state TANF funds") to NMTPC and NM DOH FPP.[46] Thus, these programs are meant to carry out the teen pregnancy prevention mission that was crucial to the passage of the PRWORA. As such, NMTPC and NM DOH FPP have utilized TANF funds to help establish the image of teen pregnancy in New Mexico as a problem of personal choices, in keeping with the National Campaign's multicultural discourse of intimate citizenship and the larger redefinition of public well-being as ensured through morality lessons rather than wealth redistribution. Therefore, they directly carry out the mission of TANF while obscuring its inevitable consequence: deepening poverty and inequality.

The landscape of federal funding related to teen pregnancy further illustrates how the politics of teen pregnancy in New Mexico is conditioned by the national discourse of intimate citizenship. Besides MOE funds and the PREP funds received by NM DOH FPP, other public funding for teen pregnancy prevention in New Mexico includes federal abstinence-only education funding, originally part of the PRWORA and TANF reauthorization, now incorporated into the Affordable Care Act of 2010. New Mexico received this funding in the 1990s and then again from 2012 to 2016 after refusing it for many years due to lack of evidence of its effectiveness.[47] This money funds "medically accurate" abstinence "education, mentoring, counseling, and adult supervision," and aims to prevent teen pregnancy by preventing sex.

Teen Pregnancy Prevention funds, part of President Obama's Teen Pregnancy Prevention Initiative, were awarded to New Mexico organizations Capacity Builders (for replication of an "evidence-based" program) and National Indian Youth Leadership Project (for a new "innovative approach"), both of which engage in teen pregnancy prevention with Native American youth in New Mexico.[48] "Evidence-based" approaches used by Farmington-based Capacity Builders include service learning projects and mentorship targeted at Navajo youth but open to all children. Their program curriculum involves "values clarification," "goal-setting," and "decision-making," among other things.[49] The Gallup-based National Indian Youth Leadership Project utilizes "experiential education" and "adventure-based" activities to promote service, leadership, and certain values such as being "safe," setting goals, and "speak[ing] your truth."[50] Their teen pregnancy prevention program involves all of these elements, including parent education and sex education.[51] These programs appear to follow the dominant logic that teenagers who are taught proper values, have high self-esteem, and perceive a productive future for themselves will avoid pregnancy and achieve success. While they may meet a real and felt need within these communities to address the effects of structural violence and erasure, these programs do not directly target the political and economic structures that condition poverty.

The Affordable Care Act established the Pregnancy Assistance Fund, which has granted funds to a partnership between the New Mexico Public Education Department, the New Mexico Department of Health, and NM GRADS to increase the effectiveness of NM GRADS in assisting pregnant and parenting teens. This work includes a "public awareness campaign" that targets teens and the public "about the importance of high school completion and other needs of pregnant and parenting teens."[52] NM GRADS served 613 teen parents in 2012.[53] The number of teen births in 2010 was 3,872.[54] While these numbers do not provide the precise proportion of New Mexico's pregnant and parenting teens that NM GRADS is able to serve, they do reflect the reality that there are far more than the money from the Pregnancy Assistance Fund (in combination with the other funding sources for NM GRADS) is able to reach.

The broader picture of federal funding related to teen pregnancy in this state, then, reflects the national mission of managing teenage sexuality by promoting "responsibility" and abstinence, but also includes assistance to pregnant and parenting teens in the form of material services, such as child care and health care. Although the exact monetary amounts going to each mission are difficult to determine, in part because of the ways that disciplinary technologies are interwoven into programs that also provide services and material assistance to pregnant and parenting teens, the situation in New Mexico shows that federal funding related to teen pregnancy shapes the programs and services on the state level. Indeed, it gears them in large part toward altering personal behavior rather than ameliorating the difficulties that condition the lives of impoverished teenagers, pregnant, parenting, or not.

The current landscape of teen pregnancy politics in New Mexico primarily denigrates and regulates pregnant and parenting teens in ways that reflect and perpetuate historical processes of colonialism, racism, and dispossession. Continuing the ongoing marginalization of New Mexico within the nation, these young families serve as symbols of the state's exclusion from and failure to live up to national standards and aspirations. They represent a "core problem," from which a number of other disquieting realities and statistical outcomes are said to originate that place New Mexico in embarrassingly low status in comparison to other states.[55]

Racism and Rights: The Public Identity of New Mexico's Young Parents

The rather clear transformation in teen pregnancy discourse that has occurred on the national level in the last twenty-five years has not succeeded fully in New Mexico. Instead, the politics of teen pregnancy in New Mexico maintains a complex and conflicting set of narratives about the nature and implications of adolescent pregnancy and parenting. The neoliberal multicultural paradigm of teen pregnancy is less potent in the context of both widespread racialized poverty and a substantial statewide contingent of critically engaged nonwhite, nonnormative adults and families. While a multicultural politics of teen pregnancy—in which colorblind and class-blind language erases the structural inequalities that affect reproduction—does exist, there is a more common focus within New Mexico on the exceptionally "high rates" of teen pregnancy among "Hispanic" teens. This focus fuels a version of intimate citizenship that portrays Latinas, recent Mexican immigrants, and sometimes Native Americans, as pathological through narratives of bad parenting, dysfunctional families, and irresponsible behavior, mirroring previous colonial discourses of non-belonging.

Alongside these racist narratives, however, is an understanding of poverty as a crucial factor in both New Mexico's teen pregnancy rates and many other indices by which New Mexico does not measure up to other states. This foregrounding of poverty at times disrupts discourses of intimate citizenship by highlighting the potential role of structural factors, but more often occurs within accounts that sidestep nuanced analyses of the occurrence of poverty in New Mexico. Another discourse that has gained increasing ground, but not in total isolation from some of these other logics, is the understanding of pregnancy and parenting as a valid choice for teenagers, and also as a trend that registers a larger set of inequalities that constrain the opportunities and choices of many teens in New Mexico. Within this context, organizations and individuals with different and conflicting views on the issue of teen pregnancy find themselves forming strategic, sometimes unexpected alliances in the service of achieving mutual goals. These temporary assemblages reveal the conditions of possibility for public action around issues of racism, poverty, welfare, and reproductive justice set by national and local iterations of neoliberal multiculturalism and intimate citizenship.

Although substantially challenged, the multicultural discourse of teen pregnancy forwarded by the National Campaign and the Candie's Foundation plays an important role in the politics of teen pregnancy in New Mexico. For example, a 2011 interview with National Campaign CEO Sarah Brown aired on New Mexico's PBS show *New Mexico in Focus* in which Brown recounts the standard National Campaign explanations and solutions to teenage pregnancy within the framework of discussing the particularly severe "problem" in New Mexico. When asked by interviewer Gwyneth Doland what "we," in New Mexico, "are doing wrong," Brown explains, "I mean in sort of a biological sense, what it means is that there is a whole lot of teenagers—a lot of teenagers—having sex, without using contraception, and getting pregnant."[56] She goes on to mention that New Mexico "may have some pockets of poverty" and has a "large Native American population, which has always had very very high rates," gesturing toward some of the race- and class-based explanations of the issue. However, the bulk of the interview revolves around explaining teen pregnancy within the frame of intimate behavior in isolation from those categories of difference.

Throughout the interview, Doland's questions seem crafted specifically to allow Brown to voice the National Campaign's usual talking points as though they are tailored to the particular context of New Mexico. A direct response to Brown's first answer, Doland's second question presents two options as strategies for curbing teen pregnancy in New Mexico. She says, "It strikes me that, in talking about teenagers out there who are having sex, but not using birth control, that there are two things to look at. One of them is, um, trying to get teenagers to not have sex, or trying to get them to use birth control. How are those things related? Which should we be doing? Both?" According to the knowledge that the National Campaign proliferates nationally, geared toward presenting a moderate, bipartisan take on the sex education debate, Brown predictably answers that both are important. She goes on to explain the ways that younger adolescents are "developmentally" more appropriate targets of campaigns to get them to "delay" sex, whereas eighteen- and nineteen-year olds are already having sex at such high rates that it makes more sense to focus on getting them to use contraception. Reiterating a logic that naturalizes constructed life-stage categories, Brown implicitly attributes New Mexico's teen pregnancy rates to the lack of proper guidance for teenagers at their various stages of development. Prompted at every step by Doland's questions, she goes on to explain the effectiveness of National Campaign–affiliated shows like *16 and Pregnant* and *Teen Mom* to convey the difficulties of teen pregnancy and presents "evidence" that these shows are not glamorizing teen pregnancy. She then emphasizes the importance of New Mexico's use of "evidence-based" practices to address teen pregnancy and the need to teach parents how to talk to their children about sex.

When asked whether school-based day care centers, which exist in New Futures High School and other facilities in New Mexico, provide incentives for teens to get pregnant or are simply tools to make the lives of teen parents easier, Brown equivocates, "Well, you know, it's a very important question, what is the effect not just on the teenage mothers themselves, but also on the young women in school who haven't gotten pregnant. You know some of them look at these teen mothers and say 'Well wait, why are they getting tutoring and all this extra support? I *don't* have a child and I'm not getting as much help as I need.' There are lots of complicated dynamics."[57] She continues, saying that although there has not been substantial research to confirm this, she "suspects" that these facilities increase high school graduation for teen mothers, which is "beneficial over time."[58] Without significantly addressing any political, economic, cultural, or other dynamics specific to New Mexico, Brown explains to the *New Mexico in Focus* audience that the state's problem has to do with adults' inability to properly guide teenagers through their adolescence to make the right choices. Overall, she applauds National Campaign–approved efforts within the state to teach parents and teens about proper behavior, while casting doubt on attempts within New Mexico to alleviate the material difficulties of teen parents, suggesting that they could even increase teen pregnancy rates. This interview thus funnels into New Mexico the multicultural politics of intimate citizenship forwarded by the National Campaign and its partners, in which the most effective way of ensuring the well-being of citizens is to manage teen sexuality, not to provide material assistance or wealth redistribution.

Similar explanations can be found in the materials generated by NMTPC and NM DOH FPP. For example, a handout created by NMTPC and provided on the NM DOH FPP website lists "10 Teen Pregnancy Facts."[59] It contains statistics about the U.S. teen pregnancy, birth, and abortion rates as highest in the "industrialized world," New Mexico's teen birth rate as third highest in the nation, and the purported negative health effects and social costs to teen childbearing.[60] The final teen pregnancy "fact" reads, "It's better for everyone when babies are born to adult parents."[61] An assumption made within the majority of discourse on teen pregnancy in New Mexico and the nation, the claim that babies should be born to adults hardly warrants a mention in public discussions of the issue. NMTPC states it here to emphasize the notion that these negative outcomes, including health problems, educational failure, child abuse, incarceration, and costs to taxpayers, are a direct result of the age of the mother at the birth of her child. This list, of course, ignores the well-founded claim that these things are, at best, correlated with each other, rather than being in a causal relationship.[62] It similarly leaves out processes of colonialism, structural racism, and neoliberal social policy within New Mexico that better explain such racialized health, educational, and income disparities. In this analysis, teen pregnancy affects each individual, regardless of race, class, nationality, gender, and sexuality in an equally painful way.

This framework of multicultural intimate citizenship in New Mexico often includes an explicit attempt to point out and propose solutions to the inadequacies of New Mexico parents. In the 1999 *Albuquerque Journal* article "Experts: Families Key to Prevention," the then-principal of New Futures High School, Sandy Dixon, explains that "knowing what your children are up to" is the way to get your children to delay "having sex and children."[63] In the same article, NMTPC's Linda Phillips Lehrer says teenage pregnancy is an "adult problem." Although she mentions poverty and education as factors, there is no elaboration on how those things matter. Instead, she states, "Teens are victims of the act of following adult patterns." In this way, she references the discourse of pathological cycles that ultimately comes to replace theorizations of poverty in the context of teen pregnancy in current national discourse. In a 2006 *Las Cruces Sun-News* "Healthy Living" piece titled "Parents: Talk with Your Kids about Sex," Julie Grenko, a health services social worker, discusses the ways that teen pregnancy has "become more normative in our communities" since she was a teenager, challenging parents to address the issue.[64] Noting that "precursors" to teen pregnancy include "early school failure, early behavioral problems, dysfunctional/distressed families, and poverty," she ultimately reiterates the solutions outlined by the National Campaign, imploring parents to provide "clear messages" about sex, supervise and monitor their children, know their friends and their friends' families, and not allow their daughters to date older men.

Another 2006 opinion piece in the *Albuquerque Journal* echoes these sentiments, explaining the implementation of NMTPC's Plain Talk / *Hablando Claro* program in the South Valley neighborhood of Albuquerque. Making no mention of the racial or class composition of this neighborhood, one of the poorest in the city, made up mostly of Latinos with a large immigrant population, the author explains that in this neighborhood and some others, "a common problem is that parents are intimidated or too shy and scared to talk about sex with their kids."[65] Ignoring any role that access to health care, stable employment, or any other structural factors may play in shaping the behaviors, relationships, and outlooks of parents and teenagers, the claim that Plain Talk / *Hablando Claro* can adequately assess and address the issue presents teen pregnancy as solely a matter of parental responsibility. At the same time, the focus on the South Valley as an area filled with particularly "shy and scared" parents displays a subtler version of race- and ethnicity-based discourses that both disallow a multicultural model of teen pregnancy and deploy a rhetoric of dehumanization so familiar in the long histories of colonialism and racism within the state.

There is a distinct focus within the politics of teen pregnancy in New Mexico and nationally on the higher-than-average rates of teen pregnancy and teen births among "Latino" and "Hispanic" youth. The National Campaign, for example, has a "Latino Initiative," which attempts to understand teen pregnancy within this group through "cultural" factors, like levels of "acculturation," "language status," and "generation status."[66] Rendering the issue mostly in terms of depoliticized cultural trends, the National Campaign is able to maintain their discourse of intimate citizenship even while fore-grounding and constructing racial difference. Their discussion largely avoids heavily racialized and pathologizing terms like "dysfunctional" and "chaotic" to describe Latino families, constructing a cleaner, more politically correct version of colorblind politics than was used to describe the racialized welfare population in the mid-1990s. On the contrary, dialogues around high rates of teen pregnancy among Latinos in New Mexico contain language more closely resembling that of welfare reform discourse.

Explicit discussion of high rates of teen pregnancy among "Hispanics" in New Mexico continues a long tradition within the state of openly deni-grating the reproductive and parenting capacities of poor racialized groups. As Lena McQuade argues, questions of the adequacy of Mexican American reproductive and parenting practices characterized debates about New Mexican statehood and continued to inform policy and public health prac-tices in the state after statehood was granted in 1912.[67] Within the politics of teen pregnancy in the 2000s, Hispanic parents and youth often appear as irresponsible, ignorant, and otherwise deficient. In the *Albuquerque Journal* in 2004, after mentioning that Hispanics have the highest rates in New Mexico and the nation, Sylvia Ruiz, executive director of NMTPC, states that "risk factors" for teen pregnancy include "low school achievement" and "chaotic" families.[68] Similarly in 2002, Lehrer is quoted saying, "It's very clear our Hispanic youths are experiencing the brunt of our teen-pregnancy problem," and goes on to reference how "serious and entrenched" the problem is, noting that it is a "core issue" contributing to "child abuse, distressed families, and poverty."[69] She ultimately concludes, as noted in the quotation in the beginning of this chapter, that the issue is one of parents needing to be "more parental." Just as Lehrer paints Hispanic parents as deeply unparental, numerous articles on teen pregnancy conclude, implicitly and explicitly, that Hispanic parents are uninvolved, do not adequately value education, are afraid to talk to their kids about sex, and convey outmoded religious and cultural values to their children in which birth control, abortion, and adoption are not real options.[70]

Within national discussions of teen pregnancy during the welfare reform debates of the mid-1990s, pathologizing narratives about poor families of color often contained at least a gesture toward the role of structural forces in the lives of these families. Such continues to be true of discussions of Hispanic teen pregnancy rates in New Mexico, despite the shift away from these tropes on the national level. Even within apparent attempts to construct a multicultural politics, experts on teen pregnancy in the state find it difficult to avoid mentioning poverty as a factor, although it ultimately remains unanalyzed. In the many articles that expressly deal with the rates of Hispanic teen pregnancy, experts attempt to describe the issue with a mixture of cultural, personal, and structural explanations that both draw on racist tropes and reference race-based social inequality. A close reading of the 2006 *Albuquerque Journal* article "Fragile Motherhood—Teen Pregnancy: Rates in New Mexico are Highest Among Hispanics," elucidates this convoluted approach to explaining Hispanic teen pregnancy.

The article begins by quoting a presumably Hispanic Albuquerque mother stating that Hispanic parents should talk to their teens about sex. The author then recounts a long list of theories about why Hispanics have higher rates. "Some say Hispanic teen pregnancy rates are tied to religious beliefs, or poverty. Others blame broken homes, a lack of role models, limited education and resources, poor teen-parent communication, peer pressure and, far too often, a combination of these factors."[71] Although "poverty" and "limited education and resources" form important counterparts to the denigrating language of "broken homes" and (backwards) religious beliefs, no mention is made of reasons Hispanic teens might suffer from these things, including heavily segregated and unequal public schools, disinvestment in public infrastructure and welfare programs, and the flexibilization of racialized low-wage labor markets.

Instead, the article continues in a vein that combines a racist discourse of faulty Hispanic culture with the logic of intimate citizenship. NMTPC's Sylvia Ruiz states that Hispanic families do not "frown upon" teen pregnancy as much, and that it is a "cyclical" problem. It is not that teens consciously try to get pregnant, Ruiz maintains, but that they are "developmentally" interested in "love, romance or affection—especially if they are coming from a dysfunctional family or lacking love and attention at home." Employing the logic of naturalized developmental stages, Ruiz suggests that Hispanic teens get pregnant because their parents do not love them adequately for the needs of their age group. Concluding that section of the article, the author references a 2005 study done by the national think tank Child Trends, which maintains that Hispanics' "lower educational attainment" and "lower income levels" than non-Hispanics put them more at risk for teen pregnancy. In this way, Hispanics are framed as suffering from heightened teen pregnancy in part due to poverty. However, since their poverty is left unexplained, the reader is able to attribute it to the various tropes of cultural and parental deficiency scattered throughout the article.

The author of "Fragile Motherhood" goes on to interview two Hispanic teen mothers, one who had "many sex education talks" with her mother, and the other, a child of parents only recently reconciled after a separation, having had none. Both young mothers are daughters of teen mothers. The article quotes them talking almost exclusively about sex: their decisions to have sex, their prior knowledge of sex, how many of their peers are having sex. The young mother who had knowledge of sex via conversations with her mother is portrayed as choosing to have sex because her boyfriend wanted to and "a lot of other girls" were doing it, thinking they would not get pregnant. These stories are followed by advice to parents offered by a former teen mom about the importance of talking about sex with your teens. Together, the stories and advice portray teen pregnancy among Hispanics to be exclusively a matter of broken homes, inadequate parenting, and peer pressure.

"Fragile Motherhood" continues by discussing the role of Catholicism in both conditioning and potentially solving the problem of Hispanic teen pregnancy rates. Next, the then-principal of New Futures is interviewed, naming poverty as the "key cause" of teen pregnancy, but then speaking at length about the importance of good "role models" and "parental involvement," and her knowledge of the "cyclical nature of teen pregnancy." The article concludes with statistics about Hispanic teen pregnancy rates and a list of "strategies to curb Hispanic teen pregnancy," which include targeting Hispanics with Spanish-language, culturally "sensitive" materials and programs that encourage abstinence, changing "attitudes" about teen pregnancy, emphasizing the importance of contraception, and "supporting" teen mothers. Although making reference to realities of race-based inequalities that structure the reproductive behavior of Hispanic teens in New Mexico, "Fragile Motherhood" ultimately reinforces the racist notions that impoverished Hispanics are dysfunctional, culturally backward, and lacking parental skills, and are therefore perpetuating a deep-seated problem that plagues the state. Accordingly, teen pregnancy prevention among Hispanics must employ a kind of "sensitivity" that allows for the active alteration and management of attitudes and behaviors around sex. The article provides no explanation of what it might look like to "support" teen mothers.

At the same time that an explicit focus on racialized poverty in the context of teen pregnancy politics in New Mexico both disrupts the national multicultural discourse of teen pregnancy and engenders racist narratives of cultural pathology, this focus has also helped to produce a substantive structural critique of social inequalities in the state. This structural critique is part of an affirmative discourse of adolescent parenthood, which both conditions and is aided by an increased presence of young parents' voices in the public discourse. Even within the dominant discourse of NMTPC, poverty is frequently mentioned as a primary cause, rather than just an effect, of teen pregnancy. For instance, in a 2011 presentation to the Legislative Health and Humans Services Committee on New Mexico's teen pregnancy situation, Sylvia Ruiz lists "teen birth rates and poverty," "per capita personal income," "children under 18 living in poverty," and "children living in poverty are at higher risk for teen pregnancy," as the first four items under "Risk Factors for Teen Pregnancy."[72] Although her presentation goes on to make the usual recommendations for programs that target parent-teen communication and service learning for youth, she also recommends increased family planning services and increased "opportunities" provided by "business."[73] A dominant public discourse like this, in which the foremost player within the politics of teen pregnancy foregrounds the important roles of access to health care and jobs in conditioning reproductive behavior, helps create the conditions of possibility for a much more trenchant analysis of social inequalities than exists on the national level.

That deeper analysis became part of the public discussion in 2012 and 2013, but has existed for decades among those who work directly with pregnant and parenting teens. In keeping with Lena McQuade's account of New Mexico's long history of reproductive health advocacy and activism on the part of women and families of color, many professionals working in the field of health care and education for pregnant and parenting teens have a sustained interest in resisting dominant narratives about teen pregnancy.[74] Evidence of a relatively long tradition of affirmative discourse around teen pregnancy can be found in the book *Teenage Pregnancy: A New Beginning,* written by New Futures educators and health professionals and published by New Futures, Inc., a nonprofit that supported New Futures High School and was dissolved in 2010. This book, originally published in 1983 and revised numerous times until its final revision in 2006, provides a guide to teen parents on how to navigate sexuality, pregnancy, birth, and motherhood. Toni Berg, one of the contributing authors and an employee of New Futures High School since the mid-1970s, notes that this book was one of the "first of its kind," being comprehensive, nonjudgmental, "supportive," and "not superficial or condescending."[75] The book incorporates the words of New Futures students talking about their pregnancies and experiences as mothers. It also contains encouraging words about dealing with the interventions of people who "still want to treat you like a child." It advises students to do "what seems best in your situation." The authors write, "We believe that you can become the person you want to be and make it in life. But it's not enough for us to believe in you. You need to believe in yourself. You have a choice about this: You can put yourself down for this pregnancy. If you do, you can expect to be unhappy . . . or you can accept it as a chance to grow. If you do, you can come out knowing yourself better and feeling more confident than before. The choice is yours!"[76] In an effort to help pregnant and parenting teens resist the negative effects of widespread denigration of their personal choices, parenting skills, and general role in society, the authors suggest that pregnancy and motherhood can actually be transformative in a productive and positive way for adolescents. This book helps represent the work of many professionals and teen parents in New Mexico working for decades to combat the politics of shame and stigma that both displace meaningful public discussion of social inequalities and help to deepen those inequalities.

The more recent work of YWU, NM GRADS, and others, including the

American Civil Liberties Union of New Mexico (ACLU–NM), has taken this agenda to more public and prominent forums, organizing to change the terms of the discussion around teen pregnancy in New Mexico. Micaela Cadena, then YWU policy and resource director, explains that YWU and its allies want to create "a more nuanced dialogue on young families in New Mexico," and "[push] back on the stigmatizing framework." Part of that effort has involved moving away from the term "teen parents," which holds decades of denigrating cultural baggage, and replacing it with "young parents" or "pregnant and parenting students," in the case of their campaign for education reform. Cadena describes YWU's emphasis on people's parenting status and their families, rather than their age, because "people of all ages deserve access to the information, education, and resources they need to make decisions about their bodies and lives."[77] Inherent in this agenda is the understanding that such information, education, and resources are lacking for young people across the state due to poverty, transportation difficulties, education discrimination, a dearth of livable-wage jobs, and environmental degradation that affects people's health and livelihoods.

In a post on the national ACLU *Blog of Rights,* YWU argues that instead of blaming teen parents for their poverty and the lower amount of tax dollars they typically pay due to their low-wage employment, the public should recognize the ways that pregnant and parenting students are pushed out of school and therefore doomed to such low wages. Advocating for education reform that will increase pregnant and parenting students' ability to graduate from high school, the authors write that "meaningful change in the lives of all young people is rooted in equal access to educational opportunities, living wage jobs, affordable health care, and safe housing."[78] This phrasing is also a part of the New Mexico Senate Memorial "Recognizing the Contributions of Young Parents in New Mexico and Designating August 25, 2012 as a Day of Recognition of Young Parents," which YWU drafted and the Senate passed on January 30, 2012.[79] This memorial is geared toward recognizing and emphasizing the humanity of teen parents, and therefore draws on categories such as "responsible" and "contributing" community members as though they are natural and apolitical (without recognizing that such categories necessarily set boundaries for exclusion). At the same time, it emphasizes the negative effects of teen pregnancy prevention programs and cuts to family-oriented public programs on young families in New Mexico. This memorial, unanimously passed in the New Mexico Senate, makes an important contribution toward the alteration of public discourses surrounding teen pregnancy, priming the legislature for the policy changes that YWU and its allies successfully lobbied for in late 2012 and early 2013 (see fig. 1).

Pioneering grassroots advocacy for the rights of pregnant and parenting teens, YWU and its allies, including Republican antiabortion Senator Alonzo Baldonado, promoted House Bill 300 (HB300), which mandates excused absences for pregnant and parenting students. Key to the passage of this bill was the bipartisan work done to ensure that it could be understood as both pro–young parents and antiabortion. For instance, Baldonado, as one *Las Cruces Sun-News* article notes, "said he would ask fourteen- or fifteen-year-old girls not to terminate a pregnancy. Therefore, he said, he wanted to make available the tools to help teenage mothers succeed in school."[80] While this successful attempt at bipartisanship in some ways resembles the consensus-building strategies of the National Campaign, the outcome is a change in the structure of public education to ensure the rights of teen parents, rather than the production of a heteronormative discourse about the morality of abortion and contraception (see fig. 2). At the same time, because YWU is an openly pro-choice organization, advocating for comprehensive reproductive freedom that involves the full range of reproductive options ensured through safe, affordable access, their partnership with Baldonado illustrates the limited horizon for an affirmative discourse of young parenthood.[81] Similar to the proposed federal Reducing the Need for Abortions Initiative, this alliance helps confirm that in the post-welfare era, perhaps the only publicly acceptable context in which to make structural changes enabling reproductive justice is an antiabortion one.[82]

The various oppositional responses to the bill make the conceivable boundaries of public discourse surrounding pregnancy and abortion even clearer. The bill's bipartisanship did not prevent politicians and community members from framing it in ways that mobilized the market-based logic of welfare reform. Just as 1990s welfare reformers on the national stage argued that an entitlement-based welfare program encouraged out-of-wedlock and teen pregnancy, critics of HB300 viewed it as creating incentives for teenagers to get pregnant due to the special treatment they would receive. Reiterating the logic that Sarah Brown gestured toward regarding day care centers in schools on *New Mexico in Focus*, Representative Dennis Roch (a Republican from Texico, New Mexico) decries the passage of HB300 in the state House, saying, "When we make it easy for people to make bad choices, they make bad choices." Teen pregnancy, he maintains, is about personal choices, and

YOUNG PARENTS

CREATING BRIGHT FUTURES
FOR OUR FAMILIES.

YOUNG
WOMEN
UNITED
www.youngwomenunited.org

FIGURE 1. "Young Parents Creating Bright Futures." Created by artist Jaycee Beyale for Young Women United as part of their New Mexico Day in Recognition of Young Parents initiative. *Image courtesy of Young Women United.*

FIGURE 2. "Education Is a Right." Created by artist Nanibah Chacon for Young Women United as part of their efforts to pass HB300, a statewide excused absence policy for expectant and parenting students. *Image courtesy of Young Women United.*

he suggests that "special considerations," as Republican representative from Albuquerque Monica Youngblood puts it, will only increase the number of, rather than improve the outcomes for, teen parents.[83] Despite the presence of this common narrative, which harks back to the specific welfare reform agendas of disincentivizing teenage childbearing through the complete denial of public assistance to teenage parents, the bill passed and was signed into law by Republican governor Susana Martinez in April 2013. Given the continued pathologization of racialized communities of poverty in New Mexico through the politics of teen pregnancy, the campaign for HB300 is notable for overcoming that discourse.

One of the most important factors in passing this bill appears to have the participation of pregnant and parenting teens, themselves, in the advocacy. In November 2012, a group of advocates reported on educational barriers for pregnant teens before the New Mexico Legislative Educational Study Committee (LESC). The group included Sally Kosnick (executive director of NM GRADS), Jinx Baskerville (principal of New Futures High School), and Carrie Robin Menapace (legislative liaison and policy analyst for Albuquerque Public Schools). Kosnick presented on national educational outcomes for pregnant and parenting teens and outlined the much-improved outcomes for pregnant and parenting teens served by NM GRADS, illustrating that this population is capable and willing to finish high school, but requires the appropriate support. She then introduced two teen mothers, Melissa Romero and Elisiana Montoya, who discussed their own experiences and what they viewed as necessary next steps. Romero, for example, said that "all students deserve respect and a good educational foundation," while Montoya said she "wants to be a good provider for her daughter."[84] Although these young parents are not quoted at length in the LESC meeting minutes, that they were present, had the opportunity to speak, and emphasized their rights and future goals as members of society and parents is crucial to the larger goal of combating the longstanding pathologizing, dehumanizing discourses that pervade public conversations of teen pregnancy in New Mexico.

Next, Kosnick introduced Micaela Cadena, who reported to LESC about the focus group YWU had formed of forty teen parents from across New Mexico. She noted that these young parents overwhelmingly wished "to be treated as members of the community, not teen parents."[85] In this way Cadena models a humanizing approach to the issue of teen pregnancy, foregrounding the experiences and desires of pregnant and parenting teens. She also emphasizes young parents' own apparent understanding of the label "teen parent" as a dehumanizing one. With its roots in the welfare reform discourse of the 1980s and 1990s—itself a response in part to the welfare rights movement of the 1960s and 1970s, in which welfare recipients organized and advocated for their own rights[86]—the label of "teen parent" was part of a broader denigration of the welfare population and devaluing of their participation in public discourse. As Holloway Sparks notes in her study of welfare reform discourse of the mid-1990s, welfare recipients made up an extremely small portion of legislative witnesses and were largely ignored in the media.[87] Ange-Marie Hancock argues that the public identity of the "welfare queen" has contributed to a wide-ranging devaluing of the public participation for welfare recipients in political debate.[88] These realities created a vicious circle in which the pathologizing rhetoric of welfare reform went largely unchallenged, which helped to discredit the input of recipients attempting to participate in public discourse. This, in turn, enforced the lack of such input, which ultimately shored up and left unchallenged the pathologizing rhetoric.

In New Mexico's more recent debate about the rights of pregnant and parenting teens, the racialized stigmatization of teen pregnancy and parenting has been significantly challenged by the kind of participation by young parents that occurred before the LESC. NM GRADS played a crucial role in facilitating such participation on the part of pregnant and parenting teens in the public discourse surrounding HB300. February 6, 2013, was NM GRADS Day and Young Parents Day of Action at the New Mexico State Legislature. On that day, over one hundred NM GRADS young parents met with legislators and media representatives in Santa Fe to discuss their lives, the challenges they face, and the ways that NM GRADS has helped them to graduate from high school and get the health care they need.[89] These parents came from all over the state, some with their children and some without, to advocate for HB300. NM GRADS and YWU publicized the event, posted photos of young families interacting with legislators on their social media websites, and promoted the participation of teen parents in the political process and public discourse relating to their lives.

Although NM GRADS and YWU ensured that pregnant and parenting teens were able to successfully advocate for themselves at the state capitol, mainstream media coverage in New Mexico of teen pregnancy during this period did not reflect this, choosing instead to focus mainly on opposition to HB300 or ignore it altogether. A report on the Albuquerque news program

KOAT Action 7 News on March 11, 2013, interviews one teen parent, Gladys Rivera, who, at the time of the interview, had not yet earned her diploma at age nineteen. She states that she would have been able to spend more time bonding with her daughter if HB300 had been in place.[90] The program then interviews another, apparently white, teen parent who opposes the bill, saying, "We need to be promoting responsibility. When I was pregnant, I didn't just get time off. I had to step up to the responsibilities." The report culminates in a progress report on an ongoing poll on KOAT.com, asking "Should NM students get maternity leave?" in which 82 percent of responders answered No. The segment presents an overall picture of the bill as having very little public support as a result of instituting special treatment for teen parents, who, if they are hardworking, do not need it. This report represents hardworking teen parents as white in opposition to undeserving teen parents of color.

A February 26, 2013, report on *KOB Eyewitness News 4,* focusing on New Mexico's status as the state with highest rate of teen pregnancy in the country, interviews one teen parent, Monique Olivas, who had been a "star student," but had to "give up a full scholarship to become a mother." Olivas states, "Your life changes in a matter of a moment that you find out you're pregnant." She goes on to state that in northern New Mexico, "you are kind of judged and put down because you are a teen mom."[91] Although Olivas may or may not have elaborated on the injustice of this judgment and the material effects of it on people's lives, her comments in the report suggest that the isolated act of getting pregnant ruins an otherwise bright future. Despite the timing of the report, it includes no discussion of rights to education for pregnant and parenting teens nor questions as to why Olivas had to give up her full scholarship.

Instead, the *KOB* report cuts to an interview with NMTPC's community liaison, Jessica Tafoya, who answers the question of why New Mexico's rates are so high by explaining, "Well, they're saying that our kids are engaging in risky behavior at a very early age. They're participating in behaviors that have really hard consequences." Listing poverty, lack of sex education, and "cultural and religious influences" as factors in New Mexico's high rates, Tafoya ultimately points to immigration as an important contributor. In regard to Doña Ana County, which has the highest teen pregnancy rates in New Mexico, she states, "Yes, it is poverty, . . . but because it's also . . . a border county, we have a lot of families that are migrating into that county." Without any further elaboration, Tafoya's comments suggest that immigrants from Mexico, with their particular cultural and religious characteristics, are (re) producing New Mexico's continued marginal status within the nation. The report concludes without mentioning HB300, NM GRADS Day and Young Parents Day of Action at the legislature, the New Mexico Day in Recognition of Young Families, or any other affirmative discourse about the rights and humanity of pregnant and parenting teens.

KOB's coverage of HB300 is similarly unconcerned with representing the pregnant and parenting teens who participated in legislative debates around the bill. Titled "Bill to Give Maternity Leave for Middle Schoolers Makes its Way through Legislature," the report focuses on the views of one apparently white male teacher, Ryan Angell of Albuquerque, who explicitly ties his rate of pay to the test scores of the students who miss school for pregnancy and parenting. He asks, "When are they going to do the make-up work?" suggesting, implicitly, that pregnant and parenting teens are not going to do that work (and ignoring the measure within the law that allows schools to enforce consequences when students do not complete make-up work within the same number of days they missed), and that this will ultimately result in their poor test scores and his lower salary.[92] Providing a logic very similar to the valorization and purported victimization of the "taxpayer" by welfare recipients in welfare reform discourse, Angell casts HB300 as a misguided punishment for hardworking teachers. Moreover, *KOB*, through its foregrounding of "middle schoolers," presents HB300 not as a bill ensuring the rights of pregnant and parenting teens, but as a perverse accommodation of deviant children.

While there are a few examples of public and alternative media coverage of issues related to teen pregnancy and parenthood that include the largely unedited voices of teen parents,[93] mainstream corporate media in New Mexico mainly chooses sound bites from pregnant and parenting teens that reflect standard narratives of hardship associated with too-young pregnancy and parenting. These sound bites are generally framed, as is evident from the *KOB* report and newspaper articles discussed above, by explanations from local experts—usually NMTPC—engaging tropes of racial and class pathology alongside discourses of multicultural and intimate citizenship. Although transformative work is being done through grassroots organizing and legislative advocacy, from these portrayals, it is clear that the public identity of teen parents in New Mexico is primarily constructed through a convoluted collision of two different themes: (1) carefully constructed, self-conscious,

National Campaign–influenced rhetoric of personal responsibility and intimate choices and (2) narratives of racial, cultural, and sexual deviance structured by both welfare reform rhetoric of the 1980s and 1990s, as well as centuries of conquest, conflict, inequality, and degradation in New Mexico.

The particular context of New Mexico as a marginalized state offers important insights about the power and endurance of local discourses of racialized pathology in the face of a national agenda to remake teen pregnancy into a multicultural issue of intimate citizenship. Equally important, the case of New Mexico shows the power and endurance of both of those discourses in the face of targeted, strategic grassroots activism on behalf of young parents. Such activism may foreclose the possibility of teen pregnancy prevention tactics similar to New York City's controversial 2013 campaign, which was based in an overt politics of shame and humiliation for pregnant and parenting teens relating to narratives of poor education, relationship skills, and parenting.[94] Nonetheless, the overall material and discursive situation for pregnant and parenting teens in New Mexico differs little from those of other states.

As in other states, the TANF program continues its very marginal and conditional support of young impoverished families. Debates about the morality of making contraception accessible in public schools prevent teens from accessing the reproductive health care they need. Larger processes of structural and environmental racism, disinvestment in public infrastructure, police brutality, and high incarceration rates continue to enforce the inequalities that are regularly named as integral parts of New Mexico's teen pregnancy "problem." The overriding formulation of that problem in the terms set by national debate, in which unruly teen sex and inadequate parenting ruin young lives and national futures, supports the ongoing extreme social stratification set in motion by the forces of colonialism and western territorial expansion. At the same time, it is undeniable that New Mexico is leading the nation in advocacy on behalf of pregnant and parenting teens. While HB300 only chips away at the structural barriers to reproductive equality, and does so at the expense of an affirmative politics of abortion, it is an approach to teen pregnancy in which attempts to alter teenage sexual behavior with values-based campaigns are eschewed in favor of tactics altering institutional circumstances that constrain the lives of impoverished young families. It both signals new possibilities for the politics of reproductive justice and points to the limits of such change within the current neoliberal context that upholds intimate citizenship, heteronormativity, multiculturalism, and market rationality as its governing logics. Ultimately, the landscape of young parenthood in New Mexico helps prove that teen pregnancy continues to play an indispensable role within the neoliberal state and its goal of public disinvestment at both the national and the more localized levels.

CONCLUSION
Neoliberal Limits and Reproductive Justice

On March 3, 2013, New York City mayor Michael Bloomberg announced a new teen pregnancy prevention campaign that sparked heated debate about teenage reproduction. Titled "Cost of Teen Pregnancy," the campaign used print ads, texting, and a YouTube PSA, attempting to dissuade teenagers from getting pregnant by sharing the "consequences" of teen pregnancy.[1] The bus shelter and subway ads each featured a distraught-looking baby with one of the following quotations:

> Honestly mom . . . chances are he won't stay with you. What happens to me?
> Dad, you'll be paying to support me for the next 20 years.
> Got a good job? I cost thousands of dollars each year.
> I'm twice as likely not to graduate high school because you had me as a teen.
> If you stay in high school, get a job, and get married before having children,
>   you have a 98% chance of not being in poverty.[2]

On the national stage, the ads were lauded for telling the "truth" about teen pregnancy and criticized for publicly shaming teen parents.[3] I conclude this book with a discussion of this campaign because it bears striking resemblance to the politics of teen pregnancy discussed throughout, while differing in some crucial and telling ways. As such, and in keeping with my analysis of teen pregnancy in New Mexico, it sheds light on the reach, endurance, and limitations of the post-welfare politics of teen pregnancy.

Drawing on the statistical magic of social scientific research such as that utilized by the National Campaign, the Bloomberg campaign suggests that dropping out of high school, single parenthood, and poverty are direct results of irresponsible teen sex.[4] As Deputy Mayor Linda Gibbs explains,

"We know that teens can be impulsive and some impulsive behaviors have greater consequences than others." She goes on to name "unprotected sex" as "one of those behaviors" that has higher consequences, because it "can lead to teen pregnancy."[5] Following the logic of intimate adolescent citizenship outlined throughout this book, the campaign was founded on a construct of adolescence as a particularly irresponsible and reckless life stage. Moreover, it relied on the notion that teens are fundamentally consumeristic and trend-obsessed. For instance, the YouTube video features a young black man explaining to the audience that teen dads do not have "money left over for new kicks and video games."[6] Portraying teenagers as volatile and materialistic, the campaign assumes that adolescents require proper instruction on achieving normalcy via the management of sex. As Robert Doar, commissioner of New York's Human Resources Administration, states, "We cannot dictate how people live their lives, and sometimes even the best plans don't work out, but we must encourage responsibility and send the right message, especially to young people."[7] Whether because young people are the easiest targets for such "encouragement" or because they appear as the most urgent subjects of sexual regulation—Gibbs suggests that teens need to be "guide[d] toward healthier decisions"—in the post-welfare paradigm of citizenship, they stand out as the prime audience for such instruction.

In the face of critiques that these ads forfeit accurate information about teen pregnancy, sex, and contraception in favor of scare tactics and public shaming, proponents of the campaign maintain that the problem of teen pregnancy necessitates such strategies. An opinion piece in the *Chicago Tribune* that is also posted on the National Campaign's corporate website reads, "Planned Parenthood's Morales says the New York poster campaign misunderstands [the] cycle. 'It's not teen pregnancy that causes poverty, but poverty that causes teen pregnancy,' she told the *New York Times*. Actually, it's teen sex that causes teen pregnancy. We're pretty sure the teens know that. There's no point in sugarcoating the challenges that follow."[8] In keeping with the popular expertise of Dr. Drew, the author blames an unsituated and abstract "teen sex" for "teen pregnancy," which appears as a problem in and of itself, whether it causes poverty or not.

Along with these important similarities to national teen pregnancy, this campaign also foregrounds the notion of the "success sequence." Bloomberg states, "By focusing on responsibility and the importance of education, employment and family in providing children with the emotional and financial support they need, we'll let thousands of young New Yorkers know that waiting to have children might be the best decision they ever make."[9] Presupposing that having children is an unambiguously free "choice," Bloomberg echoes Ron Haskins, Isabel Sawhill, and Sarah Brown in their formula for achieving the American Dream—simply plan and situate your reproductive activities properly. With the 2013 U.S. Supreme Court decision to overturn the Defense of Marriage Act, this was no longer an option that by definition excluded same-sex couples, but it nonetheless perpetuated and condoned the heteronormative structures and discourses that privilege and naturalize white, middle-class domesticity while pathologizing, neglecting, and punishing everything else.

While this campaign utilized some of the same tactics and justifications as the national teen pregnancy discourses in *16 and Pregnant,* Stay Teen, and other vehicles of national teen pregnancy prevention, it differed somewhat in its implied target audience. Rather than relying on teens to have the spending cash and leisure time for cable television, fashion magazines, and hours surfing the internet, this campaign primarily targeted users of public transit. The posters were located at bus stops and on subway trains throughout the five boroughs. In this way, given that most teen pregnancy occurs within impoverished communities that would be more likely to utilize public transit than own a car, the ads seem designed, as some critics have argued, to shame actual teen parents, as well as to acknowledge that poverty is in fact a conditioning factor in the occurrence of teen pregnancy.

Even with this implicit acknowledgement, however, and the more explicit focus on the existence of poverty and high school dropout within the ads, the campaign served as an important tool for instruction on both intimate citizenship and the privatized safety net of neoliberalism. For instance, the texting game provided teenagers who text "NOTNOW" to 877877 with a narrative about "the real cost of teen pregnancy," in which a girl gets pregnant and becomes socially isolated. Miriam Pérez, writing for the reproductive justice publication *RH Reality Check* (later dubbed *Rewire*), notes that the game was filled with scenarios about the character Anaya "being ignored by her 'babydaddy' and shunned by her parents."[10] Texters could also choose to follow a boy character through his own personal turmoil after becoming a teen dad. In order to experience the full effects of this campaign then, teens would have had to ride public transit, have access to a mobile phone, and have a text-messaging plan that accommodated multiple exchanges with this interactive service. In this way, the campaign was likely actually meant to reach a wide swath of impoverished and affluent teenagers, some of whom would simply see the posters, while others would spend the time and resources to play the texting game.

The babies in the posters provide further evidence as to whom the ads were targeting. Each ad features a different small child, one white, one black, and two others who appear to be interracial (presumably white and black). In this way, the ads could arguably be following the multicultural logic of teen pregnancy prevention, but could perhaps also be said to register the fear that poor black and white teenagers have dangerously intermingled to the point that they are now a monolithically pathological subset of the population. This harks back to the race-based fears of welfare reform rhetoric, in which pundits presented the rising rate of teen pregnancy among white teens as the most pressing reason for systemic change.[11] These ads therefore mobilize various aspects of the national post-welfare politics of teen pregnancy— public–private partnerships, the use of sensationalism and social media, a discourse of intimate citizenship—but also employ some racialized and class-based imagery and strategy that disallows the easy ascendance of neoliberal multiculturalism.[12]

It is perhaps partly for this reason that the campaign engendered such vehement critique surrounding its stigmatizing discourse in which ignorant teens ruin their babies' lives by having them too early. Some responses highlight how the information provided by the campaign inaccurately suggests that racialized poverty is the result of inappropriate sexual choices. Melissa Harris-Perry, for example, responded to the campaign on her MSNBC television show. She called on Bloomberg to explain why he would imply that teen pregnancy and poverty were linked when he "know[s] full well" that teen pregnancy has gone down while poverty has gone up, and "that poverty among African Americans and Latinos has increased even though those communities have seen the most dramatic decreases in teen pregnancy."[13] She goes on to suggest that the poster featuring an African American toddler telling her hypothetical mother that her father will leave her is part of a larger system of discourses that renders black women and girls disposable in the public eye.

Most critics of the campaign, however, focused primarily on whether shame-based tactics are effective tools of social change or simply ways of making people feel bad about themselves.[14] This generated responses by proponents of Bloomberg's efforts who claim that shame has been a reasonable strategy in anti-smoking, anti-obesity, and anti–drunk driving campaigns.[15] In fact, Richard V. Reeves, a senior fellow at the Brookings Institution, argues in direct response to attacks on the New York City teen pregnancy posters that shame plays a very important social function in deterring both illegal and undesirable legal behaviors, such as smoking (especially while pregnant), obesity, racism, homophobia, and child abuse. He goes on to state that shaming is justified in the case of teen pregnancy because "it is a fact" that teen pregnancy is "bad" for the children of teenage parents.[16] In the typical fashion of Brookings Institution and National Campaign political rhetoric, Reeves attempts to portray himself as an objective, apolitical voice of reason and science, implying that valid concerns about racism and homophobia, presumably held by those same "liberal" critics of Bloomberg, are actually met by the politics of shame. The assumption that teen pregnancy is a universally accepted problem (held even by many of those who argue against the politics of shame) is an integral part of the post-welfare projection of intimate multicultural citizenship that appears to result from a rational consensus across party lines and political factions. Reeves suggests that shaming teen parents for the harm they do to their children is simply a reasonable and scientifically sound way to prevent further social ill. As he puts it, "shame legitimately attaches to teen pregnancy." In this way, he openly embraces the normalizing function of shame that the social theorist Michael Warner points to as exclusionary and violent in his discussion of sexual shame.[17]

If children remain, as Lauren Berlant and the queer theorist Lee Edelman argue, the symbols of ideal citizenship by which the national future is secured in the era of neoliberalism, then this campaign brought sexual shame to new heights (or perhaps lows) by featuring upset children as the rightful instructors for their naïve, selfish, and impetuous teenage parents.[18] Berlant writes that the American child as a national icon is "still innocent of knowledge, agency, and accountability and thus has ethical claims on the adult political agents who write laws, make culture, administer resources, and control things."[19] Within the context of these posters, the hypothetical children of teenage parents are forced into a premature state of knowing by reckless teenage sex. Even they know better than their ignorant teen parents, who would unwittingly sacrifice their future children's health and happiness for the instant gratification of unprotected sex. Having to be publicly lectured by one's own crying baby about poor sexual choices may epitomize shamefulness in a culture that structures children as fundamentally threatened by all things sexual. Berlant shows that in the 1980s and 1990s, groups of concerned "social parents" were called on, along with the state, to compensate for bad parenting. In contrast, this New York City campaign figures children themselves as needing to step in.[20] One could argue that this replacement of policymakers, teachers, doctors, and other adult leaders with babies takes the politics of intimate citizenship to its logical conclusion: we are better off being governed by the innocent infants—who embody a good and decent America—than any form of adult political organization.

As such, the current debate about the politics of shame has directed public discourse away from what is really at stake in the post-welfare politics of teen pregnancy. The question of whether or not shame adequately prevents teen pregnancy distracts from the question of why pregnant and parenting teens are an important topic of discussion in the first place. As Melissa Harris-Perry asks, "Why in the world, as the [teen pregnancy] crisis is abating, and fewer teens are facing the challenges of early child-rearing, would the city of New York spend $400,000 on a campaign to publicly shame teen parents?" Aside from her assumption that there ever was, in fact, a teen pregnancy "crisis," and her primary concern with the campaign's shaming tactics, Harris-Perry gestures toward this most pressing question of why teen pregnancy is even an issue at all. Although she does not directly answer this question, she provides a number of reasons why the posters are misleading and points to how they "might cause people to, you know, blame young mothers for America's deepening poverty crisis, rather than putting the blame where it belongs, on a financial system that concentrates wealth at the top and public policies that entrench it there."[21] Suggesting, as this book has argued, that the post-welfare politics of teen pregnancy is a crucial counterpart to the neoliberal retrenchment of welfare, Harris-Perry and other feminist responses to Bloomberg's efforts began a national public conversation around issues that the revised image of teen pregnancy has helped to prevent since 1996—such as the systemic economic and political causes of racialized poverty.

This has been made possible, I posit, because discourses of multicultural intimate citizenship reach their most penetrable limits where the local and the national meet—in other words, where strategies developed by national organizations and disseminated on a national scale are adopted, altered, and deployed in local contexts that have their own specific politics of social inequality. In the case of this New York City campaign, the situated racial and class politics of the place became the subject of national debate. In an effort to directly target (and shame) the groups that have the highest rates of teen pregnancy in the city, New York's Human Resources Administration, like the New Mexico Teen Pregnancy Coalition, exposed (perhaps unintentionally) the social stratification within its population. The racial and class-based dehumanization that resulted thus reentered local and national discussion of teen pregnancy, despite a broader attempt within national teen pregnancy prevention to pretend that race and class have no further relevance in society.

In this book, I have argued that the post-welfare politics of teen pregnancy serves to obscure the work of punitive welfare reform and the deepening social inequalities resulting from neoliberal social and economic policies; that it helps redefine public well-being as ensured by a fully privatized social safety net; that it bolsters the heteronormative cultural logics of neoliberal citizenship; and that it does these things through the salient trope of unruly adolescent sexuality and reproduction. The degree to which the grassroots activism and news media responses to Mayor Bloomberg's teen pregnancy campaign will have breached these processes remains unclear. Months after the initial controversy, the campaign continued throughout the city and was touted by many as a revolutionary step in the battle against teen pregnancy.[22] When Mayor Bill de Blasio took office in January 2014, the city's teen pregnancy prevention efforts discreetly shifted tactics. According to *RH Reality Check,* the campaign has abandoned much of the imagery and tone that brought so much criticism, while retaining some of the gendered and shame-based content.[23]

Throughout this book, I have attempted to contextualize the contemporary politics of teen pregnancy within debates about public well-being, social policy, and citizenship over the last two-and-a-half decades. Specifically, I have looked at how teen pregnancy and welfare reform were intertwined in explicit ways in the early and mid-1990s and asked how they might still be intertwined and mutually reinforcing in the years since the passage of the Personal Responsibility and Work Opportunity Reconciliation Act of 1996. By focusing my analysis in chapter 4 on teen pregnancy prevention in New Mexico, I argued that the national post-welfare politics of teen pregnancy both endures and breaks down in the face of the specific contours of social stratification within the state. I suggested that, despite significant challenge at the local level, teen pregnancy continues to be a tool for neoliberal social and economic agendas that deepen inequalities based on race, class, gender, sexuality, and immigration status.

The Bloomberg campaign similarly illustrates both the dire potentials and the promising weaknesses of this teen pregnancy discourse. By authorizing and perpetuating a widespread denigration of teen parents so extreme that even teens' own toddlers should apparently be disappointed in and ashamed of them, the HRA's posters reached a new horizon for the privatization of citizenship, relinquishing not only the state, but adults as a whole, from any part in the securing of successful Americanness. Adolescents, in this formulation, are kept in check by the specter of their future ruined offspring. This campaign further clarifies the ultimate potentials of intimate citizenship—defined by proper sex, reproduction, and familial arrangements—for the rearrangement of state powers against any attempt at the egalitarian maintenance of social well-being and toward the securing of class power, racial privilege, and heteronormativity.

On the other hand, the juxtaposition of the New Mexico and the New York case studies reveals an important development within grassroots reproductive politics. There is a long history in the United States of activist women of color working toward reproductive rights and justice.[24] Building on this legacy, contemporary organizations are making important contributions to public discourse and public policy on reproductive issues in these states. Increasingly, these organizations are making trans-state alliances precisely around the public image and treatment of teen pregnancy and teen parents locally and nationally. Groups across the country, including New Mexico's Young Women United, the New York Coalition for Reproductive Justice, the Massachusetts Alliance on Teen Pregnancy, the Oakland-based organization Strong Families, and the National Latina Institute for Reproductive Health, are publicly networking, collaborating, and promoting each other's work on issues pertaining to teen pregnancy and teen parents. For instance, they collaborated on a project called "No Teen Shame," which targeted the Candie's Foundation for one of its recent anti–teen pregnancy campaigns (see fig. 3).[25] This project called on Neil Cole, founder of the Candie's Foundation, to meet with a group of activist teen moms to discuss his organization's tactics, mission, and impact.[26] Therefore, at the same time that the national post-welfare politics of teen pregnancy naturalizes its common sense through multiple cultural and political realms, becoming an ever-stronger presence in the national imagination as a personal problem with public consequences, grassroots responses challenging its assumptions and tactics are fortifying, cropping up, and bonding together. My hope is that this book will contribute to this process, providing insight into both the direct and indirect links between the "social problem" of teen pregnancy, the politics of welfare reform, and the project of neoliberalism.

The social theorist Roderick Ferguson explains that capitalism's demand for cheap labor has historically produced the proliferation of nonnormativity, which both fulfills and exceeds capital's demands.[27] "Teen pregnancy" is

FIGURE 3. "No Teen Shame." Created by artist Micah Bazant and Forward Together as part of the #NoTeenShame campaign. *Image courtesy of Micah Bazant and Forward Together.*

a potent placeholder in dominant U.S. culture for the various nonnormative familial formations that are brought about by advanced capitalism and which appear to threaten it. As such, it has become an important technology for the management of this contradiction in the neoliberal era of multiculturalism, intimate citizenship, and welfare retrenchment. The so-called problem of teen pregnancy indexes the increasing abandonment of the low-wage and surplus labor forces by the state in conjunction with the delayed achievement of economic stability for the middle class. Impoverished, pregnant teenagers, while likely timing their reproduction in a way that either makes little difference to their life course and economic potential or is, in fact, beneficial, appear to signal an extreme pathology in the context of a rising childbearing age for wealthier women. We must therefore understand how "teen pregnancy" marks lives for discipline, regulation, and prevention by the increasingly privatized political and economic order. Without an analysis of the relationship between the contemporary politics of teen pregnancy and neoliberal reformulations of the obligations of a state to its citizenry, concerns about stigmatizing and shaming teen parents could be understood as merely sentimental and benign. With this perspective, teen pregnancy prevention's attempt to foreclose the possibility of certain lives while humiliating and punishing others is revealed to be not only a project of disciplining the populace into normative sexual, gender, and familial roles. It can also be seen as part of an effort to eliminate any direct responsibility of the state to provide material support for all its residents to achieve the minimum standard of living—a responsibility that, although never fully realized, has been one of the theoretical functions of the modern democratic nation-state since the turn of the twentieth century.

Notes

Introduction. Preventing Equality

1. Barbara Greenberg, "Pregnant Teen Boys? Teen Pregnancy Campaign," *Huffington Post*, May 21, 2013, www.huffingtonpost.com/barbara-greenberg/pregnant-teen-boys-an-ant _b_3303310.html.
2. Daily Mail Reporter, "New Billboard Campaign Launched in Chicago Features Images of Pregnant Boys to Remind Them That a Baby Isn't Just a Girl's Responsibility," *Daily-Mail.com*, May 15, 2013, www.dailymail.co.uk/news/article-2325100.
3. Barbara Greenberg, "Pregnant Teen Boys?"
4. Claire Rasmussen, *The Autonomous Animal: Self-Governance and the Modern Subject* (Minneapolis: University of Minnesota Press, 2011), 40.
5. Media Literacy Project, "Deconstruction Gallery: Pregnant Boys and a Counter Ad," http://medialiteracyproject.org/deconstructions/pregnant-boys-and-counter-ad.
6. James Gilbert, *A Cycle of Outrage: America's Reaction to the Juvenile Delinquent in the 1950s* (New York: Oxford University Press, 1986); Regina G. Kunzel, "White Neurosis, Black Pathology: Constructing Out-of-Wedlock Pregnancy in the Wartime and Postwar United States," in *Not June Cleaver: Women and Gender in Postwar America, 1945–1960*, ed. Joanne Meyerowitz (Philadelphia: Temple University Press, 1994), 304–31; Susan E. Harari and Maris A. Vinovskis, "Adolescent Sexuality, Pregnancy and Child-bearing in the Past," in *The Politics of Pregnancy: Adolescent Sexuality and Public Policy*, ed. Annette Lawson and Deborah L. Rhode (New Haven: Yale University Press, 1993), 23–45; Elaine Tyler May, *Homeward Bound: American Families in the Cold War Era* (New York: Basic Books, 2008); Wini Breines, *Young, White, and Miserable: Growing up Female in the Fifties* (Boston: Beacon Press, 1992).
7. Kristin Luker, *Dubious Conceptions: The Politics of Teen Pregnancy* (Cambridge, MA: Harvard University Press, 1996); Harari and Vinovskis, "Adolescent Sexuality"; Deborah L. Rhode and Annette Lawson, introduction to Lawson and Rhode, *Politics of Pregnancy*, 1–19.
8. Heather D. Boonstra, "Teen Pregnancy: Trends and Lessons Learned," *Guttmacher Policy Review* 5, no. 1 (February 2002), www.guttmacher.org; Dorothy Roberts, *Killing the Black Body: Race, Reproduction, and the Meaning of Liberty* (New York: Vintage, 1997), 120; Mary Patrice Erdmans and Timothy Black, *On Becoming a Teen Mom: Life before Pregnancy* (Oakland: University of California Press, 2015), 14.

9. Harari and Vinovskis, "Adolescent Sexuality," 23–45; Deborah L. Rhode, "Adolescent Pregnancy and Public Policy," in Lawson and Rhode, *Politics of Pregnancy*, 301–35; Sue Ruddick, "The Politics of Aging: Globalization and the Restructuring of Youth and Childhood" *Antipode* 35, no. 2 (March 2003): 334–62.

10. Lisa Arai, *Teenage Pregnancy: The Making and Unmaking of a Problem* (Bristol, UK: Policy Press, 2009), 4; Diana M. Pearce, "'Children Having Children': Teenage Pregnancy and Public Policy from the Woman's Perspective," in Lawson and Rhode, *Politics of Pregnancy*, 46–58.

11. Arai, *Teenage Pregnancy*; Luker, *Dubious Conceptions*; F. F. Furstenberg Jr., "As the Pendulum Swings: Teenage Childbearing and Social Concern," *Family Relations* 40, no. 2 (1991): 127–38; Rhode, "Adolescent Pregnancy"; Pearce, "Children Having Children"; Ann Phoenix, "The Social Construction of Teenage Motherhood: A Black and White Issue?" in Lawson and Rhode, *Politics of Pregnancy*, 74–97; Melissa S. Kearney and Phillip B. Levine, "Why Is the Teen Birth Rate in the United States So High and Why Does It Matter?," *Journal of Economic Perspectives* 26, no. 2 (2012): 141–63; V. Joseph Hotz, Susan Williams McElroy, and Seth G. Sanders, "Teenage Childbearing and Its Life Cycle Consequences," *Journal of Human Resources* 40, no. 3 (2005): 683–715.

12. Erdmans and Black, *On Becoming a Teen Mom*, 3.

13. David Harvey, *A Brief History of Neoliberalism* (Oxford: Oxford University Press, 2005), 1–4.

14. Lauren Berlant, *The Queen of America Goes to Washington City: Essays on Sex and Citizenship* (1997; repr., Durham, NC: Duke University Press, 2002); Aihwa Ong, *Neoliberalism as Exception: Mutations in Citizenship and Sovereignty* (Durham, NC: Duke University Press, 2006).

15. Jamie Peck, *Workfare States* (New York: Guilford Press, 2001); Gwendolyn Mink, *Welfare's End* (Ithaca, NY: Cornell University Press, 1998); Anna Marie Smith, *Welfare Reform and Sexual Regulation* (Cambridge: Cambridge University Press, 2007).

16. Clinton promised to "end welfare as we know it" in his 1992 election campaign, a promise that he fulfilled by signing the PRWORA into law in 1996. R. Kent Weaver, *Ending Welfare as We Know It* (Washington, DC: Brookings Institution, 2000), 2.

17. Peck, *Welfare States*, 58.

18. Mink, *Welfare's End*, 65.

19. The family cap rule permanently sets a family's welfare grant at the amount specified for the number of family members it had upon entering the rolls, regardless of subsequent childbirths. For an extensive discussion of this rule, see Smith, *Welfare Reform and Sexual Regulation*, 147–58.

20. Laura Briggs, *Somebody's Children: The Politics of Transracial and Transnational Adoption* (Durham, NC: Duke University Press, 2012), 124; Mae M. Ngai, *Impossible Subject: Illegal Aliens and the Making of Modern America* (Princeton, NJ: Princeton University Press, 2004), 269; Eithne Luibhéid, *Entry Denied: Controlling Sexuality at the Border* (Minneapolis: University of Minnesota Press, 2002), xvi; Timothy J. Randazzo, "Social and Legal Barriers: Sexual Orientation and Asylum in the United States," in *Queer Migrations: Sexuality, U.S. Citizenship, and Border Crossings*, ed. Eithne Luibhéid and Lionel Cantú Jr. (Minneapolis: University of Minnesota Press, 2005), 48–51; M. Jacqui Alexander, *Pedagogies of Crossing: Meditations on Feminism, Sexual Politics, Memory, and the Sacred* (Durham, NC: Duke University Press, 2005), 227.

21. Lisa Duggan, *The Twilight of Equality: Neoliberalism, Cultural Politics, and the Attack on Democracy* (Boston: Beacon Press, 2003); Ong, *Neoliberalism as Exception*; Berlant,

Queen of America. Throughout this book, I use the term "heteronormative" to denote the complex intersection of sexual, racial, gender, familial, and class norms that structure the normative form of heterosexuality. As queer theorists such as Siobhan Somerville and Cathy Cohen have argued, the hetero/homo binary is not useful for explaining the ways that nonnormative heterosexualities are denigrated and marginalized by discourses of normative heterosexuality. Siobhan B. Somerville, "Sexual Aliens and the Racialized State," in Luibhéid and Cantú Jr., *Queer Migrations,* 77; Cathy J. Cohen, "Punks, Bulldaggers, and Welfare Queens: The Radical Potential of Queer Politics," in *Black Queer Studies: A Critical Anthology*, ed. E. Patrick Johnson and Mae G. Henderson (Durham, NC: Duke University Press, 2005), 26.

22. Berlant, *Queen of America.*

23. Philippe Ariès, *Centuries of Childhood: A Social History of Family Life* (New York: Knopf, 1962).

24. Lawrence Stone, *The Family, Sex and Marriage in England, 1500–1800* (New York: Penguin Books, 1990), 105–12.

25. Ariès, *Centuries of Childhood,* 129.

26. Ibid., 329–36.

27. Nancy Lesko, *Act Your Age!: A Cultural Construction of Adolescence* (New York: RoutledgeFalmer, 2001), 30–37; Rasmussen, *Autonomous Animal,* 40.

28. Lesko, *Act Your Age!,* 34.

29. Molly Ladd-Taylor, *Mother-Work: Women, Child Welfare, and the State, 1890–1930* (Urbana: University of Illinois Press, 1994); Sonya Michel, *Children's Interests / Mothers' Rights: The Shaping of American's Child Care Policy* (New Haven: Yale University Press, 1999).

30. Rickie Solinger, *Wake Up Little Susie: Single Pregnancy and Race before Roe v. Wade* (London: Routledge, 2000); Kunzel, "White Neurosis, Black Pathology"; Alice O'Connor, *Poverty Knowledge: Social Science, Social Policy, and the Poor in Twentieth-Century U.S. History* (Princeton, NJ: Princeton University Press, 2001).

31. Breines, *Young, White, and Miserable;* Gilbert, *Cycle of Outrage*; Harari and Vinovskis, "Adolescent Sexuality"; Alex Lubin, *Romance and Rights: The Politics of Interracial Intimacy, 1945–1954* (Jackson: University Press of Mississippi, 2005).

32. Solinger, *Wake Up Little Susie;* Kunzel, "White Neurosis, Black Pathology"; Julie Passanante Elman, *Chronic Youth: Disability, Sexuality, and U.S. Media Cultures of Rehabilitation* (New York: New York University Press, 2014); Gilbert, *Cycle of Outrage*; Anna McCarthy, *The Citizen Machine: Governing by Television in 1950s America* (New York: New Press, 2010); Lubin, *Romance and Rights.*

33. Gayle Rubin, "Thinking Sex: Notes for a Radical Theory of the Politics of Sexuality," in *Lesbian and Gay Studies Reader,* ed. Henry Abelove, Michele Aina Barale, and David M. Halperin (New York: Routledge, 1993), 3–44; Lee Edelman, *No Future: Queer Theory and the Death Drive* (Durham, NC: Duke University Press, 2005); Berlant, *Queen of America*; Kathryn Bond Stockton, *The Queer Child, or Growing Sideways in the Twentieth Century* (Durham, NC: Duke University Press, 2009); James Kincaid, *Child-Loving: The Erotic Child and Victorian Literature* (New York: Routledge, 1994); James Kincaid, *Erotic Innocence: The Culture of Child Molesting* (Durham, NC: Duke University Press, 1998).

34. Kincaid, *Child-Loving,* 5.

35. Kerry H. Robinson, "'Difficult Citizenship': The Precarious Relationships between Childhood, Sexuality, and Access to Knowledge," *Sexualities* 15, no. 3/4 (2012): 258.

36. Elman, *Chronic Youth*, 3–6.

37. Ibid., 7.

38. Ruddick, "The Politics of Aging."

39. Ange-Marie Hancock, *The Politics of Disgust: The Public Identity of the Welfare Queen* (New York: New York University Press, 2004), 4.

40. Nancy F. Cott, "Marriage and Women's Citizenship in the United States, 1830–1934," *American Historical Review* (1998): 1448 and 1452.

41. Bob Jessop, *The Future of the Capitalist State* (Cambridge: Polity Press, 2002), 169.

42. David Harvey, "Is This Really the End of Neoliberalism? The Crisis and the Consolidation of Class Power," *CounterPunch*, March 13–15, 2009, www.counterpunch.org/2009/03/13/is-this-really-the-end-of-neoliberalism/.

43. Sheila Zedlewski, Pamela Loprest, and Erika Huber, "What Role Is Welfare Playing in This Period of High Unemployment?" Urban Institute, Fact Sheet 3, August 2011, www.urban.org; H. Luke Shaefer and Kathryn Edin, "Rising Extreme Poverty in the United States and the Response of Federal Means-Tested Programs," National Poverty Center Working Paper Series #13–06, May 2013, www.npc.umich.edu/publications/working_papers/.

44. Sandra K. Danziger, "The Decline of Cash Welfare and Implications for Social Policy and Poverty," *Annual Review of Sociology* 36 (2010): 541.

45. Shaefer and Edin, "Rising Extreme Poverty in the United States"; Danziger, "The Decline of Cash Welfare," 541.

46. Shaefer and Edin, "Rising Extreme Poverty in the United States," 3.

47. For summaries of TANF teen parent rules, see Janellen Duffy and Jodie Levin-Epstein, "Add It Up: Teen Parents and Welfare . . . Undercounted, Oversanctioned, and Underserved," *Center for Law and Social Policy*, April 2002, www.clasp.org/admin/site/publications/files/0090.pdf; Smith, *Welfare Reform and Sexual Regulation*, 170–71.

48. Duffy and Levin-Epstein, "Add It Up."

49. Lingxin Hao and Andrew J. Cherlin, "Welfare Reform and Teenage Pregnancy, Childbirth, and School Dropout," *Journal of Marriage and Family* 66, no. 1 (2004): 192.

50. Liz Schott, "Policy Basics: An Introduction to TANF," Center on Budget and Policy Priorities, updated June 15, 2015, www.cbpp.org.

51. Jacqueline E. Darroch and Susheela Singh, "Why Is Teenage Pregnancy Declining? The Roles of Abstinence, Sexual Activity, and Contraceptive Use," Guttmacher Institute, Occasional Report No. 1, December 1999, www.guttmacher.org; Melissa Schettini Kearney and Phillip B. Levine, "Explaining Recent Trends in the U.S. Teen Birth Rate," Working Paper No. 17964, National Bureau of Economic Research, March 2012, www.nber.org/papers/w17964. For a summary of studies on the effects of welfare reform on teen pregnancy rates, see Sandra K. Danziger, "Welfare Policy in the U.S.: Lessons from the 1996 Welfare Reform and the Great Recession," prepared for Joint Conference WZB / Hertie School of Governance: Anti-Poverty Programs in Global Perspective: Lessons from Rich and Poor Countries, Berlin, Germany, June 20–21, 2011, 23–24, http://www.wzb.eu.

52. Jodi Melamed, *Represent and Destroy: Rationalizing Violence in the New Racial Capitalism* (Minneapolis: University of Minnesota Press, 2011), 1–2, 41.

53. Ibid., 35.

54. Ibid., 39–42.

55. David Theo Goldberg, *Multiculturalism: A Critical Reader* (Oxford: Blackwell, 1994); Avery F. Gordon and Christopher Newfield, *Mapping Multiculturalism* (Minneapolis: University of Minnesota Press, 1996).

56. Melamed, *Represent and Destroy,* 41–42.

57. Ibid., 42.

58. Harvey, "Is This Really the End of Neoliberalism?," 10. See also Jessop, *Future of the Capitalist State,* 234.

59. Karl Polanyi, *The Great Transformation: The Political and Economic Origins of Our Time* (Boston: Beacon Press, 2001, 79–80). See also Robert A. Beauregard, "Planning in an Advanced Capitalist State," in *Planning Theory: A Search for Future Directions,* ed. Robert W. Burchell and George Sternlieb (New Brunswick, NJ: Rutgers University Press, 2013), 235–53.

60. For discussions of such policies and structures, see Jacob Hacker, *The Divided Welfare State: The Battle over Public and Private Social Benefits in the United States* (Cambridge: Cambridge University Press, 2002); George Lipsitz, *The Possessive Investment in Whiteness* (Philadelphia: Temple University Press, 1998).

61. Therese J. McGuire and David F. Merriman, "Has Welfare Reform Changed State Expenditure Patterns?" National Poverty Center, Policy Brief #7, September 2006, www.npc .umich.edu/publications/policy_briefs/.

62. Jessop, *The Future of the Capitalist State,* 236.

63. Wendy Brown, "American Nightmare: Neoliberalism, Neoconservatism, and De-Democratization," *Political Theory* 34, no. 6 (December 2006): 690–714; Alison Phipps, *The Politics of the Body: Gender in a Neoliberal and Neoconservative Age* (Cambridge: Polity Press, 2014), 12.

64. Duggan, *Twilight of Equality,* 13.

65. For a comprehensive introduction to the framework of reproductive justice, see *Reproductive Justice Briefing Book: A Primer on Reproductive Justice and Social Change,* SisterSong Women of Color Reproductive Health Collective and the Pro-Choice Public Education Project, 2007, available at www.protectchoice.org.

1. Making the Political Personal

1. Lynn Harris, "The Nation: When Teen Pregnancy Is No Accident," NPR, May 27, 2010, www.npr.org (also available at www.thenation.com).

2. Jodi Melamed, *Represent and Destroy: Rationalizing Violence in the New Racial Capitalism* (Minneapolis: University of Minnesota Press, 2011).

3. Jason DeParle, "House G.O.P. Proposes 'Tough Love' Welfare Requiring Recipients to Work," *New York Times,* November 11, 1993, found in fol. 4, box 24, News Clips, Domestic Policy Council, Bruce Reed, Welfare Reform (1993–2001) Subject File, Systematic Processed Collections, William J. Clinton Presidential Library, Little Rock, Arkansas.

4. Barbara Vobejda, "Welfare an Afterthought, Teen Mothers Say," *Washington Post,* February 14, 1995.

5. Holloway Sparks, "Queens, Teens, and Model Mothers: Race, Gender, and the Discourse of Welfare Reform," in *Race and the Politics of Welfare Reform,* ed. Sanford F. Schram, Joe Soss, and Richard C. Fording (Ann Arbor: University of Michigan Press, 2003), 180–81.

6. Dorothy Roberts, *Killing the Black Body: Race, Reproduction, and the Meaning of Liberty* (New York: Vintage, 1997), 8–19.

7. Jenna Vinson, "Covering National Concerns about Teenage Pregnancy: A Visual Rhetorical Analysis of Images of Pregnant and Mothering Women," *Feminist Formations* 24, no. 2 (Summer 2012): 140–62.

8. Gayle Rubin, "Thinking Sex: Notes for a Radical Theory of the Politics of Sexuality," in *Lesbian and Gay Studies Reader*, ed. Henry Abelove, Michele Aina Barale and David M. Halperin (New York: Routledge, 1993), 3–44; Lee Edelman, *No Future: Queer Theory and the Death Drive* (Durham, NC: Duke University Press, 2005); Lauren Berlant, *The Queen of America Goes to Washington City: Essays on Sex and Citizenship* (1997; repr., Durham, NC: Duke University Press, 2002); Kerry H. Robinson, "'Difficult Citizenship': The Precarious Relationships Between Childhood, Sexuality and Access to Knowledge," *Sexualities* 15, no. 3/4 (2012): 257–76; Kathryn Bond Stockton, *The Queer Child, or Growing Sideways in the Twentieth Century* (Durham, NC: Duke University Press, 2009); James Kincaid, *Child-Loving: The Erotic Child and Victorian Literature* (New York: Routledge, 1994); James Kincaid, *Erotic Innocence: The Culture of Child Molesting* (Durham, NC: Duke University Press, 1998).

9. Berlant, *Queen of America*, 65–71.

10. Thomas B. Edsall, "Hillary Clinton Stumps before Grand Jury Date," *Washington Post*, January 26, 1996.

11. Michael N. Castle, "Republicans Really Are a Pro-Education Party but Things Got Off to a Rocky Start, Writes Rep. Castle, with Proposals to Abolish, Eliminate, and Cut," *Roll Call*, June 2, 1997.

12. Donald P. Baker, "Perot Addresses Lifestyle Issues after Debate; On 'Larry King,' Candidate Calls for Less Federal Intrusion and Greater Individual Responsibility," *Washington Post*, October 17, 1996.

13. Examples: "Teen Leaves Newborn in N.J. Bus Terminal Toilet," *Washington Post*, July 15, 1997; Katherine Boo and Leef Smith, "From Welfare, to Hope, to Tragedy; When a Child Dies a Terrible Death, a Woman's Success Story Ends," *Washington Post*, August 5, 1998; Barbara Vobejda and Hanna Rosin, "Sudden Infant Death or Murder? Authorities Reviewing Files," *Washington Post*, August 30, 1998; William Branigin, "Murder-Suicide Reflects Rising Strain on Poor Hispanic Women; Isolated and Unable to Cope, Mother Shot Triplets and Herself," *Washington Post*, September 22, 1998.

14. Katherine Boo, "Painful Choices; Denise Jordan Is Off Welfare and Loves Her Job. But What about Her Daughter?," *Washington Post*, October 19, 1997.

15. Rachel Roth, *Making Women Pay: The Hidden Costs of Fetal Rights* (Ithaca, NY: Cornell University Press, 2000); Marika Seigel, *The Rhetoric of Pregnancy* (Chicago: University of Chicago Press, 2014).

16. Examples: Kathryn Wexler, "California Cracks Down on Men to Curb Underage Pregnancies," *Washington Post*, April 6, 1996; Morton M. Kondracke, *Roll Call*, May 27, 1996; Howard Schneider, "Clarke Seeks to Put Down Tax-Cut Revolt; D.C. Council's Vote Reveals Growing Rift," *Washington Post*, February 12, 1995; Barbara Vobejda, "Welfare an Afterthought, Teen Mothers Say"; Charles Rangel, "Winning the War on Drugs Requires Education and Jobs: Addressing the Social and Economic Factors Related to Drug Abuse Is Vitally Important to Finding a Solution, Rep. Charles Rangel," *Roll Call*, June 10, 1996. Other discussions paint teen and unwed pregnancy as solely an economic, rather than a moral, issue. Tracy Thompson, "Unhitched but Hardly Independent; Having No Husband Complicates Escape from Welfare," *Washington Post*, May 13, 1995.

17. William Booth, "School Fearful That 'Johnny Can't Eat'; Congress's School Lunch Debate Worries Some in Rural Mississippi," *Washington Post*, March 7, 1995.

18. Judith Havemann and Helen Dewar, "Dole Courts Consensus on Welfare; Reform Plan Carries Tough Work Mandates," *Washington Post*, August 8, 1995.

19. Anna Marie Smith, *Welfare Reform and Sexual Regulation* (Cambridge: Cambridge University Press, 2007), 42.

20. For discussions of the racialization of teen pregnancy, see Sparks, "Queens, Teens, and Model Mothers"; Kristin Luker, *Dubious Conceptions: The Politics of Teen Pregnancy* (Cambridge, MA: Harvard University Press, 1996).

21. Rep. William Ford, "Tech-Prep Education; It's a Program That Links the Last Two Years of High School with the First Two Years of Postsecondary. Tech-Prep Can Help Relieve the Technical Skills Shortages That Are Expected to Be the Labor Problem of the Future," *Roll Call,* May 21, 1990.

22. Examples: "No Legitimate Solution in Sight," *Washington Post,* March 16, 1995; "Reformers without a Clue," *Washington Post,* January 24, 1995.

23. Michael A. Fletcher, "Immigrants' Growing Role in U.S. Poverty Cited; Advocacy Group Notes Family Size, Education Levels," *Washington Post,* September 2, 1999.

24. Other initiatives included HHS National Strategy (1997) and Second Chance Homes (a part of the National Strategy): "In response to a call by President Clinton and Congress, HHS announced a teen pregnancy prevention strategy in January of 1997 called the National Strategy to Prevent Out-of-Wedlock Teen Pregnancies. The purpose of the National Strategy is to ensure that at least 25% of communities in the United States have pregnancy prevention programs. (Annual reports were published for 1997–1998, 1998–1999, and 1999–2000.) An alternative initiative, which also forms part of the Strategy, encourages states to create Second Chance Homes with TANF and other funding. These homes are expected to provide teen parents, who might be at risk of abuse if they stayed at home, with guidance in parenting, child development, budgeting, health and nutrition; these skills are seen as a way to prevent repeat pregnancies." Carmen Solomon-Fears, *Teenage Pregnancy Prevention: Statistics and Programs,* CRS Report RS20301 (Washington, D.C.: Library of Congress, Congressional Research Service, April 27, 2007).

25. For discussions of the PRWORA in general and its punitive effects, see Gwendolyn Mink, *Welfare's End* (Ithaca, NY: Cornell University Press, 1998); Smith, *Welfare Reform and Sexual Regulation*; Jamie Peck, *Workfare States* (New York: Guilford Press, 2001).

26. Solomon-Fears, *Teen Pregnancy Prevention;* Smith, *Welfare Reform and Sexual Regulation.*

27. Clay Shaw, "'War on Poverty' Is Over. The Poor Lost. Rep. Clay Shaw: The House GOP Tries a New Approach with Its Welfare Reform Package," *Roll Call,* May 22, 1995; Judith Havemann, "Massachusetts Urged to Halt Aid to Unwed Teen Mothers," *Washington Post,* October 15, 1995; Kathryn Wexler, "For the Fiscally Interactive, California Offers Budgeting via Internet," *Washington Post,* June 17, 1995; Judith Havemann, "Gramm Proposes Tough Welfare Plan Designed to Appeal to GOP Conservatives," *Washington Post,* July 21, 1995; Judith Havemann, "Senate Enters Welfare Debate with Grab Bag of Rival Plans," *Washington Post,* August 7, 1995; "'A Real Step Forward for Our Country, Our Values and for People' on Welfare," *Washington Post,* August 1, 1996; Barbara Vobejda, "Abortions, Out-of-Wedlock Births Targeted; House Republicans Propose State Bonuses for Reductions," *Washington Post,* March 1, 1995; David A. Vise and Sari Horwitz, "GOP Leaders Seek to Change Face of District; Gingrich Panel Targets Schools, Welfare, Taxes," *Washington Post,* May 12, 1995; David A. Vise and Howard Schneider, "GOP Panel Offers Overhaul of D.C.; Foes Say Proposals Would Crush Home Rule," *Washington Post,* July 28, 1995; John E. Yang, "The Speaker Comes to Boys Town; Youth

Home Proves People Can 'Reach Out . . . to Achieve Great Things,'" *Washington Post*, October 24, 1995; Richard Cohen "Dealing with Illegitimacy," *Washington Post*, November 23, 1993 (Cohen found in fol. 4, box 24, News Clips, Domestic Policy Council, Bruce Reed, Welfare Reform [1993–2001] Subject File, Systematic Processed Collections, William J. Clinton Presidential Library, Little Rock, Arkansas).

28. Judith Havemann and Barbara Vobejda, "Senate Welfare Draft Splits with House; GOP Plan Scraps Some Limits on Teenage Mothers, Aid to Noncitizens," *Washington Post*, April 13, 1995.

29. The two hearings analyzed here are two of three that focused exclusively on teen pregnancy in the 1990s. The third, occurring after the passage of the PRWORA, also devotes significant attention to welfare reform, but focuses mostly on the abstinence-only funding written into the law. *Social and Economic Costs of Teen Pregnancy: Hearing before the House Subcommittee on Empowerment, Committee on Small Business*, 105th Cong., 2d. sess. (July 16, 1998).

30. *Teen Parents and Welfare Reform: Hearing before the Senate Committee on Finance*, 104th Cong., 1st sess. (March 14, 1995), 1.

31. *Preventing Teen Pregnancy: Coordinating Community Efforts: Hearing before the House Subcommittee on Human Resources and Intergovernmental Relations, Committee on Government Reform and Oversight*, 104th Cong., 2d sess. (April 30, 1996), 5.

32. Ibid., 12.

33. Alice O'Connor, *Poverty Knowledge: Social Science, Social Policy, and the Poor in Twentieth-Century U.S. History* (Princeton, NJ: Princeton University Press, 2001), 283.

34. *Preventing Teen Pregnancy*, 15.

35. Ibid., 16.

36. *Teen Parents and Welfare Reform*, 54.

37. Similarly, Kristin Moore, another witness in the *Teen Parents and Welfare Reform* hearing states that "we know from studies conducted throughout the world that economic opportunity and educational opportunity are associated with postponing childbearing" (10). Later in the hearing, she also notes that while the sexual revolution affected people of all socioeconomic classes, the "underclass" has "nothing to lose" and is therefore willing to engage in reckless sexual behavior (15).

38. Ibid., 54. In addressing concerns about the results of cutting teens off from cash assistance, Besharov states, "We would deny only the cash benefit until the mother turns 18. That will create financial hardship, but it is not going to create social catastrophe" (19).

39. Ibid., 6–8.

40. *Preventing Teen Pregnancy*, 67.

41. *Teen Parents and Welfare Reform*, 8–9.

42. Ibid., 10.

43. Ibid., 15.

44. Ibid., 21, 22, 24, 25, 29.

45. *Preventing Teen Pregnancy*, 59.

46. Alyosha Goldstein, *Poverty in Common: The Politics of Community Action during the American Century* (Durham, NC: Duke University Press, 2012), 81.

47. *Teen Parents and Welfare Reform*, 46.

48. *Teen Pregnancy Prevention: Hearing before the House Subcommittee on Human Resources, Committee on Ways and Means*, 107th Cong., 1st sess. (November 15, 2001), 4.

49. Ibid., 4.

50. Ibid., 5–6.

51. Ibid., 65–71.
52. Ibid., 71.
53. Ibid., 33.
54. Ibid., 10.
55. Ibid., 15.
56. Ibid., 75–76.
57. Ibid., 48.
58. Ibid., 53–54.
59. For example, Elayne Bennett, president and chief executive officer of the Best Friends Foundation (ibid., 39, 44), and Representative Benjamin Cardin (79).
60. Ibid., 17–18.
61. Ibid., 41, 128.
62. Sarah Brown of the National Campaign to Prevent Teen Pregnancy, for example, states that preventing teen pregnancy is a way of making progress on the issue of "responsible fatherhood" and that curbing "premature" fatherhood will reduce a "host of social problems" (ibid., 89, 51).
63. *Preventing Teen Pregnancy,* 98.
64. *Teen Pregnancy Prevention: Hearing,* 47, 65–66.
65. For example, in the *Teen Parents and Welfare Reform* hearing in 1995, Kristin Moore states that "sex education can encourage teens to delay sex and use contraception. But the effects today are rather small." Suggesting that solutions must go beyond sex education, she calls for increased funding for family planning and contraception, and a set of incentives and disincentives that apply to "young men as well as adolescent females" (11). In the 1996 *Preventing Teenage Pregnancy* hearing, she explains, "I think that many of us are in agreement that the causes of teen pregnancy in many cases are very profound. They are family dysfunctions, single parent families. They are poverty. They are early school failure. They are early behavior problems. The current approaches, on the other hand, are a week or two of sex education during the junior year in high school. They are short term, and they are superficial, and they are too late" (*Preventing Teen Pregnancy,* 58). Moore formulates the problem as a personal one that can be addressed by programs aimed at correcting the damage that personal and familial "dysfunction" create. Contrary to the discourse of the 2001 *Teen Pregnancy Prevention* hearing, however, Moore understands teenage pregnancy as inherently tied to the hardships associated with poverty. In 1995, she states, "Again, it is a matter of low motivation, combined with the disorder and difficulties inherent in the lives of young single parents that leads to pregnancies that are not wanted or intended, but which are not prevented either" (*Teen Parents and Welfare Reform,* 11). Moore and other hearing participants in the mid-1990s viewed "low motivation" as something that results from a perceived lack of opportunities, and the "disorder and difficulties" in the lives of these adolescents results from a complex interplay between economic, cultural, and familial circumstances. These problems, Moore suggests, fall under the purview of the federal government, requiring not just funding for sex education, but also resources that reward desired behavior, enforce child support laws, and address reproductive health and school performance.
66. David Theo Goldberg, "Introduction: Multicultural Conditions," in *Multiculturalism: A Critical Reader,* ed. David Theo Goldberg (Oxford: Blackwell, 1994), 7.
67. Ibid., 7–9; Terence Turner, "Anthropology and Multiculturalism: What Is Anthropology That Multiculturalists Should Be Mindful of It?," in Goldberg, *Multiculturalism,* 420;

Avery F. Gordon and Christopher Newfield, introduction to *Mapping Multiculturalism*, ed. Avery F. Gordon and Christopher Newfield (Minneapolis: University of Minnesota Press, 1996), 3–6.

68. Melamed, *Represent and Destroy*, 156.

69. Jasbir Puar, *Terrorist Assemblages: Homonationalism in Queer Times* (Durham, NC: Duke University Press, 2007), 24–32.

70. All aspects of TANF pertaining to teen pregnancy and parenthood were retained except the measure to reward states for reducing teen pregnancy without increasing abortion rates.

71. Anne E. Kornblut and Perry Bacon Jr., "Clinton Makeover Accents Her Midwestern Roots," *Washington Post*, June 3, 2007.

72. Scott Wilson, "'You Will Not Be Forgotten,' Obama Promises Native American Leaders," *Washington Post*, November 6, 2009.

73. Luker, *Dubious Conceptions*, 60–64; Lisa Arai, *Teenage Pregnancy: The Making and Unmaking of a Problem* (Bristol, UK: Policy Press, 2009), 4.

74. Roberts, *Killing the Black Body*, 120.

75. For mentions of teen pregnancy in these debates see *Personal Responsibility, Work, and Family Promotion Act of 2002*, 107th Cong., 2d sess., *Congressional Record* 148, no. 63 (May 16, 2002): H 2517, 2548–2552, 2565, 2588, 2590; *Personal Responsibility, Work and Family Promotion Act of 2003*, 108th Cong., 1st sess., *Congressional Record* 149, no. 27 (February 13, 2003): H 465, 470, 484–86, 493, 497, 499; *Personal Responsibility and Individual Development for Everyone Act*, 108th Cong., 2d sess., *Congressional Record* 150, no. 43 (March 31, 2004): S 3443–3444.

76. For example, during the CAA debate, Representative Barbara Lee applauds the defunding of abstinence-only programs, stating that "the health of our young teenage girls and boys" is at stake. *Departments of Labor, Health and Human Services, and Education, and Related Agencies Appropriations Act, 2010*, 111th Cong., 1st sess., *Congressional Record* 155, no. 113 (July 24, 2009): H 8779.

77. Susan Levine, "Teen Pregnancy, Birth Rates Plummet Across D.C. Region," *Washington Post*, October 29, 2007.

78. Berlant, *The Queen of America*, 22. As I discuss in chapter 2 and the conclusion, the imagined future children of would-be teen parents fill the strange role within postwelfare teen pregnancy prevention discourse of teaching their would-be parents about proper sex, reproduction, and intimate citizenship in the name of preventing their own very existence. In this way, they are portrayed as a decidedly non-innocent subset of future children, either already ruined by their imagined parents' immorality or else successful in their teaching and, in fact, never born.

79. *Congressional Record* 155, no. 113: H 8756.

80. This is exemplified by guidelines laid out by the CDC in which all such women are considered "pre-pregnant." January W. Payne, "Forever Pregnant," *Washington Post*, May 16, 2006.

81. House of Representatives, "Senate Amendments to . . . H.R. 4872, Health Care and Education Reconciliation Act of 2010—Continued," 111th Cong., 2d. sess., *Congressional Record* 156, no. 43 (March 21, 2010): H 1893.

82. *Transportation, Housing and Urban Development, and Related Agencies Appropriations Act, 2010—Conference Report*, 111th Cong., 1st sess., *Congressional Record* 155, no. 185 (December 10, 2009): S 12884.

83. *Congressional Record* 155, no. 185: S 12884.

84. Karissa Haugeberg, *Women against Abortion: Inside the Largest Moral Reform Movement of the Twentieth Century* (Champaign: University of Illinois Press, 2017).

85. *Service Members Home Ownership Tax Act of 2009*, 111th Cong., 1st sess., *Congressional Record* 155, no. 184 (December 9, 2009): S 12762.

86. Ibid.

87. *Consolidated Appropriations Act of 2010*, H.R. 3288, 111th Cong., 1st sess.

88. *Patient Protection and Affordable Care Act*, H.R. 3590, 111th Cong., 2d. sess.

89. The Support for Pregnant and Parenting Teens and Women section of the PPACA discussed above allots $25 million per year to fund programs that assess needs and the ability of an eligible institution to meet those needs, provide referrals to entities that can meet needs, and establish programs to meet needs. Needs include maternity coverage, family housing, child care, parenting classes, baby food, furniture, clothing, and postpartum counseling.

90. Anne E. Kornblut and Juliet Eilperin, "Calculated Risk with Female Voters Is Suddenly Even Harder to Calculate," *Washington Post,* September 2, 2008.

91. Kevin Merida, "GOP's Northern Lights; With Their Governor at Center Stage, Alaskan Delegates Play a Supportive Role," *Washington Post,* September 4, 2008; Keith Koffler, "GOP Base Appears Sturdy Amid Revelations," *Roll Call,* September 3, 2008; Jose Antonio Vargas, "Blog Talk: Interview with Blogger Jill Stanek," *Washington Post,* September 5, 2008.

92. Candie's Foundation, Video PSAs, "Bristol Palin and 'The Situation,'" www.candiesfoundation.org/psa_video.

93. *Preventing Teen Pregnancy,* 66–67.

94. In fact, teen pregnancy rates actually increased slightly in the mid-2000s. Rob Stein, "Teen Sex Rates Stop Falling, Data Show," *Washington Post,* July 22, 2007; Rob Stein, "Teen Birth Rate Rises in U.S., Reversing a 14-Year Decline," *Washington Post,* December 6, 2007; Rob Stein, "Abstinence Programs Face Rejection; More States Opt to Turn Down the Federal Money Attached to That Kind of Sex Ed," *Washington Post,* December 16, 2007; Rob Stein and Donna St. George, "Teenage Birthrate Increases for Second Consecutive Year," *Washington Post,* March 19, 2009; Rob Stein, "Decline in Teen Sex Levels Off, Survey Shows," *Washington Post,* June 5, 2008.

2. "Taming the Media Monster"

1. Centers for Disease Control and Prevention. "Teen Pregnancy and Social Media," Centers for Disease Control and Prevention, http://www.cdc.gov/teenpregnancy/socialmedia/.

2. William Jefferson Clinton, "State of the Union Address," January 23, 1996, U.S. National Archives and Records Administration, http://clinton2.nara.gov/WH/New/other/sotu.html.

3. "Volunteerism a Good Way to Plug the Holes in the Safety Net," Copley News Service, April 28, 1997. A reprinted version can be found in the Hazleton, PA, *Standard-Speaker,* May 3, 1997, p. 16 (newspapers.com).

4. For insight into its size and budget, in 2011 it employed forty-nine people and spent about $12 million on its operations. National Campaign to Prevent Teen and Unplanned Pregnancy, "990 Form filed for the National Campaign to Prevent Teen and Unplanned Pregnancy," National Campaign to Prevent Teen and Unplanned Pregnancy, 2011 (no longer available); National Campaign to Prevent Teen and Unplanned Pregnancy,

"Audited Financial Statements," National Campaign to Prevent Teen and Unplanned Pregnancy, December 31, 2011 (no longer available). Financial information for the year 2015 can be found at http://thenationalcampaign.org/about.

5. In 2013, these included representatives from Child Trends, the Robert Wood Johnson Foundation, Center for Equal Opportunity, Columbia University, George Washington University, and the Center for American Progress, among others. National Campaign to Prevent Teen and Unplanned Pregnancy, "Board of Directors," National Campaign to Prevent Teen and Unplanned Pregnancy, http://thenationalcampaign.org/about/leadership.

6. National Campaign to Prevent Teen and Unplanned Pregnancy, "Who We Are," http://thenationalcampaign.org/about. Although the mission does not explicitly name marriage as the appropriate confines for childbearing, National Campaign literature upholds marriage as preferable to all other contexts. Likewise, the literature presents a college education prior to having children as an important step toward "success."

7. This tradition finds its roots in 1940s liberal poverty knowledge, such as Gunnar Myrdal's *An American Dilemma,* which explained racialized poverty in terms of culture rather than biology. Through the 1960s, social scientific research into poverty worked to substantiate the "culture of poverty" thesis and forward racial assimilationism. Alice O'Connor, *Poverty Knowledge: Social Science, Social Policy, and the Poor in Twentieth-Century U.S. History* (Princeton, NJ: Princeton University Press, 2001), 10. However, this research also involved a structural analysis implicating macroeconomic policy in the persistence of poverty and assuming the importance of a broad social base. In response to the radical social movements of the 1960s and 1970s, the rise of the New Right and neoliberalism has led to professionalized poverty research that centers personal responsibility and family values at the expense of any substantive discussion of economic policy (10–11).

8. Ibid., 246–47.

9. Ron Haskins and Isabel Sawhill, "Work and Marriage: The Way to End Poverty and Welfare," Welfare Reform and Beyond, Policy Brief #28 (Washington, DC: Brookings Institution, September 2003).

10. Ibid., 6–7.

11. Ibid., 7.

12. National Campaign to Prevent Teen and Unplanned Pregnancy, "The Talk: It's More Than Just Sex" (no longer available). Some of the content and images from "The Talk: It's More Than Just Sex" can be found at www.gcapp.org/the-talk.

13. Sarah S. Brown and Leon Eisenberg, eds., *The Best Intentions: Unintended Pregnancy and the Well-Being of Children and Families* (Washington DC: National Academy Press, 1995), 1–2.

14. Ibid., 4.

15. Ibid., 4–5.

16. Kristin Luker, *Dubious Conceptions: The Politics of Teen Pregnancy* (Cambridge, MA: Harvard University Press, 1996), 152.

17. National Campaign to Prevent Teen and Unplanned Pregnancy, "What Makes Us Unique" (no longer available).

18. National Campaign to Prevent Teen and Unplanned Pregnancy, "Putting What Works to Work" (no longer available). Examples of the outcomes of this program can be found at http://thenationalcampaign.org/data/landing.

19. Katherine Suellentrop, Jane Brown, and Rebecca Ortiz, "Science Says #45: Evaluating the

Impact of MTV's *16 and Pregnant* on Teen Viewers' Attitudes about Teen Pregnancy," October 2010, http://thenationalcampaign.org/resource/science-says-45.

20. Ibid., 3.
21. Ibid., 2.
22. A different study argues that *16 and Pregnant* can be held responsible for a 5.7 percent reduction (one-third of the overall reduction) in teen births in the eighteen months following the show's introduction. Using data about geographic variation in viewership and birth rates, as well as statistics documenting changes in Google searches and tweets on Twitter, they show that teens in geographic areas where viewership is high pursued and found more information about sex and contraception immediately following the airing of *16 and Pregnant* episodes. They conclude that the majority of the reduction in teen pregnancy following the introduction of the show was due to labor market reduction and *16 and Pregnant*. Melissa S. Kearney and Philip B. Levine, "Media Influences on Social Outcomes: The Impact of MTV's *16 and Pregnant* on Teen Childbearing," National Bureau of Economic Research, January 13, 2014.
23. Sarah Brown, "Is Contraception a Code Word?," *Washington Post*, March 26, 2011.
24. Sarah Brown, "Abortion-Contraception Arguments Are Really about Teen Sex," *Washington Post*, January 26, 2012.
25. Brown, "Is Contraception a Code Word?"
26. U.S. Congress, House, *Reducing the Need for Abortion and Supporting Parents Act*, HR 6067, 109th Cong., 2d. sess., *Congressional Record* 152, no. 113, daily ed. (January 3, 2006): H 6534.
27. Heather Boonstra, "The Heart of the Matter: Public Funding of Abortion for Poor Women in the United States," *Guttmacher Policy Review* 10, no. 1 (Winter 2007), www .guttmacher.org/pubs/gpr/10/1/gpr100112.html.
28. National Campaign to Prevent Teen and Unplanned Pregnancy, "National Campaign Applauds Legislation to Prevent Unintended Pregnancies, Reduce the Need for Abortion and Support Parents," June 2009 (no longer available). A version of this statement can be found at http://archive.episcopalchurch.org/documents/Ryan-DeLauro_Bill _support.pdf.
29. Sarah Brown, "Why Aren't Faith Leaders Top Advocates for Birth Control?," *Washington Post*, March 4, 2011.
30. Ibid.
31. *Temporary Assistance for Needy Families (TANF): Hearings before the Senate Committee on Finance*, 107th Cong., 2d. sess. (March 12, April 10, and May 16, 2002), 317. This strategy is reflected in the film *Pregnancy Pact*, discussed in chapter 3, as part of the organization's efforts to, as Sawhill puts in her testimony, "work in concert with the entertainment industry to change the messages embedded in popular culture" (319).
32. Ibid., 317.
33. Brown, "Abortion-Contraception Arguments."
34. *Preventing Teen Pregnancy: Coordinating Community Efforts: Hearing before the House Subcommittee on Human Resources and Intergovernmental Relations, Committee on Government Reform and Oversight*, 104th Cong., 2d sess. (April 30, 1996), 33; M. A. J. McKenna, "Focus on TEEN PREGNANCY—Its board members include former Atlanta Mayor Andrew Young, actress Whoopi Goldberg, publisher Katherine Graham and former Surgeon General C. Everett Koop. Its chairman is Thomas Kean, former governor of New Jersey. It is the National Campaign to Prevent Teen Pregnancy, and its goal is to reduce teenage pregnancies by one-third in a decade; Group digs at root of problem;

Campaign brings in 'new voices' to answer why U.S. rate is so high," *Atlanta Journal and Constitution*, March 26, 1996.

35. Neda Ulaby, "TV Writers Script Safe Sex Product Placement," *All Things Considered*, NPR, September 6, 2012.

36. Laura Lloyd, "How Is the National Campaign Using Social Media?," paper presented at "Taming the Media Monster," National Campaign to Prevent Teen and Unplanned Pregnancy conference, Washington DC, June 26, 2009, available at www.youtube.com /watch?v=pqqO34leqoo.

37. Lloyd uses the example of the National Campaign enlisting YouTube personality Kicesie and comedian Danny Rouhier to make videos instructing viewers on sex and contraception for the website SexReally.org (later called Bedsider), which was a National Campaign project geared toward people in their twenties (ibid.).

38. These four examples are reprinted in Wanda Pillow, *Unfit Subjects: Educational Policy and the Teen Mother* (New York: Routledge, 2004), 187–90.

39. "National Campaign to Prevent Teen Pregnancy Director Sarah Brown Discusses the Use of Provocative New Ad Campaign to Convey Important Messages to Teens About Consequences of Sex," *ABC News*, October 17, 2000.

40. Shaun McCormack, "Edgy Ads Seek to Grab Teens' Attention," *Direct Marketing News*, October 20, 2000, www.dmnews.com.

41. Candie's Foundation, "About Us," www.candiesfoundation.org/aboutUs_Mission.

42. Their work has been referred to as a "public service advertising campaign." "The Candie's Foundation," *PRNewswire*, May 2, 2001. They utilize the nonprofit advertising agency Serve Marketing, which aims to bring causes that are not "sexy" or "hot" into public consciousness. "The Candie's Foundation New TV and Print PSA with Bristol Palin," *PRWeb*, April 7, 2012, www.prweb.com/releases/2010/04/prweb3843904.htm; Serve Marketing, "Serve / About," http://servemarketing.org/about/.

43. Candie's Foundation, "Video PSAs," www.candiesfoundation.org/psa_video.

44. Candie's Foundation, "Campaigns" (no longer available). Examples from this campaign can be found at http://jezebel.com/5333434/abstinence-the-sexy-way.

45. For example, Lea Michele, from the cast of the Fox show *Glee* (which features a National Campaign–influenced teen pregnancy storyline in which a cheerleader gives her baby up for adoption to a woman who had given up her daughter [Lea Michele's character] as a teenager) is a spokesmodel for the Candie's, Inc., fashion line and subject of the foundation's print ad "Don't Be a Statistic," in which she sports a Candie's, Inc., floral hair clip. Candie's Foundation, "Celebrity PSAs," http://www.candiesfoundation.org/psa _print.

46. Candie's Foundation, "Video PSAs."

47. Ibid.

48. Laura Briggs, *Somebody's Children: The Politics of Transracial and Transnational Adoption* (Durham, NC: Duke University Press, 2012), 12.

49. Alexi Knock, "Bethpage High Teen Wins Hot Chelle Rae, Karmin Concert," *Newsday*, Long Island, NY, May 22, 2012, www.newsday.com.

50. The Pew Research Center reports that the percentage of total adult Internet users (defined as eighteen and older) who use social networking sites has gone up from 8 percent in 2005 to 74 percent in 2014. Joanna Brenner, "Pew Internet: Social Networking (Full Detail)," Pew Internet and American Life Project, August 5, 2013, http://pewinternet .org/Commentary/2012/March/Pew-Internet-Social-Networking-full-detail.aspx. The percentage of teen Internet users (ages twelve to seventeen) who use social networking

sites has gone up from 55 percent in 2006 to 81 percent in 2012. Mary Madden, Amanda Lenhart, Sandra Cortesi, Urs Gasser, Maeve Duggan, Aaron Smith, Meredith Beaton, "Teens, Social Media, and Privacy," Pew Internet and American Life Project, May 21, 2013, www.pewinternet.org/files/2013/05/PIP_TeensSocialMediaandPrivacy_PDF.pdf.

51. Michel Foucault, *The History of Sexuality: An Introduction, Volume One* (1978; repr., New York: Vintage Books, 1990); Michel Foucault, *"Society Must Be Defended": Lectures at the College de France, 1975–1976* (New York: Picador, 2003).

52. Robert W. Gehl, "Distributed Centralization: Web 2.0 as a Portal into Users' Lives," *Lateral* 1 (Spring 2012) http://lateral.culturalstudiesassociation.org/issue1/content/gehl .html.

53. For example, StayTeen.org conducted a survey asking teens for their opinions of the website, offering a $25 gift card to Amazon.com. "Tell Us," National Campaign to Prevent Teen and Unplanned Pregnancy, http://stayteen.org (specific survey no longer available).

54. StayTeen.org, "About Us," National Campaign to Prevent Teen and Unplanned Pregnancy, http://stayteen.org/about-us.

55. StayTeen.org, "Games and Quizzes: Polls," National Campaign to Prevent Teen and Unplanned Pregnancy, http://stayteen.org/games/polls.

56. StayTeen.org, "Games and Quizzes: Would You Consider Dating Someone If You Knew They Believed in Abstinence Until Marriage?," National Campaign to Prevent Teen and Unplanned Pregnancy, http://stayteen.org/games/poll/would-you-consider-dating -someone-if-you-knew-they-believed-abstinence-until-marriage.

57. Ibid.

58. Nick Dyer-Witheford and Greig de Peuter, *Games of Empire: Global Capitalism and Video Games* (Minneapolis: University of Minnesota Press, 2009), xix.

59. Stayteen.org, *Crush!*, National Campaign to Prevent Teen and Unplanned Pregnancy, http://stayteen.org/games/crush.

60. Dan Melton, "'How Can We Reach Youth Using Social Media?' Video Transcript: Highlights from Dan Melton's Presentation at the 'Taming the Media Monster' Conference, June 26, 2009," National Campaign to Prevent Teen and Unplanned Pregnancy (no longer available).

61. Ibid.

62. Ibid.

63. Katherine Suellentrop, Dan Melton, and Laura Lloyd, "'Panel 2 Q and A: Using Social Media' Video Transcript: Highlights from Session 2 Q and A at the 'Taming the Media Monster' Conference, June 26, 2009," National Campaign to Prevent Teen and Unplanned Pregnancy (no longer available).

64. Although studies show that most teenagers do use the Internet, the rates at which they do so vary according to race and income. Pew Research Center, "Millennials, A Portrait of Generation Next: Teen and Young Adult Internet Use," Pew Research Center, http:// pewresearch.org/millennials/teen-internet-use-graphic.php. Lisa Nakamura argues that a binary model for understanding Internet access (access versus no access) is no longer useful in an era in which race, class, and gender permit varying degrees of access. Lisa Nakamura, *Digitizing Race: Visual Cultures of the Internet* (Minneapolis: University of Minnesota Press, 2007), 15–16, 18.

65. Teen pregnancy prevention discourse tends to construct girls as in need of tools to avoid sex and boys as in need of tools to have safe sex. For instance, in the Candie's Foundation video "Bristol Palin and 'The Situation,'" Bristol Palin and *Jersey Shore*'s Mike

"The Situation" Sorrentino discuss her commitment to "avoiding" sex (despite being a teen mom herself) and his commitment to "practicing" safe sex "a whole lot." Candie's Foundation, "Video PSAs."

66. Candie's Foundation, "Cry Baby App," www.candiesfoundation.org/crybaby.

67. iTunes Preview, "Candie's Cry Baby" (no longer available). See similar content at www .youtube.com/watch?v=0OTXU1xx1Hw.

68. For example, Planned Parenthood Federation of America (PPFA), like the Candie's Foundation, partners with the National Campaign on its teen pregnancy prevention efforts and has launched its own social media teen pregnancy–related work. Although PPFA differs in important ways from the National Campaign and the Candie's Foundation (for instance, it is a massive provider of health and medical services and also takes explicit anti–abstinence only education and pro–abortion rights stances), it produces teen pregnancy prevention work that is directly linked to those organizations and participates in the kinds of Internet-based biopolitics I have been describing. For examples, see Planned Parenthood, "About Us: Teens Are Using a Growing Number of Online and Mobile Tools to Learn About Sexual Health and Avoid Unintended Pregnancy," www.plannedparenthood.org/about-us/newsroom/press-releases/teens-using -growing-number-online-mobile-tools-learn-about-sexual-health-avoid-unintended -pregn-39255.htm; Planned Parenthood Tumblr, "Ask Us Anything. No Judgements," http://plannedparenthood.tumblr.com/; Planned Parenthood Tumblr, "Not Ready to Have Sex Yet?," http://plannedparenthood.tumblr.com/post/34517407052/read-more -facts-and-myths-about-sex; Planned Parenthood, "Info for Teens: Myths and Facts about Sex," www.plannedparenthood.org/info-for-teens/sex-masturbation/myths-facts -about-sex-33825.htm; Planned Parenthood Tumblr, "No Matter How You're Dressed This Halloween . . . Wear a Condom," http://plannedparenthood.tumblr.com/post /34666164575. While PPFA concerns itself much more substantially than the National Campaign with providing and advocating for equal access to medical and counseling services, comprehensive sex education, contraception, and abortion and focuses its sex- and relationship-affirming messages on queer youth as well as heterosexual teens, it also participates in the multicultural disciplinary politics of contemporary teen pregnancy prevention.

Another example of PPFA's participation in this discourse includes President Cecile Richards's essay in the National Campaign's interactive online project and book *Rethinking Responsibility,* in which she talks about the particular riskiness of adolescence and the responsibilities of both parents and teenagers in preventing teenage pregnancy. Cecile Richards, "Back and Forth Responsibility," in *Rethinking Responsibility: Reflections of Sex and Accountability* (Washington, DC: National Campaign to Prevent Teen and Unplanned Pregnancy, 2009), www.teenpregnancysc.org/sites/default/files/uploads /Documents/rethinking_responsibility.pdf.

69. National Campaign to Prevent Teen and Unplanned Pregnancy, "One-Third of Pregnancies in America Are Unwanted; Most Unwanted Pregnancies Occur to Women Ages 20–29," *PRNewswire,* May 9, 2007.

70. Sarah Brown, "Aunt Sarah's List: Things We All Need to Say to Teens and Young Adults," National Campaign to Prevent Teen and Unplanned Pregnancy, https:// thenationalcampaign.org/resource/aunt-sarahs-list.

71. For example, National Campaign to Prevent Teen and Unplanned Pregnancy, "Briefly . . . Unplanned Pregnancy Among 20-Somethings: The Full Story," May 2008, http://depts .gpc.edu/engage/briefly-unplanned-pregnancy-among-20somethings-the-full-story.pdf.

72. Willam A. Galston, "The Changing Twenties," National Campaign to Prevent Teen and Unplanned Pregnancy (2008), i, 1, https://thenationalcampaign.org/resource/changing -twenties.

73. Ibid., i.

74. Ariès, *Centuries of Childhood,* 329–36.

75. Galston, "The Changing Twenties," 21.

76. Ibid., 1.

77. Sharon Jayson, "Abstinence Message Goes beyond Teens," *USA Today,* October 31, 2006.

78. Ibid.

79. National Campaign to Prevent Teen and Unplanned Pregnancy, "Tips for Working with the Media," http://d3np9zinex7nzb.cloudfront.net/sites/default/files/resource-primary -download/mm_tips.pdf.

3. Televised Teen Pregnancy Prevention

1. In addition to the texts analyzed in depth in this chapter (*16 and Pregnant* [2009–], *The Pregnancy Pact* [2010], and *The Secret Life of the American Teenager* [2008–2013]), other contemporary popular shows and movies that either focus on or deal with teen pregnancy in some way include *Teen Mom* (2009–), *Teen Mom 2* (2011–), *High School Moms* (2012), *Bristol Palin: Life's a Tripp* (2012), *The Pregnancy Project* (2012), *Glee* (2009– 2012), *Gossip Girl* (2007–2012), *Raising Hope* (2010–2012), *Friday Night Lights* (2006– 2011), *Precious* (2009), *The Baby Borrowers* (2008), *90210* (2008–2012), *Juno* (2007), *Reba* (2001–2007), *Gilmore Girls* (2000–2007), *Mom at 16* (2005), *Saved!* (2004), *Boston Public* (2000–2004), *Dawson's Creek* (1998–2003), *Mom at Sixteen* (2002), *Too Young to Be a Dad* (2002), and *Popular* (1999–2001).

2. National Campaign to Prevent Teen and Unplanned Pregnancy, "Media," www .thenationalcampaign.org/media/default.aspx.

3. Some examples of texts that deal extensively with it include the film *For Keeps?* (1988) and *Fifteen and Pregnant* (1998), both of which depict teen pregnancy through white girls whose lives are turned upside down by it. The film *Losing Isaiah* (1995), while not explicitly about teen pregnancy, depicts a story more typical of the racialized discourse of impoverished unwed motherhood in which an African American crack-addicted mother abandons her infant son and then takes the white, middle-class couple who adopted him to court for custody. Additionally, as Julie Passanante Elman points out, the ABC *After School Specials* covered a variety of teen-related issues through the 1970s, 1980s, and early 1990s, including some episodes about teen pregnancy. Julie Passanante Elman, *Chronic Youth: Disability, Sexuality, and U.S. Media Cultures of Rehabilitation* (New York: New York University Press, 2014), 63. These are important antecedents to the television programming discussed in this chapter, in that they comprise an early version of edutainment aimed specifically at adolescents.

4. Marina Khidekel, "Could Hollywood Trick You into Getting Pregnant?" *Seventeen.com,* June 14, 2010; Kim Masters, "Teens, Sex and TV: A Risky Mix?" *All Things Considered,* NPR, December 2, 2008.

5. Cheryl Wetzstein, "Congress Hopes to Cut Illegitimacy at Any Age; Clinton Targets Teen Pregnancies," *Washington Times,* January 14, 1997; National Campaign to Prevent Teen and Unplanned Pregnancy, "Funders," http://thenationalcampaign.org/about/funders.

6. Joe Piazza, "What Are the Most Dangerous Shows Your Kids Are Watching Without You," *Fox News,* December 5, 2011, www.foxnews.com/entertainment/2011/12/05/what

-are-most-dangerous-shows-your-kids-are-watching-without/; Patrick Jonsson, "A Force behind the Lower Teen Birth Rate: MTV's '16 and Pregnant,'" *Christian Science Monitor*, December 21, 2010; Morgan J. Freeman (producer), *16 and Pregnant* (USA: MTV Networks), first broadcast in 2009.

7. David Theo Goldberg, "Introduction: Multicultural Conditions," in *Multiculturalism: A Critical Reader*, ed. David Theo Goldberg (Oxford: Blackwell Publishers, 1994); Lisa Duggan, *The Twilight of Equality: Neoliberalism, Cultural Politics, and the Attack on Democracy* (Boston: Beacon Press, 2003), 43–66; Rey Chow, *The Protestant Ethnic and the Spirit of Capitalism* (New York: Columbia University Press, 2002), 128–34; Jasbir Puar, *Terrorist Assemblages: Homonationalism in Queer Times* (Durham, NC: Duke University Press, 2007), 24–32.

8. Chow, *Protestant Ethnic*, 10–17.

9. Jodi Melamed, *Represent and Destroy: Rationalizing Violence in the New Racial Capitalism* (Minneapolis: University of Minnesota Press, 2011), 42.

10. Ibid., 42; Chow, *Protestant Ethnic*, 10–17; James Kyung-Jin Lee, *Urban Triage: Race and the Fictions of Multiculturalism* (Minneapolis: University of Minnesota Press, 2004), xxvii.

11. Sarah Ahmed, *The Promise of Happiness* (Durham, NC: Duke University Press, 2010).

12. Asa Hawks, "VIDEO 16 and Pregnant Season 4 Trailer," *Starcasm.net*, February 12, 2012, http://starcasm.net/archives/145011; Sarah Seltzer, "MTV's '16 and Pregnant' Exploits Teen Moms but Addresses Abortion with Dignity," *Washington Post*, December 30, 2010.

13. Laurie Oullette and James Hay, *Better Living through Reality TV* (Malden, MA: Blackwell, 2008), 12–14.

14. This section focuses only on *16 and Pregnant* because, although the series differs somewhat from *Teen Mom* and *Teen Mom 2*, these episodes exhibit important themes occurring throughout those series as well.

15. *Teen Pregnancy Prevention: Hearing before the House Subcommittee on Human Resources, Committee on Ways and Means*, 107th Cong., 1st sess. (November 15, 2001), 90.

16. For example, Katie and her boyfriend explore the option of income-based housing, but it is unclear whether they do not end up qualifying for it or do not use it for some other reason (*16 and Pregnant*, season 4, episode 2). Alex's mother worries that she might turn to the "wrong support network" if she keeps her baby, rather than giving her up for adoption (season 4, episode 5). The show never clarifies what she means by this exactly, but it would be reasonable to assume she might be referring to public assistance. Markai's boyfriend James receives unemployment in her episode, but has gotten a full-time job as a debt collector in the "Where Are They Now Special" (season 2, episode 14; season 3, "Where Are They Now Special").

17. For example, Jenelle's child's father is said to be frequently incarcerated and she says does not want him involved in the baby's life. (season 1, "Life after Labor"). Nikkole's child's father apparently has an addiction and is incarcerated. She moves in with him and his parents when he gets released (season 2, "Where Are They Now Special"). Kianna's child's father goes to prison for burglary, but she plans to be with him when he is released in fifteen years (season 4, "Where Are They Now Special"). However, according to *Hollywood Life*, Kianna was arrested and charged with aggravated robbery in August 2011. Lindsey DiMattina, "'16 & Pregnant' Mom Kianna Randall Charged with Aggravated Robbery!" *Hollywood Life*, October 19, 2011, http://www.hollywoodlife.com/2011/10/19/16-pregnant

-kianna-randall-armed-robbery/. Similarly, while not portrayed in the show, Ebony and Josh were apparently arrested on drug-related and child endangerment charges in 2011. Carolyn Robertson, "16 & Pregnant Stars Charged with Child Endangerment," *Baby-Center Blog*, September 21, 2011, http://blogs.babycenter.com/celebrities/16-pregnant -stars-charged-with-child-endangerment/. Danielle says her child's father is in jail for a drug-related offense, and Alex's daughter's father is on probation and is portrayed as struggling with drug and alcohol addiction, but in recovery (season 4, "Where Are They Now Special"; season 4, "Life after Labor 5"). Myranda's mother is also depicted as having issues with drug and alcohol addiction (season 4, episode 7). Domestic violence lands Cleondra and her boyfriend, Mario, in jail for one night, and Jennifer's fiancé, Josh, ends up in jail for one night because of a domestic dispute or possible kidnapping (season 4, "Where Are They Now Special"; season 3, episode 2).

18. Emphasis added in accordance with the speaker's emphasis.

19. Season 2, "Unseen Moments Special." Similarly, Ebony says pregnancy is "getting in the way" of things like prom in her episode (season 1, episode 4).

20. Amber's boyfriend purchases a PlayStation and then later agrees to take it back to the store (season 1, episode 3). Felicia's boyfriend purchases expensive shoes just when she apparently cannot afford the new stroller her baby needs (season 2, episode 12). Christinna's boyfriend is portrayed as purchasing new speakers for his car instead of things for the baby (season 2, episode 16).

21. Season 1, episode 2; season 2, episodes 1, 8, 9, 11; season 3, episodes 1, 4, 6, 7, 8; season 4, episode 4.

22. Season 4, episode 1.

23. Season 4, episode 2. At the end of her episode, Kailynn says that the hardest thing about being a teen mom is "the fact that you have to give up your youth, your social life—it's nonexistent" (season 2, episode 10). Many of the teen moms discuss experiencing stares, being the subject of gossip, and losing friends as a result of being a pregnant and mothering teenager (season 1, episode 2; season 2, episode 11 and "Life after Labor 2").

24. Season 2, episode 17.

25. Many scholars trace the emergence and popularization of theories of cultural pathology to describe "black family structure," "single motherhood," and "long-term dependency." O'Connor, *Poverty Knowledge;* Michael Katz, "The Urban 'Underclass' as a Metaphor of Social Transformation," in *The "Underclass" Debate: Views from History*, ed. Michael B. Katz (Princeton, NJ: Princeton University Press, 1993), 3–23; Neubeck and Cazenave, *Welfare Racism*, 152–54. All of these came to be increasingly associated with and attributed to teenage pregnancy in the 1980s and 1990s. Luker, *Dubious Conceptions*, 81–108; Wanda Pillow, *Unfit Subjects: Educational Policy and the Teen Mother* (New York: Routledge, 2004), 37–39.

26. *16 and Pregnant*, season 2, episode 17.

27. Pillow, *Unfit Subjects*, 1.

28. *16 and Pregnant*, season 2, episode 17.

29. Lisa Arai, *Teenage Pregnancy: The Making and Unmaking of a Problem* (Bristol, UK: Policy Press, 2009), 115–16; Kathleen Sylvester, *Second-Chance Homes: Breaking the Cycle of Teen Pregnancy* (Washington, DC: Progressive Policy Institute, 1995); Cynthia A. Hudley, "Issues of Race and Gender in the Educational Achievement of African American Children," in *Gender, Equity, and Schooling: Policy and Practice*, ed. Barbara J. Bank and Peter M. Hall (New York: Routledge, 1997), 115.

30. Melissa Skolfield, "Draft Talking Points," fol. 3, box 24, News Clips, Domestic Policy Council, Bruce Reed, Welfare Reform (1993–2001) Subject File, Systematic Processed Collections, William J. Clinton Presidential Library, Little Rock, Arkansas.
31. *16 and Pregnant,* season 1, episode 6.
32. Melamed, *Represent and Destroy,* 42.
33. *16 and Pregnant,* season 1, episode 6.
34. Ahmed, *Promise of Happiness,* 33.
35. Ibid., 56.
36. *16 and Pregnant,* season 1, "Life after Labor."
37. Season 1, episode 6.
38. Interestingly, Lori and Ashley, the other two pregnant teens in seasons 1 and 2 who choose adoption for their babies, are both children of teen mothers as well. According to the show's logic, Lori's birth mother could be said to have preempted Lori's potential poverty by giving her up for adoption, and Lori does the same for her baby (season 2, episode 5). Ashley's mother appears to have escaped the fate of poverty that teen moms have been said to inflict on themselves and their children and has also managed to help Ashley foreclose that possibility for her daughter (season 2, episode 19). In this way, the discourse that linked generational poverty, welfare dependence, and teen pregnancy together so tightly is even further unraveled.
39. Laura Briggs, *Somebody's Children: The Politics of Transracial and Transnational Adoption* (Durham, NC: Duke University Press, 2012), 32.
40. Ibid., 124.
41. Ibid., 145–46.
42. *16 and Pregnant,* season 2, "Life after Labor 2."
43. Season 4, "Life after Labor 5."
44. Season 2, "Life after Labor 3."
45. Season 4, "Life after Labor 5."
46. Mike Reynolds, "Lifetime's 'Pregnancy Pact' Is Cable's Most-Watched Film among Women 18–34 since 1994," *MultiChannel News,* January 25, 2010, www.multichannel .com/news/content/lifetimes-pregnancy-pact-cables-most-watched-film-among -women-18–34–1994/363541.
47. Amanda Kondolojy, "'The Secret Life of the American Teenager' Is Cable's #1 Program at 8 O'Clock in Target 12–34s," *TV by the Numbers,* June 19, 2012, http://tvbythenumbers .zap2it.com/2012/06/19/the-secret-life-of-the-american-teenager-is-cables-1-program -at-8-oclock-in-target-12–34s/138770/.
48. In some ways, this trend harks back to an earlier era of panic over teen pregnancy. As Wanda Pillow explains, the teen pregnancy discourse of the 1960s and 1970s painted the typical teen mother as "one of us," in part as an effort to prevent services for unwed mothers from being cut in a climate of racist concerns over the desegregation of public service and the over-reproduction of black women. Pillow, *Unfit Subjects,* 30–31. However, the representations of young white girls' mistakes today appear to have very different aims.
49. Chow, *Protestant Ethnic,* 14.
50. Melamed, *Represent and Destroy,* 13.
51. "About Lifetime," *MyLifetime.com* (no longer available).
52. Although pundits in the 1990s cautioned that white teen birth rates were catching up with those of black and Latina teenagers, white, middle-class girls were not considered the at-risk population. For example, *The Economist,* "Babies Making Babies," December

11, 1993, 27, found in fol. 4, box 24, News Clips Domestic Policy Council, Bruce Reed, Welfare Reform (1993–2001) Subject File, Systematic Processed Collections, William J. Clinton Presidential Library, Little Rock, Arkansas.

53. Rosemary Rodriguez (director), *The Pregnancy Pact* (USA: Lifetime), first broadcast in 2010.

54. No actual pregnancy pact in Gloucester, MA, was ever confirmed, although seventeen girls at the same school became pregnant in one year. The film was heavily criticized by school officials and community members from Gloucester. Matthew Gilbert, "Sex, Lies, and Sensationalism in 'The Pregnancy Pact,'" *Boston Globe,* January 22, 2010; Dorothy Rabinowitz, "Sex and the Schoolgirl," *Wall Street Journal,* January 22, 2010.

55. Critics of comprehensive sex education often argue that teenagers require a "single, unambiguous message" of abstinence until marriage. Carmen Solomon-Fears, *Teenage Pregnancy Prevention: Statistics and Programs,* CRS Report RS20301 (Washington, DC: Library of Congress, Congressional Research Service, April 27, 2007), 11.

56. Melamed, *Represent and Destroy,* 147–48.

57. In a National Campaign–influenced plotline, *Glee*'s teen mom is Quinn Fabray, the beautiful, blonde captain of the cheerleading squad and celibacy club. She lies to her boyfriend, telling him that he is the father of the baby (when it is really the local bad boy's child), places the baby for adoption, plots to get the baby back, then realizes the baby is better off with the adoptive mother. In *Gossip Girl*, rich, white Blair Waldorf gets pregnant and then has a miscarriage after a car accident. In the Lifetime movie *Mom at Sixteen*, Jacey Jeffries has a baby and her mother pretends it is hers so that Jacey can act like a "normal" teenager, but after everyone finds out the baby is Jacey's she eventually gives him up for adoption. In *Saved!*, Mary Cummings becomes pregnant in order to rescue her boyfriend from his proclaimed homosexuality, counting on Jesus to restore her virginity. The movie ends with the baby's birth. *Juno* portrays a young white girl's relatively carefree journey through pregnancy and adoption.

There are a few recent examples of poor white girls getting pregnant, but their teen motherhood (like some of their wealthier counterparts) is foreclosed by abortion, adoption, and even death. For example, Becky Sproles gets pregnant in *Friday Night Lights*. Her mother was a teenager when she had Becky and currently works as a waitress. Becky has an abortion, breaking "the pattern of poverty and powerlessness" in which she is embroiled, according to a *Washington Post* critic. Gloria Feldt, "On 'Friday Night Lights,' A Brave and Honest Abortion Story," *Washington Post,* July 25, 2010. In *Raising Hope,* a working-class teen dad, himself the son of teen parents, raises his daughter after her mother, with whom he had a one-night stand, is executed for being a serial killer.

As Wanda Pillow points out, examples of shows from a slightly earlier period that briefly deal with the issue of teen pregnancy include *Boston Public* (2000–2004), *Popular* (1999–2001), and *Dawson's Creek* (1998–2003). These shows portrayed wealthy or middle-class white girls either getting pregnant and having an abortion (*Boston Public*) or merely having a "pregnancy scare" that turned out not to be an actual pregnancy. Pillow, *Unfit Subjects,* 114–15. The image of the middle-class white girl getting pregnant but ultimately not becoming a parent has a long history in the popular imagination.

Not so common until now is the sustained focus on middle-class white girls carrying their pregnancies to term and parenting in full public view. Aside from the texts analyzed in this chapter, *Gilmore Girls* (2000–2007) chronicles a former teen mom in her adulthood as she parents her own teenage daughter, and *Reba* (2001–2007) follows the antics of a woman and her family, which includes her teenage daughter who got pregnant at seventeen and married the father of her baby. One of the few popular examples of this from the 1990s is Andrea Zuckerman's pregnancy and motherhood in seasons 4 and 5 of *Beverly Hills, 90210* (1990–2000), before Zuckerman is eliminated as a regular character as the series continues through five more seasons. The dominant discourse about teen pregnancy and motherhood in the 1990s came less from popular entertainment, and more from the news media and political discourse discussed in chapter 1.

An important exception to the current trend of depicting teen mothers as white and middle class is the 2009 independent film *Precious,* which chronicles the unfortunate life of a 1980s black teenager who suffers physical, sexual, and emotional abuse, lives in a household of poverty and welfare fraud, and gives birth to two children by her own father who has raped her. After learning that she has contracted AIDS from her father and watching her mother intentionally drop her baby on his head, she ultimately severs herself from her pathological childhood home to raise her second son (the first one has Down syndrome and lives with her grandmother) on her own while she works toward finishing her GED. The film received a very positive reception with the exception of some who saw it as a celebration of stereotypes of black familial pathology and an unrealistic self-improvement story.

As noted above, I focus in this chapter on those texts that both devote their entirety to representing teen pregnancy and motherhood and are explicitly part of a new set of prevention strategies spearheaded by the National Campaign. While I identify these strategies as new because of their participation in the consolidation of a dominant discourse resulting from a large network of state and private resources, these texts are reminiscent of the approach taken by a few episodes of teen-oriented after-school programming from the 1980s (for example, ABC *After School Specials,* season 9, episode 2, "Schoolboy Father," 1980; and CBS *Schoolbreak Special,* season 3, episode 3, "Babies Having Babies," 1986).

58. Brenda Hampton (creator), *The Secret Life of the American Teenager* (USA: ABC Family), first broadcast in 2008, season 1, episode 23.
59. Ibid., episode 22.
60. Ibid., episode 1.
61. Ibid., episode 23.
62. In the third season, however, another teen pregnancy occurs, this time with a slight mix-up of the original scheme. Adrian, a Latina who is portrayed as promiscuous as a result of her own familial breakdown, becomes pregnant when she has sex with Ben in order to get back at Ricky for kissing Amy. The show thus suggests that nice young white men can be the victims of bad girls, too. Adrian's pregnancy ends in a miscarriage.
63. Allison Stewart Ng and Kelleen Kaye, "Why It Matters: Teen Childbearing and Child Welfare," National Campaign to Prevent Teen and Unplanned Pregnancy, May 2013, https://thenationalcampaign.org/sites/default/files/resource-primary-download/childbearing-childwelfare.pdf.
64. *The Secret Life of the American Teenager,* season 1, episode 22.
65. David Theo Goldberg discusses the multiple iterations and consequences of multicultural politics. Goldberg, "Introduction: Multicultural Conditions," 7.
66. *Personal Responsibility, Work Opportunity, and Medicaid Restructuring Act of 1996,* 104th Cong., 2d sess., *Congressional Record* 142, no. 108 (July 22, 1996): S 8397 and 8398; *Conference Report on H.R. 3734, Personal Responsibility and Work Opportunity Reconciliation Act of 1996,* 104th Cong., 2d sess., *Congressional Record* 142, no. 115 (July 31, 1996): H 9406, 9412, and 9421; Ben Wattenberg, "Moynihan's Message," *New York Post,* January

14, 1994, found in fol. 4, box 24, News Clips, Domestic Policy Council, Bruce Reed, Welfare Reform (1993–2001) Subject File, Systematic Processed Collections, William J. Clinton Presidential Library, Little Rock, Arkansas.

4. Pathologizing and Path Breaking

1. Rebecca Roybal, "Teen Birth Rates Dip Slightly," *Albuquerque Journal,* January 30, 2002.
2. New Mexico has tended to hover somewhere within the bottom five states for teen pregnancy rates. Recent thorough data on teen pregnancy rates from the Guttmacher Institute shows that New Mexico had the highest rate of adolescent pregnancy, birth, and abortion in 2011. Kathryn Kost and Isaac Maddow-Zimet, "U.S. Teenage Pregnancies, Births and Abortions, 2011: State Trends by Age, Race and Ethnicity," Guttmacher Institute, April 2016, https://www.guttmacher.org/sites/default/files/report_pdf/us-teen -pregnancy-state-trends-2011_4.pdf.
3. Ann Stoler, *Race and the Education of Desire: Foucault's* History of Sexuality *and the Colonial Order of Things* (Durham, NC: Duke University Press, 1995); Linda Tuhiwai Smith, *Decolonizing Methodologies: Research and Indigenous Peoples* (London: Zed Books, 2012); Laura Briggs, *Reproducing Empire: Race, Sex, Science, and U.S. Imperialism in Puerto Rico* (Berkeley: University of California Press, 2002); Dian Million, "Felt Theory: An Indigenous Feminist Approach to Affect and History," *Wicazo Sa Review* 24, no. 2 (Fall 2009): 53–76; Sarah Deer, "Decolonizing Rape Law: A Native Feminist Synthesis of Safety and Sovereignty," *Wicazo Sa Review* 24, no. 2 (Fall 2009): 149–67.
4. Pablo Mitchell, *Coyote Nation: Sexuality, Race and Conquest in Modernizing New Mexico, 1880–1920* (Chicago: University of Chicago Press, 2005), 10–11; Ned Blackhawk, *Violence over the Land: Indians and Empires in the Early American West* (Cambridge, MA: Harvard University Press, 2006), 18–19.
5. James Brooks, *Captives and Cousins: Slavery, Kinship, and Community in the Southwest Borderlands* (Chapel Hill: University of North Carolina Press, 2001), 33–40; Mitchell, *Coyote Nation,* 10; Blackhawk, *Violence over the Land,* 18–24.
6. Brooks, *Captives and Cousins,* 40.
7. Blackhawk, *Violence over the Land,* 46.
8. Laura Gomez, *Manifest Destinies: The Making of the Mexican American Race* (New York: New York University Press, 2008); John Nieto-Philips, *The Language of Blood: The Making of Spanish-American Identity in New Mexico, 1880s–1930s* (Albuquerque: University of New Mexico Press, 2004).
9. Mitchell, *Coyote Nation,* 5; Sarah Deutsch also highlights the role of women and changing gender roles in the interactions and relationships between and among Anglo settlers and New Mexicans. Sarah Deutsch, *No Separate Refugee: Culture, Class, and Gender on an Anglo-Hispanic Frontier in the American Southwest, 1880–1940* (Oxford: Oxford University Press, 1989).
10. Maria Montoya, *Translating Property: The Maxwell Land Grant and the Conflict over Land in the American West, 1840–1900* (Berkeley: University of California Press, 2002), 14.
11. Jake Kosek, *Understories: The Political Life of Forests in Northern New Mexico* (Durham, NC: Duke University Press, 2006), 7.
12. Joseph Masco, *The Nuclear Borderlands: The Manhattan Project in Post–Cold War New Mexico* (Princeton, NJ: Princeton University Press, 2006), 36; Kosek, *Understories,* 20.
13. Masco, *Nuclear Borderlands,* 185–87; Kosek, *Understories,* 18–20.

14. Alyosha Goldstein, *Poverty in Common: The Politics of Community Action during the American Century* (Durham, NC: Duke University Press, 2012), 91–93; Lena McQuade, *Troubling Reproduction: Sexuality, Race, and Colonialism in New Mexico, 1919–1945*, PhD diss., University of New Mexico (Ann Arbor: Proquest/UMI, 2008 [Publication No. 3329461]), 1–31, 4.

15. Blackhawk, *Violence over the Land*, 23–34; David Correia, "'Rousers of the Rabble' in the New Mexico Land Grant War: *La Alianza Federal de Mercedez* and the Violence of the State," *Antipode* 40, no. 4 (2008): 562; McQuade, *Troubling Reproduction*, 27.

16. In 2011, NMTPC had five employees and spent $519,418 on operating costs. New Mexico Teen Pregnancy Coalition, "990 form filed for the New Mexico Teen Pregnancy Coalition," 2011, http://pdfs.citizenaudit.org/2012_12_EO/85-0310621_990_201206.pdf.

17. Angela Brauer, "New Mexico Teen Pregnancy Coalition Loses $130K in Funding," *KOAT Action 7 News*, Albuquerque, August 26, 2014, http://www.koat.com/news/new-mexico-teen-pregnancy-coalition-loses-130k-in-funding/27721120.

18. New Mexico Teen Pregnancy Coalition, "New Mexico Teen Pregnancy Coalition" (no longer available).

19. New Mexico Teen Pregnancy Coalition, "About Us" (no longer available).

20. New Mexico's Family Planning Program, "Family Planning Program 2013 Fact Sheet," New Mexico Department of Health, April 2013; New Mexico Teen Pregnancy Coalition, "New Mexico Teen Pregnancy Coalition: Pregnancy, Parenting," brochure, November 2009 (no longer available).

21. For general info on Title X of the 1970 Public Health Service Act, see Office of Population Affairs, "Title X Family Planning," U.S. Department of Health and Human Services, www.hhs.gov/opa/title-x-family-planning/.

22. New Mexico Department of Health, "Family Planning Program," https://nmhealth.org/about/phd/fhb/fpp.

23. Valerie Fisher, educational program officer for NM DOH FPP, telephone conversation with author, April 18, 2013; U.S. Department of Health and Human Services, Family and Youth Services Bureau, "2013 State Personal Responsibility Education Program Grant Awards," November 19, 2013, www.acf.hhs.gov/programs/fysb/resource/prep-2013. The NM DOH received $337,033 in PREP funds for the year 2013.

24. New Mexico Department of Health, Family Planning Program, "Teen Pregnancy Prevention Program," https://nmhealth.org/about/phd/fhb/tpp/.

25. Family Planning Program, "Teen Pregnancy Prevention Program" (specific graphic no longer available). The original graphic was a print ad created by Lindsey Schutte, who won a 2006 contest held in Washington County, MD, in which teens competed to create the best teen pregnancy prevention media. Bob Maginnis, "Teen Pregnancy Must Be a Talking Point," *Herald-Mail.com*, May 6, 2007.

26. New Mexico GRADS, "New Mexico GRADS," http://nmgrads.org/.

27. Jennifer Archibeque, "Taking on Teen Pregnancy," *Albuquerque Journal*, May 18, 2000; Rebecca Roybal, "Fighting to Save Teen Parents," *Albuquerque Journal*, February 18, 1999.

28. Roybal, "Fighting to Save Teen Parents."

29. Amy Webber, "School Programs Help Teen-Agers Balance Education and Parenting," *Albuquerque Journal*, November 3, 2001.

30. Legislative Education Study Committee, "Minutes, LESC Meeting, November 13–16, 2012," State of New Mexico, 2012, www.nmlegis.gov/lcs/minutes/ALESCminNov16.12.pdf.

31. Young Women United's Facebook page, mission statement (2013; no longer available).

32. Micaela Cadena, policy director at YWU, in-person discussion with author, April 19, 2013.

33. Debra Dominguez, "Teens & Sex," *Albuquerque Journal*, May 2, 2005.

34. New Mexico GRADS, "New Mexico Governor Signs Legislation to Improve High School Graduation Rates of Pregnancy and Parenting Students," blog, April 5, 2013, http://nmgrads.wordpress.com/2013/04/05/new-mexico-governor-signs-legislation-to -improve-high-school-graduation-rates-of-pregnant-and-parenting-students/.

35. Some of YWU's and NM GRADS's partners in their efforts to advocate for young parents include the American Civil Liberties Union of New Mexico, Strong Families New Mexico, and the Media Literacy Project, which produced a short documentary on young parents in 2012. Diana Garcia and Georgia West, "Recognition: Young Parents in New Mexico," Media Literacy Project, YouTube, October 26, 2012.

36. Milan Simonich, "New Law Allows Additional Absences for Pregnant Girls and Young Parents," *Las Cruces Sun-News,* April 5, 2013.

37. New Mexico Legislature. *School Excused Absences for Pregnancy,* House Bill 300, 51st Legislature, 1st sess., 2013, http://www.sos.state.nm.us/uploads/files/HB300.pdf.

38. Henry J. Kaiser Family Foundation, "How Will the Uninsured in New Mexico Fare under the Affordable Care Act?," June 6, 2014, http://kff.org/health-reform/fact-sheet /state-profiles-uninsured-under-aca-new-mexico/; Jane B. Wishner, Southwest Women's Law Center, to Brenda Destro, Office of Public Health and Science, U.S. Department of Health and Human Services, September 24, 2008, www.swwomenslaw.org (no longer available); New Mexico Human Services Department, "Family Planning Waiver FAQs" (no longer available).

39. New Mexico Human Services Department, Insure New Mexico! Solutions, "NewMexi-Kids and NewMexiTeens," www.insurenewmexico.state.nm.us (no longer available).

40. Dr. Mary Shepherd at the NM DOH provided an estimate at my request, based on a "population-based sample of women with a recent live birth," which comes from a New Mexico PRAMS survey (https://nmhealth.org/about/phd/fhb/prams/), using New Mexico's Indicator-Based Information System (https://ibis.health.state.nm.us/query). Mary Shepherd, e-mail message to author, October 31, 2013.

41. Medicaid covered emergency medical services for eligible undocumented people who do not otherwise meet the qualifying criteria. New Mexico Human Services Department, Medical Assistance Division, "New Mexico Medical Assistance Programs: Eligibility Pamphlet," http://www.hsd.state.nm.us.

42. Family Planning Program, "Family Planning Program."

43. New Mexico Legislature, "Keyword Search," http://www.nmlegis.gov/lcs/keyword.aspx.

44. New Mexico Human Services Department, "New Mexico Works: New Mexico's Temporary Assistance to Needy Families (TANF) State Plan, January 1, 2012 to December 31, 2014," http://www.hsd.state.nm.us/uploads/filelinks /6331671b99b34cafba9bd8cb327bc208/tanf_state_plan_2012_2014.pdf.

45. Liz Schott, "Policy Basics: An Introduction to TANF," Center on Budget and Policy Priorities, last updated December 4, 2012, http://www.cbpp.org/cms/?fa=view&id=936.

46. New Mexico Human Services Department, "Temporary Assistance to Needy Families (TANF) Fact Sheet," January 3, 2013, www.hsd.state.nm.us (no longer available). This fact sheet lists NMTPC, NM DOH FPP, and NM GRADS as organizations qualifying for MOE funds in FY2012. NM GRADS presumably receives MOE funds for its role in meeting the other two goals of TANF: providing assistance to needy families and ending families' dependence on government assistance by improving educational and

job outcomes and marriage (although NM GRADS does not claim to promote marriage and also does not appear to); New Mexico Human Services Department, "New Mexico Works." This document explains that NM DOH FPP does family planning and teen pregnancy prevention in the context of a discussion of MOE funds.

47. U.S. Department of Health and Human Services, Administration for Children and Families, Family Youth and Services Bureau, "2012 Title V Abstinence Education Grant Program Awards," October 1, 2012, www.acf.hhs.gov/programs/fysb/resource/2012-title-v-awards. New Mexico received $470,182 in FY 2012.

48. Office of Adolescent Health, "Grantee Map," U.S. Department of Health and Human Services, www.hhs.gov/ash/oah/grants/grantee-map.html. Both organizations were awarded funds for FY 2010–2014.

49. Capacity Builders, "Navajo Youth Builders Program," http://capacitybuilders.info/prevention/navajo-youth-builders.php.

50. National Indian Youth Leadership Project, "Mission and Vision Statements," www.niylp.org (no longer available).

51. National Campaign to Prevent Teen and Unplanned Pregnancy, "Key Information about New Mexico," https://thenationalcampaign.org/sites/default/files/resource-supporting-download/nm_summary_for_hill.pdf.

52. U.S. Department of Health and Human Services, Office of Adolescent Health, "New Mexico Public Education Department (NM)—Pregnancy Assistance Fund," www.hhs.gov/ash/oah/grants/grantees/paf-nm.html.

53. New Mexico GRADS, "New Mexico GRADS," http://nmgrads.org (current information posted for 2015).

54. National Campaign, "Key Information about New Mexico."

55. Archibeque, "Taking on Teen Pregnancy"; Rebecca Roybal, "Teen Birth Rates Dip Slightly"; Mike Alberti, "More than Cookies," *Albuquerque Journal,* July 18, 2004.

56. *New Mexico in Focus,* "Teen Pregnancy—Interview with Sarah Brown," New Mexico PBS, YouTube, May 20, 2011, https://www.youtube.com/watch?v=tmAQh-hH_Ec.

57. Ibid.

58. Some data does exist to suggest that in-school child care services increase graduation rates for parenting high school students. Hugh F. Crean, A. D. Hightower, and Marjorie J. Allan, "School-Based Child Care for Children of Teen Parents: Evaluation of an Urban Program Designed to Keep Young Mothers in School," *Evaluation and Program Planning* 24, no. 3 (August 2001): 267–75.

59. New Mexico Teen Pregnancy Coalition, "10 Teen Pregnancy Facts," http://www.health.state.nm.us (no longer available). Similar content and a reference to this document can be found here: https://www.nmlegis.gov/lcs/handouts/LHHS%20120111%20New%20Mexico%20Teen%20Pregnancy%20Coalition.pdf.

60. NMTPC, "10 Teen Pregnancy Facts." The list of "costs to taxpayers" that this handout uses is taken from National Campaign data on the cost of teen childbearing to taxpayers in each state. This data is calculated by taking into account the projected costs of incarcerating the children of teen parents, and the estimated lower taxes paid by teen mothers who earn lower wages, as well as other measures that assume a causal relationship between the age of the mother at the birth of a child and variety of other outcomes. While the study attempts to prove that these costs are directly due to the age of the mother at the time of the birth, the impact of systemic barriers to success for adolescent parents is taken as a given, rather than analyzed as a possible target for change. Saul D. Hoffman, "By the Numbers: The Public Costs of Teen Childbearing,"

National Campaign to Prevent Teen and Unplanned Pregnancy, October 2006, https://thenationalcampaign.org.

61. NMTPC, "10 Teen Pregnancy Facts."

62. Kristin Luker, *Dubious Conceptions: The Politics of Teen Pregnancy* (Cambridge, MA: Harvard University Press, 1996); more recently and from an economic disciplinary perspective, Melissa S. Kearney and Phillip B. Levine, "Why Is the Teen Birth Rate in the United States So High and Why Does It Matter?" *Journal of Economic Perspectives* 26, no. 2 (2012): 141–63.

63. Rebecca Roybal, "Experts: Families Key to Prevention," *Albuquerque Journal*, May 31, 1999.

64. Julie Grenko, "Parents: Talk with Your Kids about Sex," *Las Cruces Sun-News*, September 5, 2006.

65. "Teen Pregnancy Can Be Reduced," *Albuquerque Journal*, September 6, 2006.

66. Katherine Suellentrop and Molly Sugrue, "Science Says #35: Acculturation and Sexual Behavior among Latinos," National Campaign to Prevent Teen and Unplanned Pregnancy, 2008, https://thenationalcampaign.org.

67. McQuade, *Troubling Reproduction*, 13–14.

68. Ruben Gonzales, "Torrance Reduces Births by Teens," *Albuquerque Journal*, June 24, 2004.

69. Roybal, "Teen Birth Rates Dip Slightly."

70. Some examples include Andrea Schoellkopf, "Fighting Chance," *Albuquerque Journal*, November 11, 2002; Dominguez, "Teens & Sex"; Helen Gaussoin, "'Strong, Smart & Bold'—Girls Inc. Inspires Youths to Reach Their Potential, Reach Their Goals and Reach Out to One Another," *Albuquerque Journal*, January 11, 2006; Olivier Uyttebrouck, "Unmarried with Children—Single Women Gave Birth to Over Half the State's Babies in 2005," *Albuquerque Journal*, December 2, 2007.

71. Debra Dominguez-Lund, "Fragile Motherhood—Teen Pregnancy: Rates in New Mexico Are Highest among Hispanics," *Albuquerque Journal*, March 12, 2006.

72. Legislative Health and Human Services Committee, "Minutes of the Sixth Meeting of the Legislative Health and Human Services Committee," State of New Mexico, November 30–December 1, 2011, https://www.nmlegis.gov/lcs/minutes/LHHSminDec01.11.pdf; Sylvia Ruiz, "Adolescent Births and Adolescent Pregnancy Prevention in New Mexico," New Mexico Teen Pregnancy Coalition, Presented at Legislative Health and Human Services Committee Sixth Meeting, November 30, 2011, slide 5, www.nmlegis.gov/lcs/handouts/LHHS%20120111%20New%20Mexico%20Teen%20Pregnancy%20Coalition.pdf.

73. Ruiz, "Adolescent Births," Slide 9.

74. McQuade, *Troubling Reproduction*, 27.

75. Toni Berg, nurse at New Futures High School, in-person discussion with author, March 1, 2013.

76. Linda Barr and Catherine Monserrat, *Teenage Pregnancy: A New Beginning*, 8th revision (Albuquerque, NM: New Futures, 2006), 7.

77. Cadena, in-person discussion.

78. Denicia Cadena and Micaela Cadena, "What's Wrong with Blaming Teen Parents?" *Blog of Rights*, American Civil Liberties Union, August 24, 2012, http://www.aclu.org/blog/womens-rights/whats-wrong-blaming-teen-parents.

79. New Mexico Legislature, Senate, "Senate Memorial 25: Contributions of Young Parents in New Mexico,", 50th Legislature, 2d sess., 2012, www.sos.state.nm.us/uploads/files/Bills2012/Memorials/SM25.pdf.

80. Simonich, "New Law Allows Additional Absences."

81. For example, YWU has taken the lead in the "Respect ABQ Women" campaign, which was a direct response to antiabortion initiatives in the state. National Latina Institute for Reproductive Health, "Latinas Stand with New Mexico Women," October 18, 2013, http://latinainstitute.org/en/content/latinas-stand-new-mexico-women.

82. Congresswoman Rosa DeLauro, "DeLauro Touts Inclusion of 'Reducing the Need for Abortions Initiative' in Labor–HHS Appropriations Bill," U.S. House of Representatives, September 2009, http://delauro.house.gov/index.php?option=com_content&view=article&id=342:delauro-touts-inclusion-of-reducing-the-need-for-abortions-initiative-in-labor-hhs-appropriations-bill&catid=9:2009-press-releases&Itemid=25.

83. James Monteleone, "House Approves Excused Absences for Teen Parents," *Albuquerque Journal,* February 23, 2013.

84. Legislative Education Study Committee, "Minutes, LESC Meeting, November 13–16, 2012," 18–19.

85. Ibid., 19.

86. Ange-Marie Hancock, *The Politics of Disgust: The Public Identity of the Welfare Queen* (New York: New York University Press, 2004), 23–64. While welfare retrenchment was partly a response to the welfare rights movement, it is important to note that anti-welfare sentiment predated the welfare rights movement. Felicia Kornbluh, *The Battle of Welfare Rights: Politics and Poverty in Modern America* (Philadelphia: University of Pennsylvania Press, 2007), 89–90.

87. Holloway Sparks, "Queens, Teens, and Model Mothers: Race, Gender, and the Discourse of Welfare Reform," in *Race and the Politics of Welfare Reform,* ed. Sanford F. Schram, Joe Soss, and Richard C. Fording (Ann Arbor: University of Michigan Press, 2003), 171–72 and 184. Sparks writes, "Of nearly 600 witnesses . . . only 17 were welfare recipients" (184).

88. Hancock, *Politics of Disgust,* 4–5.

89. New Mexico GRADS, "February 6! Today! NM GRADS Day and Young Parents Day of Action at the New Mexico Legislature!" blog, February 6, 2013, https://nmgrads.wordpress.com/2013/02/06/february-6-today-nm-grads-day-and-young-parents-day-of-action-at-the-new-mexico-legislature/; New Mexico GRADS, "Voices of Young Parents in New Mexico Heard at the State Capitol Today!" blog, February 7, 2013, https://nmgrads.wordpress.com/2013/02/07/voices-of-young-parents-in-new-mexico-heard-at-the-state-capitol-today/.

90. "Maternity Leave Proposed for NM Students," *KOAT Action 7 News,* Albuquerque, March 11, 2013, available on YouTube.

91. Gadi Schwartz, "State Has Highest Teen Pregnancy Rate in Country," *KOB Eyewitness News 4,* February 26, 2013 (no longer available). This news clip can now be found at www.clipsyndicate.com/video/playlist/19366/3958199?title=luzerne_county.

92. Nikki Ibarra, "Bill to Give Maternity Leave for Middle Schoolers Makes its Way through Legislature," *KOB Eyewitness News 4,* March 10, 2013 (no longer available). This news clip can now be found at www.youtube.com/watch?v=GTc-t9j4T-w.

93. For example, in a teen pregnancy-focused episode of *Public Square,* a New Mexico PBS program aired in 2011, teen parents are interviewed extensively and given the opportunity to debate policy decisions with Republican state senator Mark Boitano: "Teen Pregnancy," *Public Square,* New Mexico PBS, October 27, 2011, http://www.newmexicopbs.org/educate/americangraduate/public-square-teen-pregnancy/. Other examples include the NM GRADS blog and the social media sites of YWU and the ACLU.

94. Maia Szalavitz, "Why New York's Latest Campaign to Lower Teen Pregnancy Could Backfire," *Time,* March 28, 2013, http://healthland.time.com; Miriam Pérez, "NYC Teen Pregnancy Campaign Brings Shaming to Bus Shelters and Cell Phones," *RH Reality Check*, March 5, 2013, https://rewire.news/; Miriam Pérez, "Backlash against Teen Pregnancy Campaign Brings Tweaks but the Message Remains the Same," *RH Reality Check*, March 19, 2013, https://rewire.news/.

Conclusion. Neoliberal Limits and Reproductive Justice

1. The City of New York Office of the Mayor, "Mayor Bloomberg, Deputy Mayor Gibbs, and Human Resources Administration Commissioner Doar Announce New Campaign to Further Reduce Pregnancy," March 3, 2013, Press Release No. 82, 2, www1.nyc.gov.

2. Human Resources Administration, "Think Being a Teen Parent Won't Cost You?" Department of Social Services, New York, NY, www.nyc.gov (no longer available).

3. Ruth Marcus, "Truth-Telling on Teen Pregnancy," *Washington Post,* March 22, 2013; Pérez, Miriam. "NYC Teen Pregnancy Campaign Brings Shaming to Bus Shelters and Cell Phones," *RH Reality Check*, March 5, 2013, https://rewire.news/.

4. The sources used for the posters include studies by the Brookings Institution (one by Isabel Sawhill and Ron Haskins), Child Trends, the U.S. Department of Agriculture's Center for Nutrition Policy and Promotion, and the Urban Institute. Human Resources Administration, Department of Social Services, New York, Office of Communications and Marketing, "Teen Pregnancy Campaign, OER Notes," www.nyc.gov (no longer available).

5. Office of the Mayor, "Mayor Bloomberg," 2.

6. Human Resources Administration, "NYC Human Resources Administration Teen Pregnancy Prevention Campaign," YouTube, May 3, 2013 (no longer available).

7. Office of the Mayor, "Mayor Bloomberg," 2.

8. "Kids Having Kids," *Chicago Tribune,* March 18, 2013.

9. Office of the Mayor, "Mayor Bloomberg," 1.

10. Pérez. "NYC Teen Pregnancy Campaign."

11. For instance, in a 1993 *U.S. News & World Report* editorial, Michael Ruby argues that eliminating welfare altogether might be a solution to "irresponsible behavior."

> That a crisis exists and deepens every day is beyond dispute. In an area of public policy suffering from numbing statistical overkill, a handful of numbers do nicely. The problems for many children begin early. About 375,000 babies, or 9 percent of births each year, are exposed to illegal drugs in the womb. Nearly 1 of every 3 births is out of wedlock. Two out of 3 African American babies are born to single mothers, up from 1 in 4 when Daniel Patrick Moynihan first wrote about the disintegration of the black family nearly 30 years ago; the figure for white babies is 22 percent.
>
> Black or white, these women—and many are that only biologically, given their youth— tend to be ill educated and unable to provide for themselves or their offspring.

Michael Ruby, "The Children's Crusade," *U.S. News & World Report,* December 13, 1993, 112, found in fol. 4, box 24, News Clips, Domestic Policy Council, Bruce Reed, Welfare Reform (1993–2001) Subject File, Systematic Processed Collections, William J. Clinton Presidential Library, Little Rock, Arkansas. Similarly, Richard Cohen writes in the *Washington Post* in 1993, "When it comes to illegitimacy, there's finally good news: The white rate is rising. That's an odd kind of 'good news' I bring you, but it's [*sic*] import is unmistakable: in a little while, both the problem of illegitimacy and the term 'underclass' will no longer be associated just with poor African Americans. Maybe then we'll be able to talk about these problems without charges of racism—some of them well-founded—muddying the debate." He goes on to reference Charles Murray's article, "The Coming of the White Underclass," in the *Wall Street Journal,* the proposal to make Norplant a part of welfare policy, and the need to "come to terms" with teen sexuality. Richard Cohen "Dealing with Illegitimacy," *Washington Post,* November 23, 1993, found in fol. 4, box 24, News Clips, Domestic Policy Council, Bruce Reed, Welfare Reform (1993–2001) Subject File, Systematic Processed Collections, William J. Clinton Presidential Library, Little Rock, Arkansas.

12. The campaign video, for example, features one black teen dad and one black teen mom giving testimonials as to how hard teen parenthood is and then a black man explains further, followed by a white woman asking viewers to text "NOTNOW" to 877877. In this way, the video suggests that teen pregnancy is primarily a black issue. Human Resources Administration, "NYC Human Resources Administration Teen Pregnancy Prevention Campaign."

13. Melissa Jeltsen, "Teen Pregnancy Campaign Ripped by Melissa Harris-Perry," *Huffington Post,* March 9, 2013, www.huffingtonpost.com.

14. Planned Parenthood of New York City, "New NYC Teen Pregnancy Subway Advertising Campaign Not the Answer," March 6, 2013, https://www.plannedparenthood.org. In fact, even Stay Teen (the teen-oriented website run by the National Campaign) featured a blog post written by a teenage contributor who sharply critiqued the campaign in this way: Jennifer V., "Brokering the Politics of Shame in NYC's Newest Public Health Campaign," Stayteen.org, March 23, 2013 (no longer available).

15. Marcus, "Truth-Telling on Teen Pregnancy"; Keli Goff, "Why Liberals Are Wrong on Teen Pregnancy," blog post, *The Root,* March 12, 2013, www.theroot.com.

16. Richard V. Reeves, "Shame and Teen Pregnancy," Up Front blog, Brookings Institution, March 18, 2013, www.brookings.edu. The link he provides to prove his "factual" claim has apparently been broken since he posted the article; after checking the link myself on June 27, 2013, I saw that a commenter from "3 months ago" took note of the broken link then.

17. Michael Warner, *The Trouble with Normal: Sex, Politics, and Ethics of Queer Life* (Cambridge, MA: Harvard University Press, 1999).

18. Lauren Berlant, *The Queen of America Goes to Washington City: Essays on Sex and Citizenship* (1997; repr., Durham, NC: Duke University Press, 2002), 6; Lee Edelman, *No Future: Queer Theory and the Death Drive* (Durham, NC: Duke University Press, 2005), 11.

19. Berlant, *Queen of America,* 6.

20. Ibid., 58–59, 75–77.

21. Jeltsen, "Teen Pregnancy Campaign Ripped by Melissa Harris-Perry."

22. Keli Goff, blogging for *The Root,* for example, argues that Bloomberg is simply telling teens "in poor communities" the important information they need about timing childbirth. She argues that the campaign presents factual information and that its more privileged critics (like the leadership of Planned Parenthood) take for granted that impoverished teens already understand this information. Goff, "Why Liberals Are Wrong on Teen Pregnancy."

23. Lauren Rankin, "New York's Teen Pregnancy Campaign Quietly Gets Made Over, Still Misses the Mark," *RH Reality Check,* March 21, 2014, https://rewire.news/.

24. Kimala Price, "What Is Reproductive Justice? How Women of Color Activists Are Redefining the Pro-Choice Paradigm," *Meridians: Feminism, Race, Transnationalism* 10, no. 2 (2010): 44–49.

25. National Latina Institute for Reproductive Health, New York, "No Teen Shame," www .latinainstitute.org/en/content/no-teen-shame; New York Coalition for Reproductive Justice, "NYC4RJ Launches the 'No Stigma! No Shame!' Campaign," March 12, 2013, http://nyc4rj.tumblr.com (no longer available). Similar content can be found at http:// amplifyyourvoice.org/u/brittanyywoclc/2013/03/13/nyc4rj-launches-the-%E2%80 %9Cno-stigma-no-shame%E2%80%9D-campaign/; Strong Families, "Young Parents," Forward Together, Oakland, CA, http://strongfamiliesmovement.org/young-parents. Young Women United is both active in Strong Families and participated online in forums discussing young parents and the Bloomberg campaign. Nia King, "Can New York Shame Teens out of Getting Pregnant? [Reader Forum]," *Colorlines,* March 11, 2013 http://colorlines.com.

26. Posted on May 29, 2013, the online petition for a meeting with Cole collected 881 signatures from people across the United States. Natasha Vianna, "Candie's Foundation: Stop Shaming Young Parents," Change.org, May 29, 2013, www.change.org. Although Neil Cole never granted a meeting, organizers declared a campaign victory in the successful coalition building and shifting of discourse around young parents.

27. Roderick A. Ferguson, *Aberrations in Black: Toward a Queer of Color Critique* (Minneapolis: University of Minnesota Press, 2004), 15.

Index

#NoTeenShame. *See* No Teen Shame

ABC *After School Specials,* 175n3, 179–80n57
ABC Family, 87, 101, 102, 114
abortion, 17, 27, 79, 104, 108, 110, 116, 274n68, 179n57; affirmative politics of, 147; legalization of, 3; New Mexico and, 132, 140, 147, 181n2, 186n81; religious leaders and, 61–64; teen pregnancy prevention and, 44–48, 56–57, 61–65; welfare reform and, 27, 168n70. *See also* Reducing the Need for Abortions Initiative; Reducing the Need for Abortions and Supporting Parents Act; Hyde Amendment
abstinence, 2, 168n76, 179n55; Candie's Foundation and, 68–70, 79–80; National Campaign to Prevent Teen and Unplanned Pregnancy and, 64, 67, 74–75, 101; New Mexico and, 128–29, 137; Personal Responsibility and Work Opportunity Reconciliation Act and, 10, 27, 47, 166n29; Planned Parenthood and, 174n68; *The Pregnancy Pact* and, 103–9; promotion, 74–75, 101, 105, 109, 111, 114, 129; *The Secret Life of the American Teenager* and, 114; twenty-somethings and, 83–84; welfare reform rhetoric and, 35–40
Abstinence Education Initiative of the Virginia Department of Health, 37–38
ACA. *See* Patient Protection and Affordable Care Act
ACLU-NM. *See* American Civil Liberties Union of New Mexico
activism. *See* grassroots activism
adolescence: citizenship and, 50, 88–89, 100, 116, 150; colonialism and, 6–7, 12; consumerism and, 15, 51–52, 67–71, 73, 76, 78, 87–88, 91, 150; developmental stages and, 22–23, 37, 82–84, 131–32, 136, 150; hedonism and, 67; history of, 6–7, 82; media and, 51–52, 65, 71, 73; racialization and, 25; sexuality, and 7–8, 12, 15, 21, 23, 31, 36–38, 40, 44–50, 52–54, 88, 131, 150, 153; volatility and, 1, 8, 21, 23–24, 31, 36–37, 40, 52, 82–84, 150. *See also* neoliberalism: adolescence and; popular culture: teenagers and
adoption, 3, 5, 27, 42, 45, 48, 104, 108, 110, 135, 172n45, 179n57; *16 and Pregnant* and, 94–99, 176n16, 178n38
advertising industry: teen pregnancy prevention and, 66–71, 172n42
Advocates for Youth, 54, 83
AFDC. *See* Aid to Families with Dependent Children
Affordable Care Act. *See* Patient Protection and Affordable Care Act
African Americans, 152, 175n3; social science research and, 177n25; stereotypes of, 21, 152, 178n48, 179–80n57, 188n12; welfare reform rhetoric and, 25–26, 28, 152, 178n52, 187–88n11
Ahmed, Sarah, 89, 96
Aid to Families with Dependent Children (AFDC), 7, 21, 28, 52, 55–57, 60, 94, 128
Albuquerque Journal, 118, 125, 133–35
Albuquerque, NM, 2, 123, 125–26, 135–36, 143–44, 146; South Valley neighborhood, 133–34. *See also* Media Literacy Project; New Mexico Teen Pregnancy Coalition; Young Women United
Albuquerque Public Schools, 143. *See also* New Futures High School
American Civil Liberties Union of New Mexico (ACLU-NM), 139–40, 183n35, 186n93

CLARE DANIEL was born in Winona, Minnesota. She received her BA in English and German studies with a minor in women's and gender studies from Macalester College in St. Paul. She holds an MA and PhD in American studies from the University of New Mexico. Her work appears in *Signs: Journal of Women in Culture and Society*, the edited collection *MTV and Teen Pregnancy: Critical Essays on "16 and Pregnant" and "Teen Mom"* and the library science journal *Collection Building*. She currently resides in New Orleans with her partner, Blake, and son, Milo. She works at Tulane University as assistant director in the Academic Advising Center and adjunct lecturer in the Honors Program.